Hezekiah Butterworth

Zigzag Journeys in the Great Northwest

Or, a trip to the American Switzerland

Hezekiah Butterworth

Zigzag Journeys in the Great Northwest
Or, a trip to the American Switzerland

ISBN/EAN: 9783744794015

Printed in Europe, USA, Canada, Australia, Japan

Cover: Foto ©Andreas Hilbeck / pixelio.de

More available books at **www.hansebooks.com**

TACOMA. THE BEAUTIFUL.

ZIGZAG JOURNEYS

IN THE

GREAT NORTHWEST;

OR,

A TRIP TO THE AMERICAN SWITZERLAND.

BY

HEZEKIAH BUTTERWORTH.

FULLY ILLUSTRATED.

BOSTON:
ESTES AND LAURIAT,
PUBLISHERS.

PREFACE.

HIS twelfth volume of the Zigzag books was written after a journey over the Canadian Pacific Railroad to Vancouver, the cities of the Puget Sound, and Columbia River. Its aim is to give in a picturesque way a view of the scenery, industrial opportunities, and romances of the great Northwest.

When the writer first began these books of the stories and legends of places and of travel with interpolated tales, with a view of helping home and school studies, he had no thought that the demand for them would continue beyond a few volumes. But parents and teachers have found them helpful in developing the intelligence of the young, and in creating a taste for better reading; so the series has been continued in compliance with the public wish and patronage.

The author is indebted to "Harper's Weekly" for permission to republish "Legends of the Puget Sound," and also to John Fitzmaurice for permission to use in an abridged form his excellent story of "DuLuth and the Jesuit's Sun-glass," a legend worthy of the painter, composer, and poet.

The portrait with autograph, and the biographical notice abridged from the New York "Journalist," are by their kind permission inserted by the publishers.

H. B.

28 WORCESTER STREET, BOSTON, MASS.

Hezekiah Butterworth

BIOGRAPHY.

R. HEZEKIAH BUTTERWORTH was born in Warren, R. I., December 22, 1839, his family being among the earliest settlers of Rhode Island. He grew up on the old estates where he worked, in the mean time studying and obtaining his education by teaching, and writing for the popular papers of the day. In 1870 he became connected with the "Youth's Companion" as assistant editor, a position which he has held for nearly twenty years. While engaged in his editorial duties some twelve years ago, the publishing house of Estes & Lauriat showed him a popular French work which gave an account of a French schoolmaster who took a class of boys on a journey with a view of giving them object-lessons in history. Mr. Butterworth, believing that books of narrative and historic stories interwoven would be likely to prove useful to home and school education, wrote a specimen book on the French plan. It was entitled "Zigzag Journeys in Europe." The book was immensely popular, and about forty thousand copies of it have been sold. The educational journals and the press generally saw the purpose of the book, and very highly commended it. One New York paper, however, a critical journal, ridiculed it, and said, "He threatens to go on." Mr. Butterworth did go on. Twelve books of the Zigzag series have been written, and some three hundred thousand volumes sold, proving conclusively the correctness of his theory.

Mr. Butterworth loves the quiet of country home-life; he has a farm home in Warren, R. I., one in Bristol in the same State, and a cottage and orange-grove in Belleview, Florida.

Socially Mr. Butterworth is a delightful man to meet. When he greets you, his hand-shake is cordial and his welcome warm and hearty, putting his visitor at once at perfect ease.

CONTENTS.

Chapter		Page
I.	The American Switzerland	15
II.	Planning a Trip to the Northwest	30
III.	Some Wonderful Statistics	53
IV.	The Comedy for the Holidays	71
V.	Why the Montana Girl was not surprised	97
VI.	Over the Canadian Pacific Railroad to Winnipeg.—The Beauty of the Lakes; or, the Sun-fire: a Dramatic Story of Sault Ste. Marie	118
VII.	A Thousand Miles to the Mountains	143
VIII.	Stories of the Canadian River Songs	169
IX.	Banff	206
X.	In the American Switzerland	253
XI.	Arthur Burns's Ranch	275
XII.	The New Star on the Flag	300

ILLUSTRATIONS.

	PAGE
Tacoma, the Beautiful . . . *Frontispiece*	
Portrait of Hezekiah Butterworth . . .	8
The Land of Promise	16
"Foaming with Cascades"	18
"Pinnacles clothed with Forests of Firs"	19
A Great "Wonderland of Mountain Scenery"	21
"That Immense Northwestern Empire"	23
"Sunset Skies like those which cover the Ionian Isles"	25
"Picturesque Clear-water Streams" . ,	27
"Peaks that pierced the Heavens" . .	28
On the Thames, below London . . .	31
Preparing for Sea	35
Animals of the Northwest	39
Birds of the Northwest	43
Seattle, the Indian Chief	46
Tailpiece	52
A Humble but Happy Home	54
Sheep-shearing	55
Haying on the Prairie	56
Lost Sheep	59
A Farm in the Northwest	60
"Impatient for their Breakfasts " . . .	60
Reluctant to go Home	61
"No Architect ever dreamed of such a Structure before"	63
"He would sit down on a Log by the Roadside"	69
Tailpiece	70

	PAGE
A Hardy Frontier Lad	73
Herding Cattle on the Plains	79
Gathering the Harvest	85
Modern Prairie Farming	91
In the Canadian Woods	99
A Herd of Mountain Sheep	101
A Meadow Brook	104
A Winding Mountain Stream	106
Resting for the Night	107
Liverpool on a Foggy Day	108
The Steamship "America"	109
On the Mersey	111
The Burning Vessel	113
The Banks of Newfoundland	116
The Gulf of St. Lawrence	118
Old Houses in Quebec	119
A Street in Quebec	120
Falls of the Montmorenci	121
The Chaudière Falls	122
Tobogganing	123
Cedar Bay, near Ottawa	124
Sault Ste. Marie	126
Rideau Falls, Ottawa	128
A War Canoe of the Ojibwas	129
The Parliament Buildings, Ottawa . .	132
The University of Toronto	135
A Branch of the St. Lawrence . . .	138
An Island in the Lake of the Woods .	141
A Prairie Station	144
City Hall, Winnipeg	145

ILLUSTRATIONS.

	PAGE
Rafting: breaking a Glut	148
The Thousand Islands	151
South Saskatchewan River, Medicine Hat, Assiniboia	155
A Good Harvest	158
Portaging a Canoe in the Woods of Canada	161
Early Travelling on the Plains	165
Tailpiece	168
The Nipigon	171
"Vive la Canadienne"	'73
An Emigrant Train crossing the Plains	175
Repulsing an Attack on an Emigrant Train	179
A Successful Assault on a Party of Pioneers	189
Preparing a Home in the West	193
Rat Portage, Lake of the Woods	197
The Rocky Mountains from Elbow River	201
A View on the Elbow River	202
One of the Hudson Bay Company's Stations	204
Banff Springs Hotel, Canadian National Park	207
Mount Stephen, near the Summit of the Rockies	211
Mount Stephen House	213
Hydraulic Mining in the Rockies	217
Rocky Mountains, near Canmore	221
Canoeing in the Northwest	225
A Home in the Northwest	229
Goffe, the Regicide, at Hadley	235
Glacier House, Selkirk Mountains	239
Early Settlers	244
The Great Glacier of the Selkirks	247
The Olympian Mountains	251
Yale, on the Fraser River	254
Ottertail Range, Rocky Mountains, B. C.	255

	PAGE
Cariboo Road Bridge over the Fraser River	258
Hotel Vancouver, Vancouver, British Columbia	259
On the Homathco River, British Columbia	260
Trading-ships on the Northwest Coast	263
Vancouver naming the Places on Puget Sound	267
The "Discovery" on the Northwest Coast	271
Tailpiece	274
A Settler's Hut	275
A Frontier House	276
The Great Bluff, Thompson River	277
The Peace River	279
A Cariboo Wagon-road	280
Among the Islands of the Gulf of Georgia	282
"Me and the Bar 's Coming"	285
A Vineyard in British Columbia	287
Indian Salmon Cache	288
Indian Graves	289
View from Esquimalt	291
Seal-driving	293
The Wapiti	294
On the Coast of British Columbia	295
Seymour Narrows, Canadian Pacific Coast	296
Roadway in British Columbia	297
Tailpiece	299
Sunset on the Pacific Coast	301
Mount Tacoma	307
The Oldest Church-tower in America	309
Forest Giants	311
"There is Time enough to finish the Game and beat the Spaniards too"	315
Nature's Monument, Canadian Pacific Coast	319

ZIGZAG JOURNEYS

IN THE

GREAT NORTHWEST.

CHAPTER I.

THE AMERICAN SWITZERLAND.

 PARTY of Americans on their way to Liverpool to take a returning steamer were taking a lunch in the quiet dining-room of the Golden Cross Hotel, at the West End, London. Some of them had been to Hyde Park to see the riding, some to the "Zoo," and one of them to the Guild Hall to visit the queer effigies of the giants Gog and Magog, that have been famous characters in London's history for years, and the originals of which used to appear at the Lord Mayor's shows before the great fire.

Among the party, but not a returning traveller, was a single Englishman, Henry Lette, or "Harry Lette," as he was called, who had been an explorer in the service of the Dominion government in the Northwest Territories.

Several members of the party had been to Switzerland, and the conversation turned upon their adventurous experiences in the land of the mountains, lakes, glaciers, and waterfalls; the beauties of Geneva, Interlachen, and Lucerne.

THE LAND OF PROMISE.

"However picturesque may be the high peaks of the Andes or of India," said an American teacher, whom we will call Mr. Brookes, "they cannot be as noble and impressive as the Alps. There is no land like Switzerland, and there are no mountains in the world so grand as the Alps."

"Have you ever visited British Columbia?" quietly asked Mr.

Lette, "or followed the river Wapta (Kicking Horse) down the Rocky Mountains to the Puget Sound?"

"No," said Mr. Brookes. "I have heard that the Rocky Mountains in British Columbia are very grand; of course the Rocky Mountains and the mountain systems of the Sierras are territorially much larger than Switzerland, but they do not have the sublimity and poetry of Switzerland; do you think they do? The sky of Italy does not hang over them; they do not enchant you and overawe you. So I am led to understand."

"The greater Switzerland is in America," said Mr. Lette. "A few months ago I stood at the foot of a glacier in British Columbia that was nearly forty miles square, and probably contained more solid ice than all the glaciers you have seen in Europe. Over that glacier rose a peak a mile and a half high, like a granite spire of a gigantic ice cathedral, and around it were clustered pinnacles white with snow, foaming with cascades, and clothed with forests of firs, some of the trees in which were of such wonderful size and height that you would think me a Baron Münchausen were I to describe them. The Alps, as you say, are small in extent in comparison with the great Rocky Mountain system, but I cannot agree with you in regard to their superiority in grandeur and beauty. Did you ever meet any one who had seen the Bow River and Devil's Head Lake, at Banff Hot Springs, in the Canadian National Park?"

"No," said Mr. Brookes. "The Canadian National Park, to my mind, is merely a name."

"And yet it is destined to be the Baden-Baden of America. The Hot Springs of Sulphur Mountain are the best known cure for certain rheumatic diseases. But that is not to the point. If ever you shall take a row on the Bow River, and make a study of its clear emerald waters under the great shadows of Cascade Mountains,—waters that might have been the gardens of Undine or fairy sprites,—you will be likely to change your views in regard to the beauty of the American

Alps; and should you ever see a sunset on the Puget Sound and on Mt. Tacoma, at Seattle or Tacoma, or in the violet waters of Elliott Bay or Commencement Bay, you will find that there are Italies and Floridas that yet await the poet and the painter. The fact is — pardon my plainness — you Americans do not know your own country, nor *ours;* for the Puget Sound Empire belongs partly to the Dominion and partly to the United States. No one who has been to Banff or the Glacier House, to Elliott Bay or Tacoma, will experience surprise on visiting the

"FOAMING WITH CASCADES."

Alps or Italy. A June sunset on the aerial dome of Mount Tacoma, 14,444 feet high, with its changing splendors, has no equal in beauty

"PINNACLES CLOTHED WITH FORESTS OF FIRS."

on the Italian Apennines, nor are there any skies in Europe more lovely than those of the long twilights of the Puget Sound. I have seen the Salvation Army on the plateau at West Seattle, singing from their finely printed hymn-books in the light of the red twilight at half-past nine o'clock.

"You may think me partial, but the greater wonderland of mountain scenery is not the Alps, but British Columbia,—the mighty sweep of the Rockies and the Sierras. The Columbia River with the surprise of Mount Hood is in itself, and apart from traditions, more beautiful than the Rhine; and the Wapta is the true poem of all waters."

"Then we have been visiting Europe second-hand," said an American lady, "like one who misses the date, and goes to the fair the day after the sights and scenes. We ought to have gone to the Puget Sound country before going to Switzerland."

"In that case your present visit would have made you perfectly satisfied with your own country. Europe is covered with American artists, musicians, and poets, hurrying hither and thither in search of beauty and inspiration. Your truly great artists are those who have eyes to see the wonders of your own land."

An English servant was listening eagerly to Mr. Lette.

"Beg pardon, sir; but what kind of a country would that be for a poor man to get a livin' in?"

"You are excusable, quite. I would ask that question myself were I in your place. The best opportunity in all the world for a poor man lies in British Columbia, Washington, and Oregon. The climate is a long April day. The governments will give you a farm that will produce almost everything; fuel costs nothing; there is plenty of work for industrious hands; and the future of that great empire is the future of the progress of the world. The new and the greater America is there. Vancouver is likely one day to rival Montreal, and Seattle, New York. The gods have saved the best of the feast to the last."

"Isn't your language rather Oriental?" asked a quiet-looking woman. "A son of one of my neighbors went to Seattle, but he came back again somewhat poorer than he started."

"Did he amount to anything at home?"

"No; he hadn't any great amount of force."

"People who amount to nothing at home have just the same value wherever they may go; and people who go to new places because they amount to nothing at home, will be likely to return again for the

A GREAT "WONDERLAND OF MOUNTAIN SCENERY."

same reason. But I have seen such a miracle as a shiftless man changed into an industrious one under the inspiring activities of Vancouver, Seattle, and Tacoma. Everybody is full of life and energy in those new cities, and he would be worthless indeed who did not feel their industrial force. Such a man must be either very unfortunate or a born failure.

"Think of that immense Northwestern Empire," continued Mr. Lette. "Passing by the vast plains of the Northwestern Territories and the prairie steppes, the great hard-wheat-growing empires of the Red River of the North, the Lake of the Woods, and the Assiniboine and Peace rivers, let us glance at

BRITISH COLUMBIA,

only since 1871 a part of the Dominion of Canada, but now teeming with a delighted population, and building the great port cities of the Puget Sound and the British Possessions. Here rises Mount Brown, sixteen thousand feet high. Here is the Canadian National Park, with its foaming cascades. Here are Alpine-like pastures and grand plateaus, picturesque and wonderful clear-water lakes and streams and glacial rivers. Here are natural sanitariums, and airs of life and healing. Here is a climate as lovely as Florida during much of the year, and sunset skies like those which cover the Ionian Isles. Here are stupendous forests and rich fisheries. Here are mines everywhere; the mountains are treasure-houses of gold, silver, and copper, and abound in iron and coal. Here flows the gigantic Fraser River, and here sparkles the wood-shadowed Gulf of Georgia. Here is the old city of Victoria, in a climate like the south of England, and the new city of New Westminster on the hills overlooking the calmly flowing Fraser, and itself overlooked by the white brow of Mount Baker. And here is the port of Vancouver, which is connected with all the ports of the Pacific; mountain-walled and forest-sheltered, most beautiful in situation, and gathering to itself peoples from all lands, and hospitable even to the people of China and Japan.

"And what a romantic and almost unread history it all has! Think of the names of the early explorers whose adventurous exploits would fill a story-book, — Juan de Fuca, Cook, Vancouver, Puget, Baker, Rainier, Mackenzie, and the old settlers of Victoria! This unknown land is already full of legends and traditions worthy of a poet's pen."

"THAT IMMENSE NORTHWESTERN EMPIRE."

THE AMERICAN SWITZERLAND.

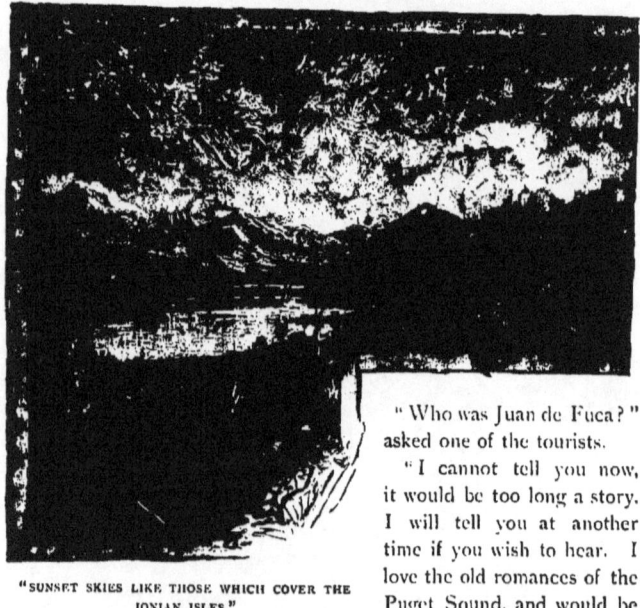

"SUNSET SKIES LIKE THOSE WHICH COVER THE IONIAN ISLES."

"Who was Juan de Fuca?" asked one of the tourists.

"I cannot tell you now, it would be too long a story. I will tell you at another time if you wish to hear. I love the old romances of the Puget Sound, and would be glad to tell them to you in the future, if you have ears to listen. I look upon British Columbia as one of the best places for a poor young man in all the British Empire; as the place that offers him the largest opportunity and the most of happiness and reasonable expectation."

It was evident that Mr. Lette had made the last thought the inspiration of his life, and that he would repeat it over and over wherever he should go. A good hobby is a good thing, and life is usually the better for one.

The waiter stood with wide eyes, and the curves of his face were all interrogation points, while Mr. Lette recounted the grandeur and the glories of the scenery of British Columbia. When the explorer came to a conclusion, the man fanned himself with his napkin, and exclaimed, —

"Hi declare! Hi will go there; hit must be a suitable place for a British subject to live hin. How far is hit from Quebec, may I hask?"

"More than three thousand miles."

"All rail?"

"Yes, all rail." Mr. Lette tilted back in his chair. The new empire was filling his vision again. "'T is the most wonderful road ever made by human hands," said he, "that

CANADIAN PACIFIC RAILROAD,

stretching from the Atlantic to the Pacific, and bridging the two oceans with an iron highway.

"I well recall the day that the great road was completed. It was the 7th of November, 1885, in the Wild Eagle Pass of the Gold Range of mountains. For five years the road had been virtually in progress, moving from Winnipeg toward the mountains and from Winnipeg toward the sea, and from the Pacific toward the mountain climbers from the steppes and plains. It had been undertaken before this period by the government; but after many delays it was decided in 1880 to surrender the stupendous work to a private company. Then it was that the enterprise was undertaken in earnest. The government put at the disposal of the company millions of money and millions of acres of land; an army of engineers and laborers mustered, armed with pickaxes, powder, and dynamite; Manitoba was soon crossed —"

"How do you pronounce that word?" was the waiter's unexpected interruption.

"PICTURESQUE CLEAR-WATER STREAMS."

"Manitoba'," said Mr. Lette, "although most people say Manito'ba. It is manitou-*ba;* that is, the manitou, or god, *speaks.*"

"I see," said the intelligent waiter; "the sheep said *baa.*"

"Yes, yes," said Mr. Lette, "so I see."

"I have a brother who lives in Minnesota'," said the luminous waiter.

"No, no," answered several of the tourists.

"I was saying," continued Mr. Lette, "that Manitoba' was soon crossed, and Assiniboia as rapidly. Then began the battle of the hills. Look on the map, and you may see the march of the army of engineers and laborers, up to Banff,—so called from the Scottish estates,—four thousand feet, then on, up, higher and higher, under peaks that pierced the heavens, over streams that for ages had been breaking the rocks in the cañons below, up to the ledge pastures of the mountain goat and the home of the eagle. At the end of the first year the engineers and navvies had advanced one hundred and sixty miles from Winnipeg. During the second year four hundred and fifty miles had been accomplished; the end of the third year found them amid the blue skies of the Rockies, and the fourth year in the snow-castled regions of the Selkirks, more than a thousand miles from the mid-ocean city, the Chicago of the British Empire. The two armies met in the Gold Mountains. Clank! The last spike was driven. The two oceans were bridged; the Rocky Mountains were conquered and bound, never to be released. England might now travel toward the Orient, to China and Japan, in the continuous lights of her own ships and homes, and in the shadow of Saint George's Cross.

"PEAKS THAT PIERCED THE HEAVENS."

"The construction of the road had not only conquered the Rockies and linked the two oceans, it had done more; it had bound the greater half of North America to England in bonds stronger than iron. That clang on the last spike had riveted the two continents of the possessions of the English crown, and made a greater England possible on this side of the Atlantic. War has its heroes, and so has peace. And among the heroes of the arts of peace, none are more deserving of honor than the statesmen, capitalists, engineers, navvies, and laborers of the Canadian Pacific Railroad."

"Hat! your honor," said the enlightened waiter, touching the bare place on his forehead where a hat-brim, had one been there, might have added grace to the obeisance.

The next morning the party of tourists left for Liverpool.

THE FOUR GREAT EMPIRES.

Russia	7,012,874 square miles
Dominion of Canada	3,127,041 " "
United States	2,999,848 " "
Brazil	2,408,104 " "

CHAPTER II.

PLANNING A TRIP TO THE NORTHWEST.

N our last volume we left Aunt Helen Mar Hampden and her nephew Charles Hampden and niece Mary Hampden at the Golden Cross Hotel, London The Hampdens, from Bristol, Rhode Island, had made an educational tour to Great Hampden, England, hoping thereby to be able to find proof that the great John Hampden, the father of English liberty, had once visited America, and the shores where they lived, in order to provide a place of refuge for the English patriots in case the cause of the people against royal tyranny should fail. In this secret service, in 1623, it is supposed that he visited the great Sachem Massasoit, who then lived at Pokanoket, now Warren and Bristol, and finding him sick, helped to nurse him back to health. The supposed place of the meeting of these two great characters of history is called Massasoit Spring, near one of the wharves in Warren. At the time when we took leave of the Hampden family in our last volume, Aunt Helen Mar had not been able to secure the positive evidence of Hampden's visit to America. She still had faith, however, that such proof existed, and that one day it would be made clear to her.

While the Hampdens were in England they stopped much at the old Golden Cross Hotel. Here they met Mr. Lette, whom we have introduced. They had chanced to overhear the description

ON THE THAMES, BELOW LONDON.

of the American Switzerland which Mr. Lette had given to the returning party of travellers from the States. It had deeply interested them.

"I would rather visit British Columbia," said Charles Hampden, "than go to Switzerland."

"And I," said Mary Hampden.

Aunt Helen Mar Hampden was not so decided at this time.

The Hampdens had intended to return to America in the autumn or early in the winter. But they had learned the strange fact which surprises most Americans, — that they could live much more cheaply in English towns than at home. So as the journey was an educational one, they resolved to remain in London, or near London, until spring, and then perhaps visit Switzerland, and return early in the summer to the States.

They often met Mr. Lette, and young Charles Hampden and the old explorer formed a very warm and intimate acquaintance. They went to amusements together, — to the Royal Albert Hall, the art galleries, and museums. They made frequent journeys in company to Sydenham Palace, Hampden Court, and other places. They would often take the boats that ply the Thames, to have a quiet outing on the river, enjoying the ever changing panorama. Sometimes they would extend their journeys and take longer sails to the mouth of the Thames, watching with interest the boats preparing for sea. Almost always after their interviews and outings Charles would say to his aunt, —

"I would rather visit the American Switzerland."

One day he added to this declaration the further information that Mr. Lette would accompany a party of emigrants in the spring to Vancouver and Seattle.

Not long after this he unfolded the following plan : —

"Let us return to Portland, Maine, with Mr. Lette in the spring, on the winter service of the Allan Line of steamers, and go with him to British Columbia and Washington and Oregon, instead of making the Swiss trip."

This plan did not meet Aunt Mar's approval, but it gained a point.

"We will not return to Portland in the spring," she said, "but we will go to Switzerland, and meet Mr. Lette at Montreal in the summer, when he is to make a second trip with a second party of emigrants to the cities of the Puget Sound. And you may go with him, if he is willing."

This seemed a most delightful plan to our young traveller. It would bring the two Switzerlands in contrast. In the mean time Charles would learn as much as possible in regard to both these lands of glaciers, waterfalls, and beautiful valleys.

One evening, at the Golden Cross, Charles asked Mr. Lette in regard to the birds and animals of the Canadian plains, mountains, and the Puget Sound. He was interested in the natural history of new places, and listened eagerly to Mr. Lette's reply.

CURIOUS ANIMALS OF THE NORTHWEST.

"Canada is the home of the finest fur-bearing animals. One still meets foxes along the line of the railroad, and it is a favorite diversion of the passengers to watch them from the windows of the train. On the plains they live in villages, hunt gophers and mice, and are very cunning in avoiding snares and traps. The coyote is often seen by the settler, though the herds of buffalo that it once followed are gone. The great gray wolf may still be seen hiding from the train or horseman. Horses are greatly afraid of this merciless animal, which will hamstring a stray horse on the plains.

"Archbishop Tache relates some anecdotes of the prairie wolf which illustrates its cunning instincts, and which I will give you from his narrative.

PREPARING FOR SEA.

"'A fisherman was in the habit of intrusting fish to one of his dogs for his master. To prevent the dog being attacked by wolves, the man attached bells to the animal. The dog performed his duty daily for several consecutive winters; but on one occasion, the bells being forgotten, the poor animal was eaten up, and the splendid fish that the delicate attentions of a poor servant intended for the chief of a post, became, with their carrier, a feast for wolves.

"'While I was staying at Isle à la Crosse, three large wolves, one black and two gray, made havoc among our train dogs, eating several of them. Their cunning in avoiding traps enabling them to escape the death planned for them, a price was set upon their heads.

"'An old Canadian, by the name of Morin, made a great effort to gain the reward, and the skins. A skilled trapper, he made use of all his experience in setting his best spring traps, which, as usual, he fastened by a chain to a very large piece of wood. All the dogs were carefully locked up, and every other precaution adopted to make the three troublesome visitors hungry. Morin visited his traps daily, and everybody was in the habit of going to meet him on his return, to learn the result of his expedition. The subject was the theme of the day.

"'There came a furious storm, during which the trapper remained at home. Calm weather followed, and the old Canadian went to visit his traps; in the distance he saw snow covering one of the three thieves that had been caught; a second trap had been set off unsuccessfully, and the third had disappeared; disorder reigned in the pack of wolves; the others never appeared again.

"'Morin, after long and vain searching, was regretting the loss of his trap, when, a month having elapsed, the people of Green Lake, about ninety miles from Isle à la Crosse, saw a wolf walking on one of their lakes, apparently with difficulty. Several dogs were sent after him; he was caught and killed. He was no other than one of the rogues from Isle à la Crosse, for the trap was still attach.. o his leg. The chain and log of wood were detached at the time of his companion's death; he had wandered in every direction through the forest for a whole month, dragging this heavy and cruel encumbrance in the midst of the most intense cold. This wolf was reduced to a mere walking skeleton, but the occurrence indicates a power and tenacity of life in the animal, difficult to understand.'

WOLVERINES.

" The wolverine is noted for its great strength and its skill in feats of strategy. Its cunning indicates the faculty of reason, or what is like it. Archbishop Tache relates some anecdotes to the point; the first, of a wolverine that had robbed a hunter's hiding-place of a gun and some food. The archbishop says: —

"'After a long search we first found the leathern gun-case, which had been taken off the gun, for it had been carefully put on to protect and conceal the piece. Then, in another direction and farther away, we found the gun under the trunk of a tree; leaves had been thrown over it, and scattered for some distance around as if to conceal the tracks of the thief. We should certainly have concluded that a man had been at work, had not the deep solitude of the forest obliged us to recognize the acts of a wolverine, of which traces were everywhere visible in the neighborhood.

"'If the skilfulness of the wolverine sometimes insures him success, here is an incident that proves his mischief frequently brings punishment. An Indian had left his lodge without any one to look after it. A wolverine presently entered the deserted habitation, brought out, one by one, all the things he found inside, and hid them here and there, and even far away from the lodge. There remained only a bag of gunpowder. This the animal seized between his teeth, and concealed among the cinders in the fireplace. Some fuel still unextinguished soon burnt the bag, and caused an explosion, of which the roguish wolverine was the first victim; for it stretched him dead on the spot, scattering the brains of the thief right and left.'

"The black bear of Canada is harmless, and runs from man. The grizzlies are of course a source of terror to man and beast. They have been known to carry away Indian women, like the tigers of India. An Indian sometimes has escaped from a grizzly after capture by feigning death.

"The beautiful prog-horned antelope has almost wholly disappeared from the buffalo plains. Moose still abound in the region of Peace River, and the caribou in the north. The Big Hor: or Rocky Mountain sheep grazes on the wooded slopes of the mountains. The bones of the bison are found everywhere, but the great herds are gone forever."

ANIMALS OF THE NORTHWEST.

BIRDS.

"The birds of Canada are chiefly the inhabitants of the woods, lakes, and thickets. They consist of thrushes and finches, robins and swallows, white-winged blackbirds and rose-breasted grossbeaks. The prairies abound with meadow larks and bobolinks. The Canadian jay and cow-bird are the travellers, and the woodpeckers the stay-at-homes. Owls hoot in the dark recesses of the forests, and ospreys and eagles wheel over the forests near the coasts. The game-birds are the grouse, partridge, and prairie-hen. Herons, cranes, snipes, and plovers are common near the coast and about the lakes and ponds, and wild geese and ducks of many kinds furnish abundant game in the same marshy places. Grebes, or water-hens, build their nests on the sedges that rise and fall with the water. The Avi-fauna of the Northwest Territories numbers some two hundred and fifty species."

Among the many places of interest that Mr. Lette and young Charles Hampden attended was a school of working-boys, to which free instruction was given evenings. These boys were for the most part the orphan sons of English sailors, to whom a home had been given until they were prepared to enter the trades. The school was called the Grace Darling Institute. The boys of the Institute were as greatly interested as Charles Hampden in Mr. Lette's Canadian experiences. In fact, so interested did they become, that several of them wished to go to America and take homesteads, on their becoming of age, in Manitoba, Assiniboia, Alberta, or British Columbia.

Mr. Lette had delivered before the Institute a course of lectures on these provinces, and the opportunities for settlement which they offered. No topics could excite a more eager ear than these new lands.

One of these lectures related to the stories and legends of the new cities on the Puget Sound. It was a record of facts gathered during his own travels from Vancouver, B. C., to Olympia, Washington, and up the Oregon or Columbia River. It contained some very curious incidents, and we give it here, as a preparation for the interesting journey which young Hampden had decided to make, in hope that it may awaken a desire in our reader's mind to follow him.

STRANGE LEGENDS OF PUGET SOUND.

New America is rising on the shores of the vast and romantic fiord called by the Indians the Whulge, but known to modern geographers as Puget Sound. Already the prophets of Seattle claim that their city will one day be the larger New York. "We shall be," they say, "the port of the Pacific and of Asia. We shall distribute our commodities through the vast empire west of the Mississippi as New York does through the east. We are to be the lumber-yard of the world. Pennsylvanias of coal and unknown mountain treasure-houses of all kinds of ores lie behind us, and the quiet waterways to all lands before us, and one of the three great cities of modern times must here lift its domes of industry over the sunset sea."

Tacoma, the beautiful, makes the same claim, and argues that she not only has the port on which are to ride the ships of the world, but the Northern Pacific Railroad as the direct route to the shop towns and cities of the East. The most beautifully situated of all American cities, the Naples of the North, on the new Mediterranean, with Mount Tacoma spread out like a celestial tent above her, the most splendid and poetic peak in the American atmosphere, Tacoma has literary and artistic as well as commercial aspirations. These ambitions are well founded, if we may trust the modern prophets. Says the author of the "Vestiges of the Natural History of Creation," Robert Chambers, "When the populations of America shall reach the Pacific, the literary period of that country will begin."

Theodore Winthrop, drifting down the Puget Sound in a canoe, prophesied that religion would find its new spiritual development and evolution among the nations that were to gather there. The march of progress here holds her steeds in the blaze of the sunset, with the crystal tent of Tacoma like a deserted abode of the gods of the golden age in the sky. The axe and hammer

BIRDS OF THE NORTHWEST.

have begun their work everywhere in all these lands of the woods. Troy was, and Troys are to be. The Puget Sound laborer, with faith in the future, smites the giant trees. But let the prophets pass and the poets come, here surely is to be a great political empire, and the literary sense is awakening to the fact, and beginning to inquire about the old romances and traditions of these new-created scenes.

The Puget Sound country is rich in legendary lore, and here new School-crafts and Longfellows, new poets and composers and painters and artists, may find a field worthy of a higher inspiration. The religion of the Puget Sound Indians is spiritualism: every tree has its soul, and all the mountains are the abodes of invisible gods; personification, as in ancient Greece, is everywhere, and all the truths of life are taught in parable.

The student from the North unrolls his map, and asks, "Who was Juan de Fuca?" He finds that the strait that opens this new world was named after an Italian romancer and pretended discoverer. And he next asks, "Who was Puget, and why was that name given to the Indian Whulge?" Even the cyclopædias are silent here, as are Wilkes, Swan, and Victor; but the old pioneer will tell you that Puget was the chivalrous lieutenant of Vancouver, and that he measured the one hundred and twenty miles of the winding sea, and fathomed its sea-green waters, and saw the celestial tent of Mount Tacoma spread in the sky, and dreamed in the bright days of 1792 that he would soon enter a marvellous river that would run from the Pacific to the Atlantic. So he drifted on in the wonderland anywhither; but although the sky was domed with crystal, the open river to the Atlantic did not appear. The way to the Atlantic was to come; but it was to be iron and steam. Puget's old camping-ground is still shown to the tourist on the Whulge. His body should be brought there, and his monument bear the name of the sea. But his name is already written eternally on the waters, like Vancouver's on the island, where also infant cities are at play with the axe and hammer. Puget's romantic dreams, like that of the old adelantado of Florida and Bimini, were allegorical: the types of stupendous realities, like a child's visions of life.

TACOMA'S FIRE BATTLE.

Theodore Winthrop, in his "Canoe and Saddle," fixed the Siwash name of Tacoma on Mount Rainier or Regnier. The Seattle people still call the mountain Rainier; and you may know a Seattle man by the emphatic use that he makes of this word. "Rainier" is never allowed to be so much as uttered in Tacoma. The legend of Tacoma evolved through the lively and picturesque imagination of Theodore Winthrop may be found in "Canoe and Saddle," a Rip Van Winkle medley of little classic importance, and we will not repeat it here. The Siwashes have a nobler legend of the mountain, growing out of the probable view that it was once a volcano. Once, in times dim and distant, the tamanouses, or guardian spirits, of the mountain became enraged with the tamanouses of Mount Hood, who were acting unruly, and tossing, as we may imagine, stones and smoke and fire into the air. To teach Mount Hood a lesson and make him more quiet in his manners among the monarchs of the air, Tacoma began to stone the rival peak. Some of the stones thrown by Tacoma fell short, and a terrible accident happened, the bad effects of which remain to this day. Some of the rocks thrown by Tacoma fell into the Columbia River and turned it aside, and caused the Cascades and Dalles. You may see them there today. That is why the steamboat from Portland, Oregon, cannot go all the way up the New Rhine.

SEATTLE, THE INDIAN CHIEF.

Tacoma has learned the arts of peace since then, and buried under mighty glaciers her spiteful fires. Mount Hood smokes a little at times, but he too is becoming quiet. Men will soon blow the rocks out of the Columbia, and illumine Mount Tacoma and Mount Hood with red fires on Fourth-of-July nights, and then all the land of the new empire will be peace. This legend has grand outlines. Like many of the Siwash tales, it is stupendous, and the proofs of it are wonderfully visible.

STORY OF ANGELINE SEATTLE.

Poor old Angeline Seattle,—the Princess Angeline! Her flat, tan-colored face, fiery black eyes, and black hair are a familiar picture in the streets of the new city, where she sits down daily on some log or shoe-box to marvel at all that is going on. Now and then she hies away to beg " one bit " or " two bits " of Henry Yesler or some other old pioneer. She is a very happy mortal if you please her, and very ugly if you tease her. She is the daughter of Seattle, the chief who gave the name to the lively and ambitious city whose prophets claim the earth. Her legend is: Once upon a time the town of Seattle was surrounded by a union of the war tribes bent on its destruction. Warriors were hiding in every bush. Angeline, the princess, the daughter of the chief, discovered the plot and the plans to murder the town, and she stole away from her lodge under " the moon and stars," and came to the imperilled place, and gave the old settlers warning. Was her warning true ? Many laughed at it. The war-ship " Decatur " lay in the harbor. The captain determined to shell the woods. The Indians understood the " one shot " of the cannon-ball, but not the " two shot " of the shell. The sight of a ball that would *shoot again* was to them a miracle. The " two-shot" balls caused such an astonishment in the woods that a hideous yell arose, and the Princess Angeline's warning was proven to be an episode of heroism.

It seems a pity to doubt so desirable a story, especially as old Angeline is a very benevolent soul, and gives away to others nearly everything she has or begs. But Mr. Yesler, the old pioneer and mayor, has recently written an article, in which he claims that it was old Curley, a friendly Indian, who gave the warning and caused the shelling of the woods. We visited Mr. Yesler, and he denied the heroic claims of the Princess Angeline. Veto. We must know the truth, so went to the palace of the princess herself.

The palace of this daughter of the hero-chieftain of the new New York consisted of a hovel or tent of boards on the side of a hill, among other hovels and pans and kettles, and stumps innumerable. We knocked at the door. A dog came to meet us. One dislikes to meet a dog at the door in an Indian town. We went away cautiously, and looked over the bay, and listened to a thousand hammers, which one may hear anywhere. Then we came back again over the charred stumps. The palace door was open, and on the step sat the dumpy form of the daughter of the great Seattle.

" Are you Angeline, the daughter of the chief? "

A nod, — a bow nod. Triumph!
I gave her one bit. Her face beamed.
"*Nika attle copa mika.*"
"Did you save Seattle during the war?"
A low bow. There, Henry Yesler, that settles it. She herself said, and it is greatly to her credit. We gave her another bit.
"*Mitlite.*"
"Yes, I will sit down;" and I did, and she "shooed" away the suspicious-looking dog, and there on the palace step I had a talk with the venerable princess, the once lovely heroine of Seattle. Paint her picture, somebody; she will not be here long to watch the progress of the city from the log or shoe-box.

The "great Seattle," — who was he? The lord of all the Indians, one would suppose. Veto again. He came with Dr. Maynard, the pioneer, to Seattle, and was true to the interests of the whites; and so Governor Stevens, the great territorial governor, made him a titular chief, and the new town received his name.

THE COPPER CANOE.

Long, long ago, say the Siwashes, in the splendid sunsets of the Whulge, or Puget Sound, there came a canoe of copper, sailing, sailing. The painted forest lords and feathered maidens saw it from the bluffs, — in the sunrise at times, or in the moonsets, but ever in the red sunsets, sailing, sailing. The gleam of copper in the red sunset is more beautiful than gold; and ever and anon on the blue wave was seen the burnished gleam of the copper canoe.

On it came, and the solitary voyager in the copper canoe landed at last on the Whulge, under the crystal dome of Mount Tacoma, and he shadowed among the cool firs of the headlands there the boat that flashed out the rays of sunset light.

He called together the tribes. They came in canoes from everywhere. He began to teach and preach. "I come among you as a preacher of righteousness," he said, or thoughts like these. "All that men can possess in this world, or any other, is righteousness. If a man have that he is rich though he be poor, and his soul shall rise, rise, rise, and live forever.

"O Siwashes," he preached, "the unseen power that thinks and causes you to act is the soul. It does not die when the breath vanishes. It goes away with the unseen life, and inhabits the life unseen. You have never seen the soul or life; but death is only the beginning of a longer life, and the soul with righteous longings shall be happy forever.

"But war is wrong, — the spear, the arrow, and the spilling of human blood. Man may not kill his brother. The soul was meant for peace."

He preached these or like doctrines, a beautiful gospel, like the Sermon on the Mount.

The warlike tribes rejected the word. They nailed to a tree the Saviour who came gleaming over the violet sea in the copper canoe, and he died there. They took down his body; but, wonder of wonders! it rose from the dead, and appeared to all the tribes, and the risen Saviour preached the same doctrine of righteousness and immortality as before. The legend may have been derived from the preaching of some forest priest in some distant place, for the Catholic missionaries were on the coast of California before 1700.

THE STORY OF THE STONE SHOES.

As curious and wonderful is the Siwash tradition of the flood, which may have had a like origin. There once fell upon the earth a long and terrible rain; the Whulge arose; it filled the mountain walls, and all the tribes perished except one man. He fled before the rising waters up the sides of Mount Tacoma, or Rainier, or Ranier. The waters rose and covered the mountain. They swept over his feet; they came to his knees, to his waist. He seemed about to be swept away, when his feet turned to stone. Then the rain ceased. The clouds broke and the blue sky came again, and the waters began to sink.

The one man stood there on the top of Rainier. He could not lift his feet; they were rocks. Birds flew again, flowers bloomed again, but he could not go.

Then the Spirit of All Things came to him. "Sleep," said he. And the one man with stone feet slept.

As he slept there the Spirit of All Things took from him a rib and made of it a woman. When he awoke, there stood his wife ready-made on the top of Mount Tacoma. His stone shoes dropped off, and the happy pair came down the mountain to the wooded paradises of the Whulge on the sunset sea. Here sprung the human race at the foot of Mount Tacoma, or Rainier, or Ranier. Hear that, O ye builders of the new cities! The golden age began with you, and it is yours to bring it back again. The ark, however, did not rest on Mount Tacoma; we are sorry for that. Yet this legend is worth any two traditions of the ark; it is the story of Adam, Eve, and Noah all in one. Are the stone shoes yet on the top of the mountain, like the rocks tossed by the tamanouses in the cascades of the Columbia? It is a hard climb up the mountain. The traveller begins to bleed from eyes and ears at the height of eleven thousand feet; and it is very hot in the thin air, although the glaciers lie beneath. But these stone shoes would be worth going up to get. Who shall find them, the "Rainier" man or the "Tacoma" man of the rival cities?

THE INDIAN POTLATCH.

The devil dance has been forbidden by the British government among the Canadian tribes. It was once the great feature of all the potlatches. The potlatch is a feast of gifts. The wealthiest man of the tribe makes a potlatch, or feast, and gives away to his own tribe or a neighboring tribe all that he possesses, and whoever gives a potlatch becomes an Indian grandee or lord. The inspiring plan of this Northern feast is benevolent, though somewhat vain; but the ceremonies used to be of the most horrid character, especially the tamanous dance, or spirit dance, and the devil dance, which was a dance of blood.

"I once witnessed a potlatch," said a pioneer missionary, "and I hope I may never see such a scene again. I had landed among a tribe of northern Siwashes on the Whulge, where I had gathered a little church some months before, and I expected to hold a meeting, on the night I came, in one of the cabins. The place was deserted; the woods were all silent. Sunset flashed his red light along the sea, — such a sunset as one only sees here in these northern latitudes, — a wannish glare of smoky crimson lingering long into the night. As soon as the sun went down I began to hear a piping sound like birds in all the woods around. One call answered another everywhere. I had never heard a sound like that. I tried to approach one of these sounds, but it receded before me.

"Suddenly a great fire blazed up and lit the sky. I approached it; it was built on a little prairie. Near it was a huge platform, covered with canoes, blankets, pressed fish, berry cakes, soap-olalely, or berry soap, wampum, and beads. Not an Indian was in sight save one. She was an old squaw bound to a stake or tree.

"'What is this?' I asked in Chinook.

"'Cultus tee-hee,
Cultus hee-hee,
Dah-blo!'

she wailed in Chinook.

"'When, — *tamala*' (to-morrow)?
"'Ding, ding —
'Cultus tee-hee,
Cultus hee-hee,
Dah-blo!'

"Then I knew that all was preparation for a potlatch, and that there was to be a devil dance — ding, ding — at that very hour.

"It was a night of the full moon; such a night would be selected for such a ceremony. The moon rose red in the smoky air, and the sounds like the bird-calls grew louder and wilder. There was a yell; it was answered everywhere; and hundreds of Indians in paint and masks came running out of the timber upon the prairie. Some were on all fours, some had the heads of beasts, fishes, and birds, some had wings, and many had *tails*.

"Then came the biters, attended by raving squaws. The biters were to tear the flesh from the arms of any who were not found at the dance after a certain hour.

"Now the drums began to beat and the shells to blow. Indians poured out of the woods in paint, blankets, and beads. A great circle was formed; the tamanous, or spirit dance, was enacted. Great gifts were made at a powwow, or wahwah. Then the great dark crowd grew frantic, and under the full moon gleaming on high came the devil dance.

"The first victim was a live dog. He was seized, torn in pieces, and eaten by the dancers, so as to redden their faces with blood. The yells were now more furious; the dancers leaped into the air, and circled round the old woman tied to the tree. I will not describe the sickening sight that followed; I will only say that the old hag who was accused of 'casting an evil-eye' shared the same fate as the dog.

"'Why do you worship the Devil?' I asked an exhausted brave the next day.

"'Good spirit always good; him we no fear. Please the Devil, and him no harm you. All well, happy; good tamanous, bad tamanous. See?'

"It was plain, — the old philosophy of the sinking sailor, who prayed, 'Good Lord! good Devil!' The tradition was — it came out of the long past — that the Devil must be appeased."

They are vanishing, — the tribes, — and it is time to gather up the old legends. The Southern Pacific Railroad is to run *up* to Seattle, and the Canadian Pacific *down* to Seattle, and the city will sit like a jewel in the great ring of iron that runs round the coast of North

America. Tacoma's triumphal road strikes at once the States, and here the past is forever to go and the future forever to come; here on the woody shores of the sunset are the castellated headlands of the Whulge. One of the old legends states that the tamanous once stole the sun and hid it. It was happily found, and the theft is not likely to occur again in the new empire of the North and West, that will one day largely dominate the States, and perhaps lead the thoughts of mankind.

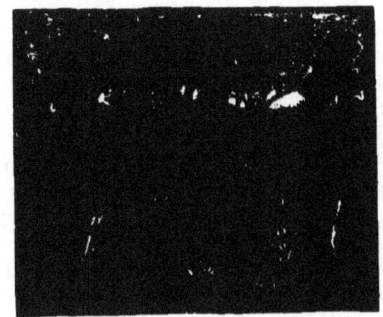

CHAPTER III.

SOME WONDERFUL STATISTICS.

T one of his lectures before the Grace Darling Institute Mr. Lette made a tabular statement which greatly surprised young Charles Hampden as well as the sons of the sailors. He pronounced the words of this statement so slowly and evenly and impressively that it made even statistics interesting. He said:—

"The Island of Great Britain has about 90,000 square miles. New England, in the United States, which includes six States, has 65,000 square miles. The great State of New York contains 47,000 square miles, and the State of New Hampshire, the New England Switzerland, about 9,000 square miles.

"Now, boys, listen. The original British Columbia, the real American Switzerland, contains 220,000 square miles, and is not only much greater than the United Kingdom of Great Britain and Ireland (32,000 square miles), but would make four countries as large as old England, three countries larger than New England, four countries larger than New York, and more than *twenty* countries as large as New Hampshire. Yet British Columbia is not so large as the State of Texas, which has an area of 274,000 square miles. The most wonderful American province of the English crown is British Columbia, and it must one day rise to one of the great maritime powers of the world."

Mr. Lette delighted to repeat this prophetic statement.

There was another tabular statement which he made in regard to the Swiss Alps and the American Rocky Mountain systems of British Columbia and the Californian Sierras, which as greatly astonished Aunt Mar.

"The superficial area of Switzerland," he said, "not including the Lakes, is about 15,000 square miles. The mean elevation of the highest range of mountains is from 8,000 to 9,000 feet. The highest point of the St. Bernard Pass is 7,190 feet, and of the Great St.

A HUMBLE BUT HAPPY HOME.

Bernard, 8,170. The loftiest pass in the Alps (Col of Mont Cervin) is 11,200 feet. This is the highest pass in Europe. Mont Blanc is 15,744 feet high, — a little higher than Mount Tacoma; the Jungfrau is 13,716 feet high. But Mount Brown, in British Columbia, is 16,000 feet high; and there is a single plain in Montana which is as large as the States of Ohio and Indiana combined, and in which four Switzerlands might be placed and be overlooked by the American Alps around them. As I find myself often saying, there is a single glacier in British Columbia that probably contains more ice than is to be found on all the Alps. But the ranges of the Rockies which run through the Sierras south, and to Alaska north, form a system that leaves the Alps a mere child in comparison. Let me make an arithmetical table of the two Switzerlands on the blackboard.

British Columbia	220,000	square miles.
Switzerland and Alpine Provinces	20,000	"
	200,000	" "

"I have included the Lakes and the old boundaries in this statement. How does it look? Would you not think that an American traveller would wish to see his own land before seeing Europe?"

The free use of such statistics as these so greatly interested the boys of the Institute in this wonderful empire of the Northwest, that they began to make inquiries how an emigrant from Europe could go there, and what were the terms of obtaining land and making settlements. Mr. Lette appointed an evening for a very curious lecture, which should consist of answering such questions in regard to emigration and homesteading as any of the boys might like to ask. Among the questions asked were these:—

SHEEP-SHEARING.

Question. Who are entitled to government lands, and how may such lands be obtained by the emigrant?

Answer. Any male person over twenty-one years of age can obtain a homestead of one hundred and sixty acres free on the public lands in Canada by paying ten dollars, or two pounds, as an entrance fee. Farms may be purchased at any price, from one dollar, or four shillings, per acre, upward. The Canadian Pacific's grant of government lands consists of twenty-five million acres stretching through a large portion of the Dominion. These lands are offered at $2.50 per acre, with a condition of rebate in case of immediate cultivation. Each male member of a large family, if of age, might secure one hundred and sixty

HAYING ON THE PRAIRIE.

acres of the government, and purchase other lands of the railroad, and so secure an immense estate for a very little money. A family of four might obtain a farm of one thousand acres at less cost than as many dollars, including a house and sheds. Aliens may acquire lands the same as British-born subjects.

Q. What would be the probable cost of settlement on a one hundred and sixty acre grant for the first five years, and what the gain?

A. According to Magoun's "Manitoba" it would be nearly as follows. I quote the figures of Magoun, as his estimates are intelligent, and as nearly correct as such calculations can be made.

SOME WONDERFUL STATISTICS.

First Year.

Expenditure of settler with family of five, for provisions, etc., one year	$250.00
One yoke of oxen	125.00
One cow	35.00
Breaking-plough and harrow	35.00
Wagon	80.00
Implements, etc.	25.00
Cook-stove, etc., complete	25.00
Furniture	25.00
Tent	10.00
Sundries	50.00
Outlay for First Year	$660.00

At the end of the year he will have a comfortable log-house, barn, etc., cattle, implements, and say twenty acres of land broken, ready for seed.

Second Year.

Will realize from twenty acres, 600 bushels of grain at 60 c. (which is a low figure)	$360.00
Expenditure	300.00
Profit	$60.00

And he will have an additional twenty acres of land broken.

Third Year.

Forty acres will give him 1,200 bushels of grain, at 60 c.		$720.00
Will pay for land	$160.00	
Expenditure, including additional stock and implements	500.00	
		660.00
Profit		$60.00

And he will, with his increased stock and other facilities, be able to break at least thirty acres.

Fourth Year.

Seventy acres will give him 2,100 bushels of grain at 60 c.	$1,260.00
Less expenditure for further stock, implements, and other necessaries	600.00
Profit	$660.00

And another thirty acres broken.

Fifth Year.

100 acres will give him 3,000 bushels of grain, at 60 c.	$1,800.00
Less same expenditure as previous year	600.00
Profit	$1,200.00

At the end of the fifth year he will stand as follows: —

Cash, or its equivalent, on hand	$1,980.00
160 acres of land increased in value to at least $5 per acre	800.00
House and barn, low appraisal	250.00
Stock, including cattle and horses	600.00
Machinery and farm implements, 50 per cent of cost	200.00
Furniture, etc.	150.00
	$3,980.00
Less outlay first year	660.00
To credit of farm	$3,320.00

Q. What is the United States law in regard to the securing government land?

A. Any citizen or intending citizen can take government land, and the same with unmarried women. All the adult members of a family, except wives, can obtain quarter sections. These lands may be obtained, first, by homesteading, for which the fee for one hundred and sixty acres is fourteen dollars; by pre-emption, for which the fee for filing papers is five dollars; and by planting trees. A single person may secure four hundred and eighty acres.

Q. How are these lands to be found?

A. By application to the government land-offices in the Dominion or in the United States, which will furnish free circulars of information. Immense tracts of land in the Western Canadian provinces, and in Montana and the Northwestern States, are still subject to homesteading, pre-emption, and tree claims.

Q. What is the climate of this Northwestern Empire?

A. In the regions of the Chinook winds, which include British

Columbia, and the States of Washington, Oregon, and Montana, the climate is an almost continuous April.

Q. What are the Chinook currents of air and water?

A. The Chinook current is a warm stream of air and water that flows from Japan along the coast of Alaska and down to California. It causes warm rains, prevents severe frosts, and melts snow. There is but little winter weather in the Provinces and States that border on the Puget Sound. Near the Pacific coast roses bloom out of doors at Christmas. Winter here is usually a rainy season, like early April in England and New England, and it rains chiefly at night.

LOST SHEEP.

Q. What is likely to be the future of these Provinces and States?

A. They are likely to become the most populous, rich, and powerful political divisions of the world.

There was one plan of biographical and historical education adopted by Mr. Lette for the use of the Institute, which he called Audience Lectures, and which proved so successful that we must depart somewhat from our narrative to commend it here. It made the boys in reality their own lecturers. Mr. Lette would give the school a topic, and explain it, then ask that on a certain evening the boys relate as many illustrations of it as they could secure. The boy who brought the best illustration was offered a prize, and what was the best illustration was decided by a vote of the school. For example, Mr. Lette would say, on announcing a topic, something as follows: " Next week on Thursday evening we will have an audience lecture on ' Boys who were Laughed At.' Let me advise you to read ' Martyrs of Science,' the works of Samuel Smiles, and the popular books that relate to early struggles, such as ' Men who have Arisen,' and ' Turning-Points in Life.' "

A FARM IN THE NORTHWEST.

"IMPATIENT FOR THEIR BREAKFASTS."

We will give a specimen of one of these audience lectures as conducted by Mr. Lette. The plan is worthy of imitation in schools. On the evening of the lecture on "Boys who were Laughed At," the following illustrations were presented by the boys; and we will ask the reader to decide which is the best, before we give the result of the vote of the Institute on the subject.

COLUMBUS.

"Do you suppose that there is a part of the world where trees grow upward, and people stand upon their heads?" asked a learned ecclesiastic of Salamanca of the council assembled to consider the claims of a young man named Colon, to be sent on a voyage of discovery.

FULTON.

"Let us go and see that crazy man try to sail a boat by steam," said one to an idle crowd in New York. They hurried off to the Hudson. Thousands were there to see *that* crazy man's novel experiment. That boat went.

RELUCTANT TO GO HOME.

DISRAELI.

When Disraeli first attempted to speak in Parliament, he pitched his voice too high, and the Commons roared with laughter. "You will not hear me now," he said, "but the time will come when you *shall* hear me." That time came.

JOHN HUNTER.

Science is one long record of the ridicule of new discovery. Dr. John Hunter's discoveries in anatomy were the gibes of the medical profession. When one physician laughed at him because he did not publish his investigations in Latin, Dr. Hunter sharply returned, "I would teach him on a dead body what he never knew in any language, Latin or Greek." Jenner (who first vaccinated) was both ridiculed and abused.

While the first steamboat was crossing the Atlantic ocean, a pamphlet was being circulated, showing how futile and visionary was such a plan, and that it could never be accomplished. Edison's inventions have even in recent years been treated in the same manner.

POETS.

The early poems of Wordsworth were criticised as being next to idiotic. Byron says that this poet wrote so naturally of the "Idiot Boy," that he must be the hero of his own tale.

Tennyson's early volume, "The Poems of Two Brothers," was a failure, and some twelve years passed before he began to publish those ideal poems which were at first received as lunacy, but which have made him the poet of the age.

Longfellow's early poems were laughed at by the imaginative Poe, who found in them only mediocrity, with little indication of genius or promise.

Near the close of the last century there came into an editor's office in London a young man of diffident manners and rustic appearance.

"Is the editor in?"

"I am the acting editor."

"I have a poem on country life which it would please me to have published. I am inexperienced, but I thought perhaps you would read it and give me some friendly advice."

Any gentleman would have received such a contribution in the true spirit of courtesy. But this editor was one of those men without double sight, and he took the manuscript as a joke, to use it as a joke. He read it with immoderate laughter after the friendless young man had gone, and violated every law of good-breeding by reading it to a friend, in order to show what ridiculous creatures there are in the world.

The author had come from the fields. His home was now a London garret, and in that dreary place he had fondly dreamed of the old rustic cottage, the hedge-rows and trees, the flocks, herds, and farm life.

The poem found a publisher at last, despite some bad spelling, which is a minor defect in the manuscript of a good poem. It was called "The Farmer's Boy." It went over England and made the writer famous. That man was Robert Bloomfield.

AN ARCHITECT.

When prizes were offered in England for the best models of an industrial palace for all nations, there came into the day-dreams of an unknown man of genius a plan of such a palace, that haunted him night and day. "That is the way the world's palace should be built," he said; "iron and glass, iron and glass." He worked out his plan on iron and glass, and sent it to the royal commissioners. People thought him a fool. Architects thought him a fool

"NO ARCHITECT EVER DREAMED OF SUCH A STRUCTURE BEFORE."

The commissioners themselves hardly knew whether he was a fool or a genius. It was an Aladdin's palace that he had sent them, a poet's dream, a thing of air.

But the plan haunted every eye that saw it, as it had haunted the inventor. Iron and glass, — the light frame of iron throwing the great mountain of glass, like a great crystal hemisphere, into the air. Would the world laugh at it, or admire it? No architect ever dreamed of such a structure before.

Men laughed and laughed, but the plan was accepted. The crystal structure rose like a thing of fancy that would dissolve in the twilight and depart with the daylight. The old architects shook their heads, and criticised, and laughed.

But London began to admire the poet-like structure as it grew, the architects began to discuss the matter, and the world to wonder at a building that "should not have been so." The stupendous covering stood at last, a thing of light and air, glimmering in the sun. The obscure architect, a common workingman, was called forth to be knighted, and to receive the admiration of the world. The building that ought not to be, *was*. Every intelligent eye in the world now sees it in imagination, — the London Crystal Palace.

THOMAS CARLYLE.

Something over half a century ago there lived a young man in the "loneliest nook in Britain," as he said in a letter to Goethe, "among the granite hills and the black morasses which stretch westward through Galloway almost to the Irish Sea." He had been a laughed-at boy, a prodigious devourer of books, a silent thinker; and a terrible conflict in regard to the truths of life at last agitated his soul. On a moorland farm he gave expression to this agitation in a manuscript which he named "Sartor Resartus," — the tailor reclothed, or, after the manner of the old Scottish song, "the tailor done over." The manuscript was sent to various London firms and was rejected, with the wise opinions of the critical readers.

Finding a publisher at last in "Fraser's Magazine," and also in America, the "reclothed tailor" went forth to the view of the world to receive its valuable critical opinion. It is said that when John Stuart Mill, held to be the most competent authority even at that time, first read the work, he pronounced it "the stupidest piece of stuff that he ever set eyes on." The young writer himself, in after years, published many of the bad things said of the redressed tailor. Among them are the following: —

"The author has no great tact; his wit is frequently heavy, and reminds one of the German baron who took to leaping over tables, and said that he was trying to be lively."[1]

"'Sartor Resartus' is what old Dennis would call a 'heap of clotted nonsense,'" etc.[2]

"An author who treats of dress, appeals, like the poet, to young men and maidens, and calls upon them to buy his book. When, after opening their purses for this purpose, they have carried home the work in triumph, expecting to find in it some particular inspiration in regard to the tying of their neck-cloths or the cut of their corsets, and meet with nothing better than a dissertation on things in general, they will — to use the mildest term — not be in very good humor. If the last improvements in legislation which we have made in this country should have found their way to England, the author, we think, would stand some chance of being lynched."[3]

STANLEY.

The influence of Henry Stanley has touched the heart of humanity. In some respects the African explorer transcends all the men of the age. Africa will be likely to owe her civilization in the future largely to him.

Brought up in a parish workshop in Wales, he landed on our shores all alone in the world. A New Orleans merchant pitied the boy, and gave him a home and his own name, Stanley. The boy's soul longed for a worthy life and noble achievement. The world listened only to laugh. Rejected by a young lady to whom he had offered his hand, he is reported to have said one day to a friend, "It does seem that the world has no place for me, and I am tempted to commit suicide."

But he found a way into the ranks of men. He offered his life for Livingstone. It was accepted for Africa, and the world has it. His first offer was made amid a storm of ridicule, and the world long refused to believe his story of the marvellous exploration. But he is to-day the companion of kings, statesmen, and the greatest scientists. The public had nearly laughed his highest convictions out of him, but on the wings of his inspiration he rose over all. Entering the great arena of the world like Melchizedek or Elijah, without even a name, his faith has set his deeds among the stars.

Mr. Lette added to these illustrations Keats and Wagner, and then related the following incident, with inferential remarks.

[1] Bookseller   [2] Sun Newspaper, 1834.   [3] North American Review, 1835.

Young Lincoln.

Some years ago I visited Springfield, Ill., and stood at the tomb of Abraham Lincoln. The country had already placed the hero's fame among the greatest apostles of democracy, and that fame has steadily grown, until Lincoln's name stands to the world for the genius of free and progressive America. The monument with its heroic figures and emblems stood in the sun, amid the sea of cornfields and wheat-fields. The city, like a new Troy, was building beyond it, piling up its honest wealth. The living spirit of Lincoln seemed to be everywhere, — in the old home, the half-finished State House, the flag, and universal prosperity.

I met at Springfield an old man who had been an intimate friend of the great commoner President in his boyhood. I will repeat, very nearly as I heard it, one of his reminiscences.

"You ought to have seen Lincoln when he was a young man, and just beginning to study law. He was the curiousest-lookin' fellow one ever saw. He used to wear blue jean trousers, and he was so tall that they only came down a little below the knees. The folks used to laugh at him, but everybody knew he had an honest soul.

"We boys used to sit down on a log at early evening, and how he used to talk to us and tell stories!

"The world laughed, but there was a power in him even then. He used to walk ten miles to borrow law-books, and people must have thought it rather queer that Abe should take to the law. On his return home, after going to borrow the books, he would sit down half-way on a log by the roadside and study, he was so eager to make the most of everything. The world laughed then; it does not laugh now."

Here, indeed, is a picture of a law student. Walking ten miles to borrow law-books, and studying them on wayside logs in pioneer Illinois! It is said that he believed he would one day be President, even when he made a log his rostrum and the weary emigrant boys his senate. Who would have dreamed that in that laughed-at youth God had chosen his prophet of humanity, who would call to the battle-field a million of men, who would emancipate a race, and who, over a mighty graveyard of dead heroes, would speak words that would live and breathe through the ages?

Do not be discouraged by a sneer. A sneer is a small weapon, which strong men never use. Follow your highest inspiration, holding to God, blind to ridicule and deaf to all the auction-bells of "Vanity Fair." Never did a man gain the celestial knighthood without passing the slender spears of ridicule. Faith is success, no matter what the world may say.

To sum up: Any young man who has an original purpose in life will fall under ridicule; but if it be a right purpose and an inspiration, and he pursue it, he will be respected in the end, and that in proportion to the courage of his convictions. "He laughs best who laughs last."

The boys voted that Mr. Lette's illustration was the most effective. The story of President Lincoln's struggle to read law seemed to touch their hearts.

Among the most studious boys in the Institute was Arthur Burns. His father had perished off Faroe. On hearing Mr. Lette describe the opportunities for the emigrant in British Columbia and in the United States, he desired to return to America with the explorer, and to secure a farm by homesteading or pre-emption. He was introduced to young Charles Hampden by Mr. Lette, and the two boys became friends.

"I would go to British Columbia and settle, if I had the means," said Arthur to Charles one day. "How could I earn the necessary money?"

"I do not know," said Charles. "I would be glad to go to Washington and find employment in Seattle or Tacoma, and take a homestead in that State or in Arizona when I become of age."

"I wish we might visit the Northwestern Empire together," said Arthur. "I dream of America continually, and I like you because you are an American boy."

Charles told Mr. Lette of Arthur's dream and ambition.

"Could we not in some way raise the money for Arthur to emigrate?" asked Charles. "What would a second-class passage to Quebec be?"

"About £7, or thirty-five dollars."

"And how much the fare from Quebec to Vancouver?"

"About as much more, emigrant fare."

"Seventy dollars, or £14," said Charles. "How much would it cost to settle him on a claim?"

"HE WOULD SIT DOWN ON A LOG BY THE ROADSIDE."

"About ten dollars for fees, and twenty dollars for a log house; and he should have some one hundred dollars for provisions, board, farming implements, and early emergencies. Two hundred dollars, or £40, would give him a start for the first year."

"Could you not earn this money for him through the school?"

"How?"

"By giving an entertainment."

"What? Will you suggest one?"

"A comedy for the holidays."

"What shall it be?"

"Oh, you could write it. The most humorous story that you ever heard."

"The oddest incident I ever heard of for a platform comedy was an experience of some impoverished travellers in the old Hôtel de Batteau."

"What was that?"

"They thought that a French costumer's room in the hotel was a den of thieves, and one alarmed another until the scene became very comical, and ended ridiculously but agreeably. I have often thought that the incident might be made a pleasing tableau for exhibitions."

"Write it out, will you not, and read it to the school, and if the boys like it, ask them if they will give it as an exhibition for Arthur, to help him emigrate. A good exhibition by the boys would yield two hundred dollars, or £40, profit, would it not?"

"Yes; entertainments given by the boys are popular. I will write out the incident in the form of a dialogue for the tableau, and will read it to the school."

CHAPTER IV.

THE COMEDY FOR THE HOLIDAYS.

HEN he next met the boys of the Institute, Mr. Lette said : —
"My boys, several of you have expressed a wish to emigrate to the Canadian Provinces or to the United States, and to settle on the government free lands. But only one of you is of age, and he has not the means to emigrate. I have a plan that I wish to bring before you. It is to give a holiday exhibition of a humorous dialogue with tableau, and give the proceeds to Arthur Burns, who is of age, to enable him to go to British Columbia and make a settlement there. If the plan proves successful, it can be repeated as others come of age. Arthur would correspond with you, and so you would have one of your own number on the field. How many of you approve of the plan?"

The proposal met with instant favor. To have one of their own number go to British Columbia and prepare the way for others was a matter of intense interest to them. Every boy in the school was ambitious to have the exhibition take place, to make it a success, and send Arthur Burns to America.

"You have shown a truly generous spirit," said Mr. Lette. "The next thing will be to decide what the exhibition shall be. I have written a humorous dialogue, or comedy, which will admit of some curious historical tableaux. I would like to read it to you, and illustrate its action; and if you like it, we will at once assign the parts to the speakers and begin the rehearsal."

Mr. Lette then read the following odd comedy, which the boys liked, and were unanimous in favor of putting upon the platform as the means of raising money for Arthur.

THE HÔTEL DE BATTEAU;

OR, LADY BLESSINGTON'S CHARITIES.

A Comedy for the Holidays.

CHARACTERS.

MR. TROTT, an American traveller, returning.
MRS. JOHNS, an American traveller, returning.
MONSIEUR LA PLACE, a French traveller.
PATRICK AND BIDDY, Irish laborers.
HANS LISTMAN, a German violinist.
LADY BLESSINGTON, a London philanthropist.
CURATE.
A FRENCH COSTUMER.
Characters for a series of historical tableaux.

PART I.

SCENE I. *A platform representing parts of two rooms having a partition between them, with a door, and over the door a transom, which may be looked through by a person standing in a chair. One room represents a traveller's bedroom, and the other the apartment of a French costumer. The latter contains masks, wigs, costumes, face paints and powders, and a large chest.*

Thomas Trott (alone). Here I am in London again, and London is the world. This room does look uninviting, I must confess, but it will answer for a week in winter, when the skies are all clouds and the streets rivers of fog. When I was in London in the summer, and took rooms at Charing Cross, and passed my afternoons at Rotten Row and my evenings in St. James Park, how delightful it was! But now my letter of credit is exhausted, and I have only £2 left for a week's board, and to pay my fare to Liverpool for the returning steamer, and I shall have to practise the closest economy. Mr. Bound, whom I met at Lucerne, said that the Hôtel de Batteau was an excellent lodging-house. Lodging-house! How cheap that sounds after my summer and fall life in the great hotels of the Continent; weeks at Basle, Geneva, and Lucerne, in apartments fit for lords and ladies, and, for that matter, often occupied by such grand people!

A HARDY FRONTIER LAD.

Hark, hear the water run! The river Thames, I suppose, though it might be a canal for aught I could tell in the fog. The Hôtel de Batteau. What a place for a tragedy this would be, for a robbery, and the body to be thrown into the river below! An American all alone — no moon, no stars, only misty lamps in the fog! I have read of such things in such places. Just as likely to be me as any one else. Papers have accounts of such things every day, and Heaven only knows how many crimes the night waters of the Thames cover. Bodies may have been thrown out of that very window, — splash, that would be all. Oh, it makes me shiver! Where's my pocket-book? Here, in my under pocket. Let me see how much — Oh yes! I haven't anything in it, like Lucy Lockett, - only £2; that relieves me. But how would a robber know that? English thieves think that Americans are as rich as the old Incas of Peru; but as little as I have, I have nothing to spare. If I were to lose my £2, I should have to walk from London to Liverpool, and beg my food along the way. It is well that I have a return ticket to New York. (*Looks up.*)

What's that over the door, — a transom — lattice — ventilator? The door is locked. I wonder what's in the other room. Let me try the door; fast. Let me get up into the chair and see what's there. No, that would not be honorable, — spying. This is the first time that I was ever afraid of thieves; but the room does look bare and scary, and the water under the balcony goes gurgle, gurgle, gurgle, and I can hear cabs rattling, and boatmen swearing, and the city is as black as the shores of oblivion. Oh, that gurgle, gurgle, gurgle! I *must* know what's in there if it is spying. I'm suspicious. (*Mounts a chair and looks through the transom. Starts back with open mouth and staring eyes, steps down from the chair, and clasps his forehead in his hands.*) What a place is *that*, — false faces, scalps, dead men's clothes, all hanging on the walls! I do believe it is a den of thieves. I should be safer to go right out into the night, and wander the streets in the fog and slops, and dodge among the lamp-posts. I might just as well jump out of the window and despatch myself at once. No! I will get my pistols and will watch. They'll come home by-and-by. (*Rap, tap, tap!*) Who is there?

Caller. Monsieur la Place, a friend.

Mr. Trott. What can I do for you, Monsieur?

Caller. Will Monsieur the Americanne lend me a match?

Mr. Trott. Yes, yes. You occupy the room next to mine, I suppose?

Caller. Yes, those be my lodgings.

Mr. Trott. Yes, yes, come in; this is an awful night! Shocking time for a tragedy, or a ghost, or —

Caller. Was you expecting one of doze, Monsieur the Americanne? I hopes not. I haf never been disturbed in the Hôtel de Batteau.

Mr. Trott. Here — matches. (*Hands him matches.*)

Caller. Merci ! now I will go. I beg your pardon for the interruption. Monsieur the Americanne looks nervous to-night.

Mr. Trott. Stop! (*Makes signs for silence.*) Listen! (*A noise is heard in the adjoining room, into which the costumer enters, followed by two young men.*) Thieves, I do believe. Put your ear against the door and listen. Don't you leave me! I know that you are an honest man, if you are a — French — a foreigner. There's something wrong in this house.

Caller. The same by you, Monsieur the Americanne; I think you be honest. I hears nothing strange. Monsieur is nervous.

Mr. Trott. Listen — here — close to the wall. Do you hear that? (*Both listen, and Mr. Trott acts in pantomime his surprise and horror at what he hears.*)

ROOM NO. 2. *A room with a window.*

Costumer. So you would be Gog and Magog, and represent London's legendary period. You will be rather hard to make up. But I have made up thieves and assassins and goblins, and even centaurs, and I will try to serve you. (*Pantomime of suspicion and horror in Room No. 1.*) Let me see who you are.

1st Masker. You know that the thirty-three daughters of the Emperor Diocletian all despatched their husbands —

Mr. Trott (*in Room No. 1*). Hear! hear! (*In a whisper.*)

1st Masker. And were sent to sea in a ship, and came to London. We are their descendants. Our fathers were giants. We stand in the Guildhall. We used formerly to appear in all the Lord Mayor's shows. We were burned in the great fire. We used to stand on London Bridge, and after that at Temple Bar, giants.

2d Masker. We ought to be fourteen feet high; ten will do.

Costumer. You will have to stand on two barrels.

ROOM NO. 1.

Mr. Trott. Thirty-three of them!

Frenchman. Stand in the Guildhall!

Mr. Trott. Used to rob people on London Bridge and at Temple Bar. I have n't anything left. This is all very mysterious.

Frenchman. It is very mysterious.

Mr. Trott. What is your theory, Monsieur?

Frenchman. I think that is one place of thieves, where they make over peoples; change der color, hair, eyes, and teeth; shorten der legs, put a hump on der back, make tall peoples short and short peoples tall; put the small-pox on the face; make white peoples black, and black peoples white, and the Englishman a Frenchman, and the Frenchman an Englishman. That ish my theory, Monsieur the Englishman.

Mr. Trott. Do they — do they have such places as that?

Frenchman. Oh, *oui* — in Paris, we do. Make one all over another man.

Mr. Trott. This is a wicked world indeed. They make over thieves?

Frenchman. Oh, *oui* — der own mothers would not know them. Don't you know? Didn't you never hear? Make over one thieve into another — all just the same.

Mr. Trott. This is awful. What was it he said? Thirty-three daughters of the emperor, somebody despatched all their husbands, and he ought to stand ten feet high. Say, if you were in my place, what would you do? Open the window and cry "Police," or run? Thirty-three daughters! Do you think that I am in my right senses? I never drink, nor take opium, nor nothing. Hark! There are more people in there now, — women's voices, too. Thirty-three daughters. I hope it isn't any of them. Let me look through the transom again. You be quiet, and I will make signs to you. There!

ROOM NO. 2.

Costumer. I will have the Gog and Magog transformation all ready on the afternoon before the act.

ROOM NO. 1.

Mr. Trott. He is talking about the *act*.

Costumer. And now, ladies, who are you?

Ladies. We are weeping queens from the Vale of Avallon. Arthur is wounded. Shall we bring him in? We shall need to make a study of positions.

Costumer. Yes, bring him in, and lay him on the rug, just as he will be.

(*Gog and Magog bring in the body of a man, and lay him on the rug.*)

ROOM NO. 1.

Mr. Trott. They have waylaid a man. They are bringing in his body. He is dead, or dying, with his eyes rolling about, *so.* Oh, it is awful; I tell you it is awful. We must call the police. They are the most distraught looking set of people I ever saw. Let me step down. (*Steps down. Rap, tap, tap!*)

Mr. Trott. Come in.

(*Enter Patrick and Biddy.*)

Patrick. And would you be after lending us a match, would ye? Sorry a one have we got, an' they don't furnish no matches at the hoffice at all.

We've taken a room adjoining ye, we have, in the Hôtel de Batteau, and it has got a taller dip, and nothin' but stick of wood to light it with. We would n't be after goin' to bed in the dark, in a strange place, too. There might be spooks there, or a secret room, or —

Mr. Trott (pointing to the transom). Secret room. There's one there now. Oh-o-o! They've waylaid a man, — Arthur is his name, — wounded in the Vale of Avallon, wherever that may be. Gog and Magog killed him. Just you get up in that chair and look through that transom, and tell me what you see.

Patrick (looking through the transom). They've fetched him, sure. Lot of women cryin' over him, with their hair all streamin' down their backs. I'd like to have my shillalah, and go right in among 'em. Oh, Biddy, we must get out of this house straight.

Biddy. An' niver a wink of slape will I take now, after all the 'orrid sights you are tellin' me. I knew the house was no good, when I heard the water runnin' under it all so lonesome like. The saints preserve us! What are they doin' now?

Patrick. The man is dyin', kind o' ginteely like, as though he did n't care, and the women are all tearin' their hair. I niver see the loikes o' that. Are we all crazy now, or is it them? They told me this was the Hôtel de Batteau.

Biddy. f I only had that ould broomstick of mine now, — the one I left in Sligo; you know about that, Pat, the one I used to have to kape me home affairs all so stiddy in Sligo; you remember that, sure you do? And what are they doin' now?

Patrick. Ther's comin' a man with a stuffed cat under his arm, and another man, and they are payin' no attention at all to the dyin' Arthur, but are bowin' and bowin', and sayin' and sayin', " Did ever a subject have such a prince?" and " Did ever a prince have such a subject?" and the women are all smilin' and callin' him " Whittington, thrice Lord Mayor of London." The Lord Mayor has come, sure, with a stuffed cat under his arm, and now they say that the bow-bells all are goin' to ring. It does seem to me that I must have gone out of my senses. Where are we, Biddy? Sure, did n't they tell us that this was the Hôtel de Batteau?

(*The scenes seen through the transom are to be acted in Room No. 2, as indicated by the dialogue.*)

Biddy. I think that you have gone daft, sure, Patrick. Step down now, and let me look again. (*They change positions. Rap, tap, tap!*)

Mrs. Johns. Pardon, friends; the lady of this establishment is a particular

HERDING CATTLE ON THE PLAINS.

friend of mine, and as she takes a few genteel lodgers, I have come here among all these tradespeople on my way home to America. My letter of credit is running close, and my friend the English Madame is not so exacting in her charges as my friend Madame of the Golden Cross. Can I borrow a match or two? I occupy a room that was rented by the late Lady Carroll. Very ancient, I am told, is this same Hôtel de Batteau.

Biddy. Hush — tisl. — thieves, another tragedy, — 'orrid! No — they're goin' to have a weddin' instid of a funeral, and a big woman is singin' — list — tish — whurra!

(*Song is heard from Room No. 2. Solo:*)

"The mistletoe hung in the castle hall,
The holly branch shone from the old oak wall,
And the baron's retainers were lively and gay,
A-keeping their Christmas holiday.
And the baron beheld, with a father's pride,
His beautiful child, young Lovell's bride,
And she with her bright eyes seemed to be
The pride of that merry company.
  Oh, the mistletoe bough,
  Oh, the mistletoe bough."

Biddy. Now they are all dancing, and the wounded Arthur, he's better, I guess.

(*Song.*) "I'm weary of dancing now, she cried.
Here — tarry a moment, I'll hide, I'll hide.
And, Lovell, be sure thou art first to trace
The clew to my secret hiding-place.
Away she ran — "

Biddy. Whurra! There she goes. What doin's and actions! And now she is hidin' in a great big chest, right before their eyes, too. Pat, you don't think we've been takin' a drop too much, now, do you?

Mrs. Johns. What does this mean?

Biddy. Mane? The other room is full of thieves and crazy folks and ghosts. There's a wounded man named Arthur, and the Lord Mayor with a stuffed cat, and we'll all be arrested and tried in the High Court of Chauncey, like other great folks for more than a hundred years. What now? There comes a tall saplin', and he is after sayin', "Remember, remember the 5th of November." Tish — be still! Do I hear my own ears? He says. 'Gunpowder Plot." Tish — he says, "One hogshead and thirty barrels of powder," and — oh that I should ever live to see the sorry night! — he's goin' to blow up the Parliament. It's conspirators they be, dynamites, Nihilists from Rapscalia or some foreign parts. We'll all be blown up, and all go down, down, down into the river, the Hôtel de Batteau and all. Oh that I should ever see the loike o' this! There, he said "Slow match!" Whurra! Let the American Madam look and see. Here, get up here, and see a sight that will turn your eyes to ice and your heart to stone. (*Mrs. Johns mounts the chair.*)

Mrs. Johns. This is very extraordinary. I only came here because Madame is, or was, a particular friend of mine. She's gone away. I don't know what I shall do. We ought not to stay in this dreadful place. It's an awful night outside. I've heard terrible things of these great lodging-houses — establishments — that hang over the water. There comes a little fat man into the room — looks clever — they're going to paint him! They're putting a (*pause*) hump and a pack on his back, and a fool's cap (*pause*), and furs (*pause*), and bells (*pause*), and a wig (*pause*), and a long false nose. Let me get down. (*Steps down. Scenes in Room No. 2, acted as before.*)

Mr. Trott. What is your theory, Mrs. Johns?

Mrs. Johns. We're in an asylum.

Mr. Trott. Is it we that are crazy, or they? What is your theory, Biddy?

Biddy. Me theory? Seems as though 't was a wake; I've seen double at wakes. But I tell ye they be conspirators; I heard it with my own ears. Did n't he say "gunpowder plot," and "thirty barrels of powder," and a "slow match"?

Monsieur la Place. I tell you, Monsieur the Americanne, they are thieves; it's a place where they make over robbers, I know. A man goes in there an helephant like and comes out a mouse. They have such places in the Seine; this is the Hôtel de Batteau. How that sounds, — Hôtel de Batteau!

Mr. Trott. An awful name! Why did I come here? Oh, I know now, my pocket-book. I suppose the Hôtel de Batteau is known to all the thieves in Europe. The geese and the foxes have met.

Mrs. Johns. Known to all the thieves of Europe.

Biddy. And sure, did n't you say that Madame Hôtel de Batteau was your particular friend?

Mr. Trott. This is awful, awful! What shall we do?

Mrs. Johns. We must stand by each other. We are all unprotected strangers.

Mr. Trott. We will sell ourselves as dearly as possible.

Biddy. Yes, and sure we will all die together, and have one piece in the papers about us all, 'orrid murthers it will be, in great letthers. How the people will stare at it! My name is Biddy McQueen.

Monsieur la Place. No, there will never be anything about it in the papers, Madame Biddy McQueen. This is the Hôtel de Batteau.

Biddy. And what is that, — such as they had in Paris among the unsane?

Monsieur. Don't you know? The hotel of the *boat*, of the water, where all bodies sink into the water, down, down, down, and nothing more is ever said or heard, except — listen!

Mr. Trott. Gurgle, gurgle, gurgle!

Mrs. Johns. Gurgle, gurgle, gurgle!

Biddy (*in deep tones*). Gurgle, gurgle, gurgle! All the saints protect us! Gurgle, gurgle, gurgle!

Mr. Trott. Let us arm ourselves and all stand up in row and await our fate, and we will see what will happen before morning. I will stand here *so*, and hold my pistol *so*. (*Attitude.*)

Monsieur. Let me get my loaded cane (*Goes and returns stealthily*), and I will stand beside you, *so*, Horatius like, I will. (*Attitude.*)

Biddy. I feel horratious like, but I have n't any weapon at all.

Mrs. Johns. I will get my umbrella (*Steals away timidly and returns*), and I will stand beside Monsieur. (*Attitude.*)

Patrick. There's a stick of wood in my room; I'll get it, and hold it aloft, Paddy me whack. (*Goes, returns, and attitude.*)

Biddy. And I'll scream "Murther!" and "Police!" I know how; I can out-scrame a whole neighborhood.

Mrs. Johns. I once read a story called "The Tavern in Spessart," and the lodgers — the occupiers of apartments — were put into just such peril as we are in now. They found that there was a plan to rob them. So they armed themselves, and to keep awake, each one related the most dreadful story one had ever heard. We might edify one another and cheer us up in this way. Did you ever hear the story of "The Living Eye in the Portrait"?

Biddy. Did you ever read about the lively doin's of Jack Shepherd? We've got that book in Sligo.

Patrick. I know a story of Captain Kidd that would keep ye all awake.

Monsieur. Did you ever read the "Mysteries of Paris"? There's no need of it. This is the last night I will ever pass in London.

Mr. Trott. True, true; the last, no doubt. This is an awful situation.

Monsieur. Awful it is, — de Hôtel de Batteau.

Mrs. Johns (*shaking*). Very awful, awful!

Patrick (*shutting his eyes*). Extramely awful it is. Hear the water there. All the saints help us!

Biddy (*in deep voice, and shaking*). Don't say another word, or I will

scrame. This is what they would call a predicament in auld Sligo. It is never a such will I get into again!
Monsieur. Never. This is the Hôtel de Batteau.
(*A strain of music on the violin is heard in the entries.*)
Monsieur. That is Hans Listman; he has returned from the concert rehearsal. (*In a loud whisper.*) Hans, Hans, come here. Tragedy!
Violin. (*Tune "Silent Night," by Haydn.*)
Biddy. Tish, tish, you German boy; this is no hour for fiddlin'. Come in, ye saplin' of the wind, and stand there. Ye'll be wanted before morning.
Hans. Wat ish this?
(*All point to the transom and assume attitudes of horror.*)
Mr. Trott. Tragedy.
Monsieur. A robbers' den.
Biddy. An' sure it's a conspē-racy.
Patrick. An' piracy it is.
Mrs. Johns. There are some insane people in there. They are dangerous.
Hans. But wat, I say, does ish all mean? Ish you crazy?
Biddy. Arra, boy, put away your fiddle now, an' you'll never need it again. Ye'll never see any more Zarmony over the Rhine, ye won't. This is the Hôtel de Batteau.

PART II.

SCENE II. *While the above dialogue goes on in Room No. 1, the costumer in Room No. 2 arranges a row of historical and allegorical tableaux. They are the giants Gog and Magog of the Guildhall; King Arthur wounded at Avallon and wept by women; Whittington and his cat; Guy Fawkes; the Waits; Santa Claus; and the Angel of Christmas. The Waits are boy carol singers. The Guy Fawkes should be a frightful figure, tall and leering, and stuck full of weapons and burglars' implements.*

Costumer. It is now quarter to ten o'clock, and Lucy Blessington said that she and the Rector would call before ten on her way from the Charity Lodge. Hark! that is her carriage. The tableaux are all ready for inspection, and I hope she will like them; she is so good as to arrange all this surprise for the poor children, and come to this out-of-the-way street to see the rehearsal. She is coming on the stairs. Gog and Magog, get into position; and wounded King Arthur, and Whittington and his cat, and Ginevra and Guy Fawkes, and the Waits, and Santa Claus, and the Angel of Christmas,—all. There, I will turn a soft red light on you now, through the glass reflector; ready!

GATHERING THE HARVEST.

Lady Blessington. I hope I find Monsieur the Costumer well to-night. Oh, how lovely! Don't you think so, Rector Bonney? Charming! Gog and Magog, the old London giants, — how they will please the little orphans to-morrow night! I will tell them the story; why, the anticipation of it makes me happy now. How I do love Charity Lodge! All places are pleasant where one makes others happy. Yes, Costumer, Gog and Magog are just as I would have them; and the wounded Arthur wept by the wives of knights. I must get you, Rector, to relate to the children one of the Arthurean romances, — the story of the Holy Grail, perhaps. Whittington? Ah, yes, I see. Rector Bonney, you must also tell the story of Whittington and his cat, and I will pretend to punish wicked Guy Fawkes with a whip. An excellent Guy Fawkes; fantastic! I know it will please them so much! And Ginevra! here is the beautiful bride about to hide in the old oak chest. I will read Rogers's poem to-morrow night. I will hear the Waits sing soon. The Santa Claus is very good, and the Angel of Christmas beautiful. I congratulate you, Costumer; you have provided an excellent treat for the Charity School, — excellent. I am more than satisfied with your work; and you will be at the chapel early to-morrow night, and I know that you will enter into the spirit of the entertainment, and help make us all very happy.

Rector. Your plans all please me very much, Lady Blessington. They are such as lead others to follow their best selves. I have a kind of theory, Lady Blessington, that the world would be much better if people followed their better hearts. I have some plans of sympathetic work for the holidays, and I would carry them out if I only had the means, Lady Blessington.

Lady Blessington. And what are they, Father Bonney?

Rector. I would like to give each poor family in the parish a little home library for the children, — a little library of books that inspire to high ambitions. I have a theory, Lady Blessington, that character is formed largely by right models in youth, and the right books furnish the best models. What do you think of my plan, Lady Blessington?

Lady Blessington. Oh, excellent, excellent! Do it by all means. Your plan is after my own heart.

Rector. But how shall we secure the means, Lady Blessington?

Lady Blessington. Oh, Father Bonney, I know that you will let me pay for that. What were your further thoughts? "The valleys are being exalted."

Rector. Rents; there are so many people who are troubled about their rents. They would have a happier Christmas with their families if their rents were paid. Don't you think so, Lady Blessington?

Lady Blessington. Such thoughts as these ought to be turned into gold.

as the cakes in the basket of Hungary's margravine were changed into roses. I hope you will let me pay for that I am sure you will allow me this happiness. It would so prepare the way for Christmas.

Rector. "The crooked is being made straight." And shoes,—I think that there is a great blessing in shoes. Don't you think so, Lady Blessington? Good shoes are health, and there are many people in the parish in poor shoes. They all ought to have good shoes for Christmas.

Lady Blessington. Surely, surely, they ought. Now, I hope that you will be willing to let me pay for those.

Rector. "And the rough places plain." Now, pardon me, good lady, if I have one thought more. It always makes a mother's heart happy to have the baby remembered at Christmas. And a mother's heart is a sacred thing.

Lady Blessington. I have no doubt that the Virgin herself was glad to hear the tinkling of the camel-bells of the Magi. I would like to have all the babies that have come to live in the parish this year have a little gift, in remembrance of the gold and myrrh and frankincense of life. I would send them all a few shillings to be spent by their mothers. It would prepare their mother's hearts for the better enjoyment of the festival. Don't you think so, Lady Blessington?

Lady Blessington. Now, I like that, and I hope you will let me bless myself by doing that. It is so good to have a rector that sees these things. But sympathy is the real gold of charity. If you think my thought a good one, I will go and carry the shillings to the mothers myself, and so give my heart with them. I have been given time, and I ought to turn it into good. I shall need sympathy myself some day. This is a beautiful, beautiful world, but the shadow falls sometimes on us all, and we need sympathy then.

Rector. And I know of a certain lady who ought to be remembered in ivy, holly, and mistletoe.

All present. And so do we.

Lady Blessington. Be quiet, Pygmalions. Statues ought not to speak.

Rector. I would have our good people fill her windows with evergreens, and her heart with happiness and gratitude.

Guy Fawkes (*taking out his pocket-book, comically*). And let me pay for *that*.

Costumer. I will now turn on the golden light with another reflector, and then you shall hear the little Waits sing.

(*Three boys, carollers, sing the old English carol.*)

"God rest you, merry gentlemen,
Let nothing you dismay;

> For Jesus Christ, our Saviour,
> Was born on Christmas day,
> To save us all from Satan's power,
> When we had gone astray.
> O tidings, O tidings of joy for all astray,
> For Jesus Christ, the Saviour,
> Was born on Christmas day."

ROOM NO. 1.

Biddy. Do you hear that, — "God rest you, merry gentlemen"? Let me look through the transom once more now. (*Mounts the chair.*) The saints above! If there ain't an angel come down from the heavins, and a mighty foine lady, and a priest. Now I am beat, sure. What do you think now, eh? Let me step down; what is your theory now? (*Biddy steps into the room again.*)

ROOM NO. 2.

First Wait. I just saw a face at the transom.
Second Wait. And I. It was watching us.
Third Wait. I saw it there before the lady came.
Costumer. It is not good breeding to look into people's rooms; but, Guy Fawkes, suppose you see if all is right in the other room. Here, get up in a chair. (*Obeys.*)
Guy Fawkes. There's a mob there, — thieves, conspirators (women among them), dynamites, all around, prepared to attack us. The leader has a pistol. Oh, what shall we do?
Gog (*jumping down from his barrel*). Let me look. 'T is so; this is the Hôtel de Batteau.
Magog. Let me look. 'T is so; this is the Hôtel de Batteau.
Lady Blessington. I hope that name bodes no evil. It has a mysterious sound.
Guy Fawkes. A very ominous sound.
Costumer. I assure you all that this is a most respectable lodging-place Guy Fawkes, ask the people in the other apartment who they are.
Guy Fawkes (*through the transom*). Good people, who are you?
Biddy. We've found you out, and we're all ready for you, that we be. We'll have you all arristed, we will. Who are *you*? We know you, but don't you dare, or I'll holler.
Guy Fawkes. We are rehearsing for Christmas, arranging our costumes and tableaux for the charity festival.
Mr. Trott. Beg pardon, beg pardon. We thought you were — were — dan-

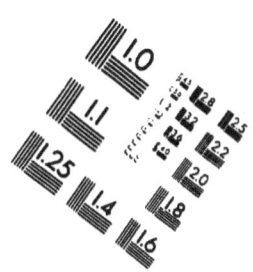

**IMAGE EVALUATION
TEST TARGET (MT-3)**

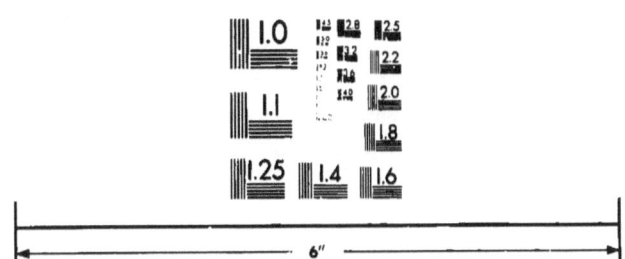

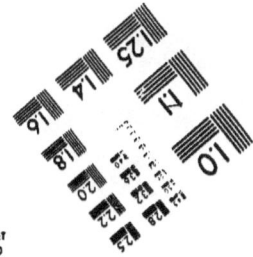

Photographic
Sciences
Corporation

23 WEST MAIN STREET
WEBSTER, N.Y. 14580
(716) 872-4503

gerous people. We are lodgers; we armed ourselves for protection. Beg pardon, beg pardon.

Guy Fawkes (*to the Rector*). These people are lodgers; they thought we were dangerous people, and have armed themselves through fear.

Rector Bonney. Very funny, very funny. Tell them we are friends. Ask them to come in and meet Lady Blessington, and hear the Waits sing. Unlock the door. (*The door is opened by Guy Fawkes.*)

Mr. Trott. Beg pardon — we thought you were —
Guy Fawkes. Beg pardon — we thought you were —
Monsieur la Place. Beg pardon — I thought you were —
Gog and Magog. Beg pardon, we thought you were —
Lady Blessington. I am quite sure that you are all honest people.
Biddy. Honest, is it? I 'm quite sure I am an honest woman, and I know Pat is.
Mrs. Johns. And Madame, my particular friend, keeps this lodging — this establishment. That 's why I came here among these tradespeople. I 'm an American *lady.*
Lady Blessington. Well, well, the coming of Christmas ought to make us all very equal and friendly, I 'm sure. (*To Costumer.*) Kindly arrange the tableaux, and turn on the white lights, and we will have one more carol. My good woman, what shall it be? (*To Biddy.*)
Biddy. The Irish carol, sure. There never was any carol like that. Don't you know, — the three ships that sailed right into Bethlehem on Christmas day in the mornin'. I 'll just sing it to you myself. (*Bridget sings.*)

> "I saw three ships come sailing in
> On Christmas day, on Christmas day;
> I saw three ships come sailing in
> On Christmas day in the morning."

Lady Blessington. This is very pleasing, — don't you think so, Rector? — to meet people of so many different nationalities in the Hôtel de Batteau, — French, German, Irish, American, our brothers and friends of all the world. The true Christmas spirit is in it.
Biddy. Och, and so it is. I'm always glad to mate me friends anywhere. I 'm not particular, me and Pat ain't, now; we 've seen too much of the world.
Mrs. Johns. I knew I should meet excellent people here; but to find you here, Lady Blessington, is an unexpected pleasure. This is a lovely establishment, with grand old Father Thames running under it.

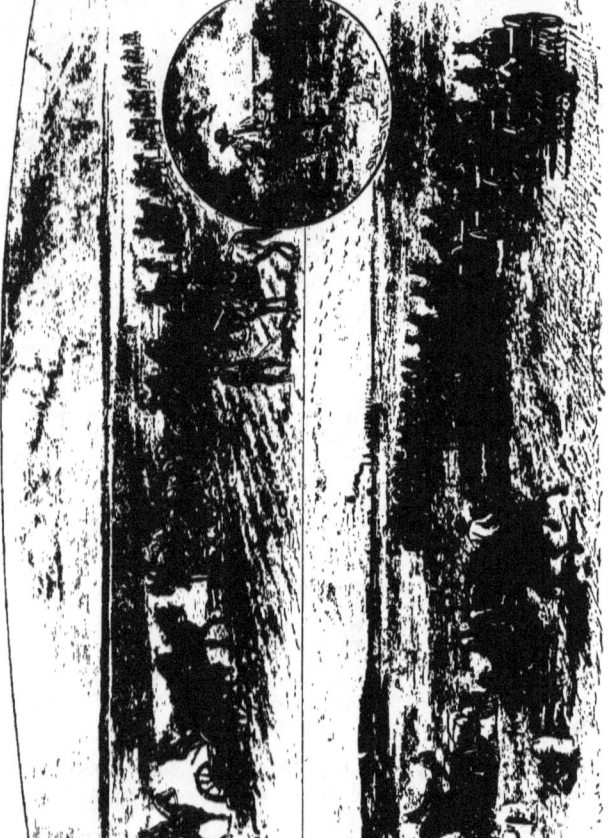

MODERN PRAIRIE FARMING.

Biddy. An' who is he runnin' *under* it? Madame Grinders, the fish-market woman it is that runs this two-penny lodging-house. Never mind, we 're all on an equal here. It 's a foine time we 'll all be havin'.

Mr. Trott. I knew that you were all of the better class of people, with artistic tastes, though I did not quite understand your movements at first.

Monsieur. Yes, *oui,* I was sure you were all superior people, or you would n't have been here, at the Hôtel de Batteau.

Lady Blessington. It is the mission of music to create harmony, and of poetry to express the soul of things ; don't you think so, Rector? We have had the old Irish carol; perhaps our friend here, Monsieur, will give us the old French carol, " The First Noël." You all seem like one family here, in the Hôtel de Batteau.

> " The first Noël, the angel did say,
> Was to certain poor shepherds of old, as they lay
> In the fields where they were keeping their sheep,
> On a cold winter's night that was so deep.
> Noël, Noël, Noël,
> Born is the King of Israel."

(*Let the Waits repeat the chorus pianissimo, to the accompaniment of Hans's violin.*)

Lady Blessington. I think that one of the most beautiful Christmas carols in the world is Haydn's "Silent Night." I thought I heard a strain of it a little while ago on the violin. Will not our German friend here give it to us? Perhaps the Waits will sing it to the violin.

(*Waits sing to the violin, very softly.*)

> " Silent night! holy night !
> All is calm, all is bright
> Round yon virgin mother and Child !
> Holy Infant, so tender and mild,
> Sleep in heavenly peace,
> Sleep in heavenly peace."

Mr. Trott. Well, well, I declare, if everybody only was like Lady Blessington, everybody would be good to everybody, and Heaven would be good to everybody, and then —

Costumer. Everybody would have a merry Christmas inside and out —

Mr. Trott. Of the Hôtel de Batteau.

Lady Blessington. Thank you, gentlemen. I wish I were more worthy of your kind compliments. Now we must surely have one more carol, and the sentiment of it, I am sure, will meet the spirit of this most delightful occasion.

Biddy. Most delightful occasion (*bowing*).

Lady Blessington. You seem to have been somewhat alarmed, some of you, when you first came here. The fine old English carol, "God rest you, merry gentlemen," contains a sentiment which we shall all share on parting. What is the night? Let me look out of the window. Oh, I see something very, very beautiful! I will lift the curtain, and show it to you at the end of your song. Let us all sing, "God rest you, merry gentlemen." One of the Waits will lead, and we will be the chorus.

(*Song — one verse. During the chorus Lady Blessington lifts the curtain and reveals a star, while Hans plays "Silent Night" very softly on the violin.*)

Lady Blessington. It is all clear again; the stars have come back. May you all have a quiet and happy night, and all the world be blessed inside and outside of —

All. The Hôtel de Batteau.

(*Star — magnesium wire touched with flame — low light, and tableaux If the window be artificial, the magnesium wire star may be burned inside of the window under a very low and diminishing light.*)

The dialogue, tableaux, and pantomimes of the medley called the "Hôtel de Batteau" were well studied and prepared for, exhibition, and the entertainment attracted a full audience, who asked to see it again. There was a novelty about it that was pleasing, and some of the parts were admirably taken and very humorously presented. The two exhibitions secured for Arthur Burns more than the £40 needed for emigration. The boys entered into the business part of the matter, such as the sale of the tickets, with great enthusiasm, and the delight of the audience at the final tableaux made the exhibition an episode of joyous life long to be remembered.

The entertainment was closed by an impromptu patriotic expression. The audience sang, "God save the Queen!" and three cheers were given for British Columbia, three for Mr. Lette, and three for Arthur Burns, the young emigrant.

Aunt Mar continued her investigations in regard to the supposed visit of John Hampden to America in 1622-23. She found a record of one Phineas Pratt, who sailed from England in the "Sparrow," in 1622. He was one of Weston's colony, and he left a "Narrative" of his adventures. News came to Weston's Colony that Plymouth was about to be attacked by the Indians.

"I said," writes Pratt, "that if the men of Plymouth were not informed of this plot, they and we would all be dead men."

Who should go and give them warning?

No one would volunteer to set out on such a perilous expedition through the woods, filled, it might be, with lurking enemies.

At last Pratt resolved to go himself, when the following incident occurred. We quote from Pratt's own narrative. The spelling of Hamdin was to have been expected if indeed the person he met were the English patriot: —

"I came that part . . . Plimouth Bay wher ther is a town of later time . . . Duxbery. Then passing by the water on my left hand . . . came to a brock & ther was a path. Having but a short time to consider . . . ffearing to goe beyond the plantation, I kept running in the path; then passing through James Ryuer, I said in my thoughts, now am I as a deare chased . . . the wolfs. If I perish what will be the condish . . . of distressed Englishmen. Then finding a peec of a . . . I took it up & caried it in my hand. Then finding a . . . of a Jurkin, I caried them under my arme. Then said I in my . . . God hath given me these two tookens for my comfort; yt now he will give me my live for a pray. Then running down a hill J . . . an English man coming in the path before me. Then I sat down on a tree & rising up to salute him said, 'Mr. Hamdin, I am Glad to see you alive.' He said, 'I am Glad & full of wonder to see you alive: lett us sitt downe, I see you are weary.' I said, 'Let . . . eate some parched corne.' Then he said, 'I know the caus . . . come. Masasoit hath sent word to the Governor to let him ( ) yt Aberdikees & his confederates have contrived a plot,' etc., etc."

Was this Mr. Hamdin, John Hampden the patriot?

Aunt Mar could not be sure, though it seemed probable. In 1631, John Hampden the patriot, with Lords Say and Brooke, Pym, and others, purchased a large tract of land on the Narragansett River within the limits of the present State of Connecticut. Did Hampden see this country across the bay when he visited Massasoit at Warren?

Aunt Mar found in the correspondence of Sir John Eliot many things that would make it probable that Hampden had secretly visited America, but the proof was not direct and positive. The study of the lives of Eliot, Pym, and Cromwell occupied the winter evenings of the Hampdens in London, and one of the noblest biographical studies it was. If one would know the really great characters of England, let him read the lives of the patriots and pioneers at the period of the Commonwealth and Charles II., — Hampden, Eliot, Pym, Milton, Williams, Vane, Penn, Lord Baltimore.

Aunt Mar still believed that more positive evidence of the great historic episode of the visit of John Hampden to America, and his interview with the great chief Massasoit, would be found.

"I would not wonder," she said, on giving up her studies in London, "if we found all we have been looking for some day right at home. Now, remember what I say; I have a presentiment that it will be so."

Arthur Burns often called on the Hampdens. He gave all his leisure time to the study of America, reading the great books on the Northwest, such as Lord Ravenswood's "Great Divide," Magoun's "Manitoba," "The History of the Hudson Bay Company," the journals of Vancouver, magazine articles on Lord Selkirk, and articles on Victoria, B. C. He found but little fiction on the subject, and no poetry at all, although the Northwestern Empire would seem to be the most poetic of all new lands, and to invite the highest inspirations of the novelist, poet, artist, and musician. The greater literature and art of America are likely to be associated with this new country. The Augustine age of America is yet to come.

CHAPTER V.

WHY THE MONTANA GIRL WAS NOT SURPRISED.

UNT MAR went to Switzerland in the spring. The party consisted of Aunt Mar, Charles Hampden and Helen Hampden, and a young lady named Helena Earl, from Montana. Their course was from London to Basle by swift train, and from Basle to Lucerne.

They arrived at Lucerne early one spring evening. The glaciers were gleaming like palaces in the sky; Mount Pilatus was dark in twilight shadow, and the lake lay in deep purple under a sky cerulean and amber, pink flowered and gold walled. The sight of a glacier excited Aunt Mar; it filled Charles and Helen with wonder and delight; but it did not seem greatly to interest the Montana girl.

"This is the most beautiful place on earth," said Aunt Mar to Helena.

The Montana girl looked greatly surprised, but merely said, "Is it?"

"Yes," said Aunt Mar. "So travellers and guide-books say. You certainly never before dreamed of a scene as beautiful as this."

The Montana girl was politely silent.

"Look at Pilatus," said Aunt Mar. "The legend is that Pontius Pilate came a wanderer to that mountain and committed suicide there in one of the lakes of the sky. His ghost arises and summons the storms. They used to ring the bells to appease him. Near us are the Lakes of Uri, and the scene of the William Tell legend. Did you ever see a forested mountain as sublime as Mount Pilatus?"

"Yes," said the Montana girl, "I think I have."

"Where?"

"In Montana, British Columbia, and Washington."

"Mr. Lette used to speak of the mountain scenery there as being very grand, and give cold statistics, but I supposed he spoke from the enthusiasm of an explorer. Switzerland, I think, comprises some fifteen thousand square miles of this beautiful scenery, and these ranges are some two hundred miles long. How long are your ranges?"

"I think some two or three thousand from Mount St. Elias to Popocatepetl." The Montana girl spoke rather indifferently, as though a thousand miles of mountains were not a matter to be exact about where the territory was so large.

"You live in a valley in Montana?"

"Yes."

"How large is it?"

"I think it has an area of some seventy thousand square miles. It has not been very well surveyed."

"Seventy thousand miles! Four times as large as all Switzerland, as Mr. Lette said. Your scenery may be more extensive and loftier than this, but it cannot have such beauty. This is the most beautiful place in all the world."

"But why? The long Northern sunsets on the peaks overlooking the Puget Sound are as brilliant as this, and the twilights, which last late into the hours that we call night, or past ten o'clock, are as soft, and have as spiritual a tone of color. I would not like to seem boastful of my own country, but all the splendor of the sunset around us does not surpass the beauties of an early evening in the Selkirks, or at Banff, or near Mount Tacoma or Shasta. The east side of our mountains may lack a certain spirituality of sky tone, but the evening skies of

IN THE CANADIAN WOODS.

Puget Sound seem to me as beautiful as this. I hope I am not prejudiced. This is *a* beautiful scene."

After supper the party went out and sat down by the lake. Helena stepped into the old church for a time to hear the monk play "The Organ Tempest of Lucerne." When she returned to the Hampdens, the sunset fires in the glaciers seemed dying, bells were ringing in the distance, and lights were glimmering on the Righi. Aunt Mar had been purchasing some minerals from a peasant child, and began at once to talk with Helena on the chamois, the mountain goats, and the flowers of the Alps.

The quicksilver mines of the Alps did not seem at all remarkable to the Montana girl, nor would Golconda itself have surprised her. As for Alpine flocks and pastures, had not her father ten thousand sheep and cattle? It was the chamois that Aunt Mar was most pleased to describe, — its adventurous habits and poetic mountain ways.

A HERD OF MOUNTAIN SHEEP.

"It reminds me of the Big Horns," said the Montana girl.

"The Big Horns! What are they?"

"The Rocky Mountain sheep."

"I suppose that they are as big as elephants, and fly through the air, bodies and all," said Aunt Mar, losing all patience at having the wings of her fancy clipped at all points by the Montana girl. "But you wait until we get to Berne, and we shall see some famous animals."

"What, may I ask?"

"Bears."

"I have seen some bears,— grizzlies."

"Yes, but you have never seen those of Berne. They are historic bears."

"No, but I have seen some unhistoric bears."

The Montana girl was very weary, and retired early, leaving the Hampdens overwhelmed with all the mingling splendors of sky, glacier, and lake. There was a poem on the scene that Helena had found in an American paper or magazine, and which she repeated to Aunt Mar. The dark night fell; stars mingled their silver fires in the ice palaces, and Mount Pilatus grew black and the Righi a shadow. At Chamouni the Montana girl entered into the spirit of beauty and seemed at home. Stupendous Mont Blanc thrilled her like the rest of the party; but at Berne her want of interest again provoked Aunt Mar.

They went to the historic bear-pits. Berne was founded where Berthold had slain a bear, so the Bernese keep a bear-pit in memory of the exploit of the hero.

"Poor innocent creatures!" said the Montana girl. "They remind me of our bears of the blueberry-bushes."

"These are historic bears," said Aunt Mar, "as I told you. Did you ever see any as noble?"

"Why — yes. Did you ever see a grizzly bear of the Rocky Mountains?"

"No, I never did."

"It is well you have not; you can enjoy this exhibition the better for it.

'Where ignorance is bliss, 't is folly to be wise.'"

This was too severe a reflection to go unrebuked. "You repeat the same stories as Mr. Lette, the Canadian explorer," said Aunt Mar. "I did think that our Yankee nation exceeded all others for boastfulness, but they are of small account beside a Rocky Mountain Canadian explorer or a Montana girl."

"I beg your pardon. I did not mean to be disrespectful. I could hardly help saying that—"

"What?"

"That these historic bears do not quite meet my expectations."

"Oh!" and Aunt Mar added sharply, "I wonder what would quite meet the expectations of a girl from a ranch in the Rockies!"

"I do not know; I do not mean to be boastful. Will you not come and pay me a visit? You may have free use of my horses, and I will go with you into the Selkirks, and then you will understand what I mean. Your nephew talks of visiting the Northwest; I hope we may have the pleasure of entertaining him. I am sure that he will regard ranch life a very free and noble one, and will think that our mountains and valleys and even bears are not inferior to these. I am sorry if I have seemed rude."

Arthur Burns became acquainted with Helena on the return of the party from Switzerland. Nothing gave him so much pleasure as to question her about life in the great Northwest, partly on account of his growing interest in the great empire, and partly because the very agreeable girl seemed pleased to answer his questions, and enter into the spirit of what he wished to know.

It pleased Helena to so answer his questions as to excite surprise. Once, when he had asked her how long a horseback ride it would be from one end of Montana to the other, she said:—

"Oh, five hundred and forty miles. Do you want to know how large Montana really is? Well, we will call it a great trundle-bed. Come, England and Scotland, get in first; come, Ireland, you will need plenty of room, so we will leave a long space between; come, Denmark, here is a wide space for you; and here, little Holland, you can creep in too. Now you can all go to sleep and not jostle one another."

"How many inhabitants have you?" asked Arthur, one day.

"Oh, less than one hundred and fifty thousand, perhaps."

"I should think one would be rather lonesome in a country of one hundred and forty-five thousand square miles, with only one inhabitant to a mile."

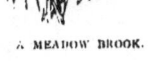

A MEADOW BROOK.

"But," answered Helena, "nearly all of our people are rich, and our poorer cousins from over the sea are coming in flocks, like Sir Joseph Porter's numerous relatives, to keep us company. Our keeping-room is large enough for them all, and we have plenty of grain to feed them all, and plenty of coal to warm them all. I declare, I do pity the poor of London every time I go into the streets. I do not wonder that they become hard, and sick at heart, and ask why they were called into being. They do not know that God has provided a world for them; they think that London *is* the world. You could not find ragged children enough to make a school interesting, in all Montana, or in British Columbia."

Once when Arthur asked her how it was the steamers came loaded every year to Liverpool with visiting Americans, Helena said, with the free air of her own mountains and plains, —

> "Let your people all remember
> Uncle Sam is not a fool,
> Where the people do the voting,
> And the children go to school."

"Are not the settlers troubled with wild animals?" asked Arthur on one occasion.

"Yes, sometimes," answered Helena.

"What kinds are most troublesome?"

"Catamounts in the story-books, cats in reality. I once knew an old lady from Boston who had a fearful adventure on a Montana ranch."

"What was it?"

"She went to the mountains to make a surprise visit to her son-in-law. When she arrived he was not at home; he had gone to Tacoma. So she entered the house and concluded to pass the night there alone with her little grandchild and an emigrant servant. In the night she heard a scratching on the roof.

"'What is that?' she asked of the child.

"'Nothing but old Catamount,' said the sleepy boy.

"'A catamount!' exclaimed the old lady, rising in the greatest terror, and awaking the servant, whom she informed that a great catamount was breaking into the house.

The servant, who had read boys' books of the far West, was as greatly terrified. The scratching continued, and the two terrified souls sat up all night, expecting every moment that the catamount would break in and devour them.

A WINDING MOUNTAIN STREAM.

In the morning the little grandson awoke.

"Oh, my little innocent, such a night as we have had!" said the grandmother. "You said it was a catamount."

"Yes, old Catamount, *the cat*. There she is now at the door. Listen—"

"Mieu!"

Miss Helena imitated the inhospitably treated cat with a most comical expression of the face, her eyebrows lifting, and her lips protruding with a pout of woe. She evidently was not troubled about the wild animals of Montana.

Charlie Hampden and Arthur Burns continued their intimacy until March, when Arthur sailed for America with Mr. Lette, in an Allan Line steamer to Halifax. They were there to take the

RESTING FOR THE NIGHT.

Intercolonial Railroad for Montreal. Charlie promised to meet Arthur in British Columbia in June. He was to return in early summer to Quebec, and had arranged to meet Mr. Lette at Montreal, and to go with him to British Columbia and Washington on his second trip to Vancouver. Mr. Lette made several trips between Montreal and Vancouver during the summer.

A farewell meeting was given to Arthur Burns at the Grace Darling Institute. It was made the occasion of a patriotic entertainment, and many people were invited who were not connected with the school.

The entertainment consisted of Dr. Mackay's cantata, called "The Emigrants," and some original songs written by Mr. Lette. Dr.

LIVERPOOL ON A FOGGY DAY.

Mackay's song, "To the West! to the West!" was sung with great spirit, and "Far, far upon the Sea" was beautifully rendered as a solo. But the most inspiring song of all was "Cheer, boys, cheer!"

THE STEAMSHIP "AMERICA."

WHY THE MONTANA GIRL WAS NOT SURPRISED.

ON THE MERSEY.

"Cheer, boys, cheer, the merry breeze is blowing
To waft us onward o'er the ocean's breast;
The world shall follow in the path we're going,
The Star of Empire glitters in the West.
    Cheer, boys, cheer, for country, mother-country;
    Cheer, boys, cheer, for the willing, strong right hand;
    Cheer, boys, cheer, there's wealth for honest labor;
    Cheer, boys, cheer, for the new and happy land."

This was sung by all the boys, and the chorus shook the old building.

Mr. Lette sang a song of his own composition. It was —

THE PLOUGHSHARES OF THE WEST.

Heart of the West, I love thee, —
 Thy pulses grand and free,
Thy sails of progress as they move
 Across the floral sea.
The pen of art, that song indites,
 May stir the gentler breast;
But history's noblest pages writes
 The ploughshare of the West.
  Good cheer, my boys,
  Cheer, cheer, my boys,
  The ploughshares of the West.

The world's best hands now drive the plough,
 The soil-king's freedom-crowned,
And man's imperial chariots now
 Are those that break the ground.
The rime, the rune, the saga old
 May be the hermit's quest,
But man's best promise writes the bold,
 Brave ploughshare of the West.
  Good cheer, my boys, etc.

Plough on, plough on, till justice rule;
 Plough, for the ages wait;
Plough for the church, plough for the school,
 Plough for the hall of state;
Plough, like the hand of Lincoln, plough,
 Like Garfield, for the best,
And map the fields of nations now,
 Ye ploughshares of the West.
  Good cheer, my boys, etc.

Then hail forever, sons of toil,
 And hail the work ye do,
Thy field the mighty empire's soil,
 And brown thy royal hue!

THE BURNING VESSEL.

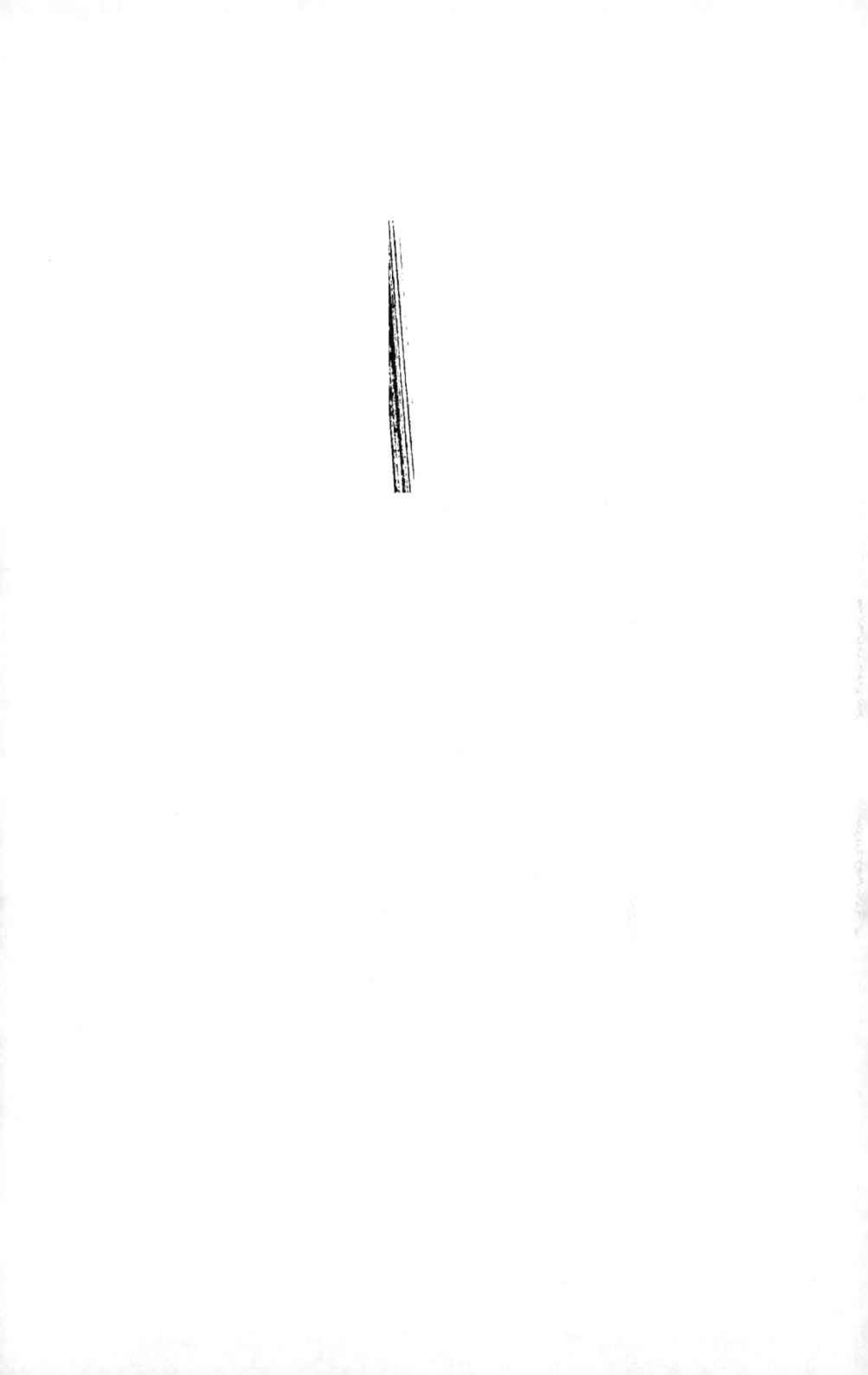

> And hail ye cabin-palace gates
> That ope to every guest;
> All hail! Heaven's noblest blessing waits
> The ploughshares of the West.
> Good cheer, my boys,
> Cheer, cheer, my boys,
> The ploughshares of the West.

Helena Earl took part in the entertainment. She represented America. She stood beside Arthur in the last tableau, dressed in white, holding the American flag in such a way that the folds fell over her shoulders. She looked very beautiful and noble, and the boys called her the Princess Montana. She sang an American song composed by one of her friends in Boston, and set to rearranged music of the old war-tune "Maryland, my Maryland," itself rearranged from an operatic air.

THE AMERICAN KNIGHT.

> LET other lands of knighthood sing!
> Thou art my song, America;
> In thee each free-born soul is king,
> In freedom and America!
> Strong were the hands that planted thee,
> Grand was the "Mayflower" on the sea,
> That bore the seed of liberty
> To thee, the world's America!
>
> The ages waited long for thee,
> Our own, our own America;
> Then rose the pilot of the sea,
> America, America!
> He saw the stars prophetic shine,
> And dreamed the earth a star divine,
> And found, beyond the horizon's line,
> Thy happy isles, America!
>
> Let other lands of knighthood sing!
> Thou art my song, America;
> Each free-born soul is crowned a king,
> In my own land, America!
> I love thy homes, where honor dwells,
> The honest toil that commerce swells;
> I love thy old New England bells,
> My own, my own America!

THE BANKS OF NEWFOUNDLAND.

Arthur ended the entertainment by singing "God Save the Queen," under the folds of the British flag, which he held in his hand. The audience responded with: —

"So say we all of us,
So say we all of us,
So say we all," etc.

Several months later our party were on board the great steamship "America," sailing down the Mersey. Liverpool on a foggy day, when the smoke does not rise above the chimney-tops, is indeed unpleasant; but on this morning the city put on its best appearance, the weather being fine, and the sail down the Mersey was very enjoyable and full of interest.

When but a day out, they saw what is a terrible sight at sea, — a ship on fire. The burning merchantman was clearly beyond control; and the sailors, seeing that their vessel was doomed, were rapidly rowing toward an inward-bound steamer that was waiting to take them back to England.

The time on board passed quickly, and almost before our travellers knew it they were in sight of the Banks of Newfoundland.

CHAPTER VI.

OVER THE CANADIAN PACIFIC RAILROAD TO WINNIPEG. — THE BEAUTY OF THE LAKES; OR, THE SUN-FIRE: A DRAMATIC STORY OF SAULT STE. MARIE.

HE lights of the old French city of Jacques Cartier glimmered on the Heights of Abraham, on the Fortress, and over the Terrace, as the great ocean steamer came calmly to rest. It was late in the evening.

"Passengers who wish to land at Quebec to-night can now go ashore," said the officer of the boat.

THE GULF OF ST. LAWRENCE.

Our tourists were tired of the sea, though the passage had been a smooth one, and they hurried to the tender, and were soon landed at the American city of 1535.

The next day they were on the Canadian Pacific Railroad bound for Montreal. It was a charming ride,—past the ancient settlements, past Lorette of the Huron Indians, founded nearly two hundred and sixty years ago, past beautiful churches and pastoral homes.

Montreal is a surprise, a splendor, a veritable wonder.

OLD HOUSES IN QUEBEC.

It seems to be a city of churches. Situated on an island formed by the junction of the St. Lawrence with the Ottawa, and connected with the mainland by a bridge which is held to be one of the wonders of the world, overshadowed by Mount Royal, overhung with melodious bells and gray bell-towers, hospitable with palace hotels and public buildings, the traveller at once wishes to stop here, and is slow to go. Old Montreal, or Hochelaga, is one of the earliest settlements in America.

Here our tourists met Mr. Lette, and the meeting was a glad one.

Aunt Mar and her niece were to return to Rhode Island after a few days in the city. Charles and Mrs. Earl and Helena were to go to Vancouver with Mr. Lette, after which Helena was to return to her home in Montana by the way of Puget Sound, Tacoma, and the Northern Pacific Railroad.

The first questions that Charles and Helena asked Mr. Lette were about Arthur Burns.

"I left him delighted on a homestead which he had taken near the Gulf of Georgia," said Mr. Lette.

"All alone?" asked both.

"No."

"Who is with him?"

"Wilhelmine."

"Who is *he*?" asked Charles.

"Who is *she*?" asked Helena.

"Arthur joined a party of Swedish emigrants at Vancouver. He had met them on the train. Among them was a girl named Wilhelmine. She was an orphan, and was dependent upon one of the families.

A STREET IN QUEBEC.

Arthur became greatly interested in her. On arriving at Vancouver, and going to the Government Land Office, he found, as I had told him, that this young lady could secure a homestead of one hundred and sixty acres as well as himself, and they thought it would be social to take their claims together. Then Arthur saw that it would be better for them both to have one log-house, and so Wilhelmine consented that the minister should be called to make the matter legal and agreeable. They were living in a tent when I left them, but they will have a log cabin before you arrive. As soon as the cabin is built, Arthur is to obtain work in one of the lumber-mills. A place is promised him at good wages for a beginner."

"How does the place look?" asked Charlie.

"Like a thousand-years-old forest," said Mr. Lette. "They are clearing with fire a place for a garden. They expect to have a clearing for a prune-orchard before fall, and to build a good house when Arthur has earned enough money. The woods are full of game, and the waters will soon abound with wild geese and ducks. They will have a rough time for a year or two, but their three hundred and twenty acres of land will grow in value as the population increases, and they are likely to be well-to-do before ten years. I am glad that Arthur came to Canada."

FALLS OF THE MONTMORENCI.

That evening, Charles, Mrs. Earl and Helena, and Mr. Lette

were on the train for Vancouver, — a train that bridges the continent and makes the Atlantic Ocean a ferriage.

The cars were solid and comfortable. This road is generally level between Montreal and the mountains. Wood is much used

THE CHAUDIÈRE FALLS.

on the engines, so that the black coal-smoke of travel is avoided, and one can sleep as comfortably on these cars as at a palace hotel. Indeed, a humorist has said that a bride could make a tour across the continent by this railroad without so much as soiling her veil. The train stops at least three times a day for meals, and has a fine dining-car attached, or dining-cars that are attached at regular intervals. The road between Montreal and Winnipeg is not so interesting beyond Ottawa as is the rest of the way, the last four hundred miles of which have no equal in the world.

Ottawa is a poem, especially as viewed from the river. It would be even more sightly if the waters were freed from the sawdust of the mills. The government buildings here are among the most beautiful in America, and the views of the river from the parks around these buildings are a summer delight. Here our tourists were met by another Mr. Lette, who has been the city clerk of Ottawa for some thirty years, a local poet and orator who loves his country with real patriotic fervor, and knows how to express the sentiment in prose and verse. With him our tourists hastily visited the Parliament Park, the City Hall, and the wonderful Museum containing the most interesting specimens of minerals and natural history. If you visit Ottawa, reader, be sure to see the curious animals, birds, and Indian masks in this museum. Out of the beautiful Ottawa valley the train swept on its sunny way to Mattawa, and thence to North Bay, a city leaping into life out of the woods on rolling Lake Nipissing; thence to Arthur's Landing, or Port Arthur, nearly one

TOBOGGANING.

thousand miles from Montreal, on the sounding shores of Thunder Bay. The scenery is wild and desolate in places beyond Port Arthur.

CEDAR BAY, NEAR OTTAWA.

The Lake of the Woods offers the most interesting views at its outlet, at Rat Portage. At noon on the third day our tourists were at Winnipeg, 1424 miles from Montreal.

They were now on the Red River of the North and romantic Assiniboine.

From old Fort Gerry of the Hudson Bay Company, on the great Lone Land of the mid-ocean territory, Winnipeg, the metropolis of the Northwest, suddenly began to attract the ears of the world. The Hudson Bay Company's license over the country ceased in 1859. Pioneers began to flock at once to the old Company's post. In 1862 a village had been formed, and England began to hear of the grain-growing ocean of land, in which it rose like an island. In 1870 there were some thirty buildings outside of the fort. In the fall of 1880 the Dominion of Canada and a syndicate of capitalists agreed to begin the construction of the Canadian Pacific Railway. Clear-sighted people were not slow to discern that the situation of Winnipeg must make it a great city if the road should be built. In 1881, speculators reached the town; real-estate agents filled it, and its history is involved in one of those transient excitements called a boom. The town soon became a city; the railroad, after some changes of management, was built, and the city enlarged and is enlarging. Its spires rose over the Lone Land, and its many bells rang over the vast grain sea. It is a very beautiful city to-day, and has a great history before it.

The early history of this vast region of the Lakes has many romantic traditions, and there are few legends of early times that are more worthy of the attention of musician, artist, or poet than one we are about to give the reader. Every nation has a few great legends, as the Anglo-Saxon Chronicle and Arthurean heroes of England, the Rhine-gold and Faust of Germany, and William Tell of Switzerland. Such stories become literature, music, and art. They represent national history and characteristics.

America is yet young. Her great legends have hardly been recognized. When they shall be husbanded for art treasures as in other lands, the following tale of Sault Ste. Marie (itself a beautiful name for art work), is likely to become conspicuous, as it has the largest dramatic possibilities. We may call this legend "The Beauty of the Lakes." The version of it that we give here is furnished us by Mr. Fitzmaurice, a well-known Michigan editor and writer. We abridge

SAULT STE. MARIE.

it from a serial story published by him, and use it by his special permission. The dramatic scene is entirely from Mr. Fitzmaurice's picturesque pen.

THE BEAUTY OF THE LAKES;

OR, THE SUN-FIRE.

A DRAMATIC STORY OF SAULT STE. MARIE.

One afternoon in August, 1670, the Chippewa village at Ste. Marie's Falls was thrown into great commotion. The cause was the simultaneous arrival of what may be termed the representatives of the Cross and the scalping-knife.

To explain; the great Chippewa nation had several branches, the greatest of which were the Hurons and Objibwas. The branch retaining their original name of Chippewa had their principal town at Sault Ste. Marie. North of them was the nation of Iroquois, and south the Objibwas extended their hunting-grounds from Lake Superior to the headwaters of the Mississippi.

Waboegonas, "White Otter" (so called from his light complexion), was chief of the Objibwas. His principal headquarters was upon the largest of the Apostle Islands, near the south end of Lake Superior. His father, a Frenchman, had deserted his mother, a Chippewa chief's daughter, while he was yet a babe. Upon the desertion, his mother, being a high-spirited woman, committed suicide; first, however, intrusting the child to the care of the chief, with the request that he should be brought up and trained to hate white men and avenge his wronged mother. The old chief was faithful to his trust, and White Otter's hostility toward the whites was well known.

Père Marquette, a Jesuit missionary, — born 1637, died 1675, — had labored among the Chippewas at the Sault for two years. He had been largely instrumental in bringing about a treaty between them and the Hudson Bay Company, who, as a result, were about to establish a large trading-post at Sault Ste. Marie.

This gave offence to the great war-chief of the Objibwas, and he made this his excuse for declaring war upon the Chippewas. So he sent Otonogas, "Gray Wolf," his most powerful lieutenant, to convey his message of disapprobation at their harboring the "black coats" and "white snakes," as the missionaries and traders were respectively called.

By a coincidence, the great war canoe arrived at the mouth of the St. Mary River at the same time that the French *coureurs de bois*, with goods to stock the trading-station, arrived at the Falls a mile below. Hence the commotion. It was the knife and the Cross meeting face to face.

The great war-drum began to beat, calling the chiefs and warriors to a grand council.

When all were assembled, Gray Wolf, who was decked in all the barbaric splendor of his high station, with a rich head-dress of gayly-colored eagle-feathers, a gray wolf-skin robe trimmed with black scalp-locks, and a painted face, proudly delivered his message, to the effect that if peace was to continue between the Objibwas and Chippewas, the "black coats" and "the lying white traders who steal Indian maidens" must die; and then with the war-cry of the Objibwas he whirled his tomahawk around his head and launched it with unerring force at the trunk of the pine forming the centre of the lodge, to signify that a refusal meant war to the death.

To this the Chippewa chief with his own tomahawk gave an equally defiant answer, which was received with a shout of approval by the assembled braves: "Let it be war to the death! I care not and fear not! Take thou back my answer to thy chief, and depart in peace."

At this critical moment Père Marquette, followed by Greysolon DuLuth, the brave leader of the traders, pushed his way through the mass of warriors to the open space in the centre. There he stood, silent for a moment, gazing

RIDEAU FALLS, OTTAWA.

upon the multitude surging around him, astonished at his audacity. His eyes blazed with the fire of heroic enthusiasm. Fearlessly he stood, and fearlessly in the name of God he called upon them to cease their bloodthirstiness, and learn to love and forgive; and urged them to conciliate the Objibwa chief and teach him kindness and peace, and turning to the Objibwa, he said that God could so soften the heart of his cruel chief that it would be like the heart of a little child, and, upon being dared, offered to go and tell Waboegonas so to his face.

The Chippewas tried to dissuade him, knowing it was sure death; but he

A WAR CANOE OF THE OJIBWAS.

was firmly convinced of his duty to go in the name of his Master and preach the gospel; whereupon DuLuth announced his intention to accompany the holy father.

At early dawn they entered the war canoe of the Objibwas, and started upon a voyage from which the assembled Indians and *coureurs de bois* felt assured they would never return alive.

They were conducted into the presence of the White Otter, who having been informed by Gray Wolf of what Marquette had said, was speechless with rage. He had them bound hand and foot with tough rawhide thongs, and thrown into the Cave of Death to await the morrow's sacrifice.

DuLuth, for attempting to resist, was knocked senseless by a war-club. During the night he recovered consciousness and found himself in the impenetrable darkness. Soon the stillness was broken by the voice of song and prayer. It was Marquette. He began to comfort DuLuth, and assured him of their certain deliverance. " Stand thou still and behold the glory of God in the rescue." And so it came to pass.

Waboegonas had killed his wife that night because she had interceded in behalf of the two white strangers. His favorite daughter, Wanena, a beautiful girl, and known as the Beauty of the Lakes, actuated partly by the same spirit as her mother, and partly to avenge her mother's death, thereupon determined to rescue them. Under cover of darkness she crept into the cave, freed them from their bonds, and guided them by a secret tunnel to the shore of the lake, amid a thick cluster of cedars, where they were enveloped in a dense fog. She launched a small birch canoe, and at the same time disclosed her identity, and her motive in liberating them. She bade them lose no time, but enter at once and paddle for their lives, and she would pilot them to the Holy Isle.

This island, which they reached about an hour after sunrise, lies nearly in the centre of the great lake, midway between Sault Ste. Marie and the opposite shore. Here the medicine priests of the Objibwas had established the home of the Great Spirit, and woven every possible legend, fable, and myth about it, to beget fear and reverence. Here the Objibwas at stated intervals made pilgrimages to render homage and present offerings to the Great Spirit, or Manitou, whose image was on the island. It was because it was held so sacred that she deemed it a safe hiding-place. The canoe was hidden among the trees. She told them that her plan was for them to hide on the island until they could see if they were pursued, and then continue on their way as soon as they were out of danger, while she would remain and gladly sacrifice herself if need be.

To this DuLuth responded: "No, my girl, if we escape you go with us; and God do so to me as I deal with the woman who has so nobly risked her life to save us. Where shall we hide?"

She led them through thickets and over bowlders, till near the centre of

THE PARLIAMENT BUILDINGS, OTTAWA.

the island they began to descend precipitous, steep rocks. Passing through a narrow chasm between two gigantic pillars, they found themselves in a semicircular space of some fifty feet in diameter, the perpendicular walls reaching up fully seventy-five feet.

Near the centre, on a flat stone, stood the uncouth image of the Manitou, a rudely carved pine trunk, six feet high, and dressed in all the possible Indian fantasy of bark, colored grass, feathers, and beaded buckskin strips. Scattered about were the offerings in the form of war and hunting weapons, broken and disordered.

"I wonder if that murdering ruffian will think to look for us here?"

"I think not, my son; but if directed by the Power that hath led us, he will come."

"I sincerely trust not, father, else our case would be as hard as before, were he to find us here."

"He has found you, and no escape is now possible!" exclaimed a deep voice.

Starting to their feet, the two men beheld with dismay the dreaded form of Waboegonas, with eight of his warriors, standing at the entrance to the sacred enclosure.

They were lost! The Cross and the scalping-knife had at last met face to face! Light and darkness had joined issue! DuLuth grasped an old war-club and stood on the defensive, prepared to sell his life dearly. The Jesuit fell upon his knees and began to recite the prayers for the dying. The Indian girl covered her head with her robe and sank down by the edge of the brook, mournfully chanting her death-song, and awaiting the final stroke, which was sure to come. The Objibwa chief with folded arms stood and gloated upon the victims before him with a fiendish grin upon his face, while behind him stood grouped his warriors, ready at a word to begin the slaughter.

The sun was upon the noon hour, and shot its burning rays directly into the gorge where the awful tableau was being exhibited. For fully five minutes the actors in the tragedy about to be consummated were silent, till at last Waboegonas spoke in sneering sarcasm: "And so the 'black-coat' and the white woman-stealer have come to die at the feet of the god of the Objibwas?"

The priest arose from his kneeling position, and looking the savage full in the face, replied: "Yes, heathen, if so be our hour has come, we can die defying both thee and thy god."

So sure was the chief of his prey, that like the cat with the mouse, he could afford to torment before slaying them. Advancing close to the priest, he hissed: "Can the 'black coat's' god save his scalp from the knife of Waboegonas?"

"He can, if it is His will, thou pagan wolf," replied Marquette, "and I defy thee to do thy worst. We fear not death."

"'Black coat,' you lie!"

"I lie not, Objibwa; for as sure as yon sun shines down upon your hideous idol here, just so sure can the God we serve deliver us out of thy cruel hands!"

"Ha, ha, ha! Waboegonas and his braves would be glad to see how your god can deliver you."

"Come on, you great hulking coward, you slayer of helpless women, you murderer of unarmed men! Come to me if you dare, and I will show thee how a man can fight," said DuLuth, whirling his club.

The savage gazed at him with a momentary feeling of admiration: "The woman-stealer is a brave when he knows he has to die, but Waboegonas will not soil his hands with a dog's blood. The torment and the fire are for him."

"Do your worst, you cowardly snake; I defy you!" retorted the Frenchman.

"Man's extremity is God's opportunity, chief," said the priest, raising his crucifix on high.

The monotonous chant of the girl's death-song filled in the silence which ensued.

It was a spectacle of sublimity, worthy to be perpetuated, a sight for gods to admire. The sun glared down with still greater intensity, till the interior of the heathen sanctuary glowed like an oven.

"Ere yonder sun shall reach the top of that hemlock, 'black coat,' thou diest," said the chief, pointing upward.

The priest followed the direction indicated by the long, lean, cruel hand, with finger pointing, and saw that not more than five minutes would elapse ere the top of the tree would shade the orb.

"Chief," said the priest, turning to the Objibwa, "thou hast often been dared to deadly strife, and hast dared others to the same. I am a poor, weak, unarmed man, and thou a mighty warrior, and still I will dare thee."

"To what combat, 'black coat'?" asked the chief with a sneer.

"To a battle between my God and thine. If the God I serve can conquer thy god, thou wilt agree to spare our lives, and become, thou and thy warriors, Christians. If, on the contrary, thy god shall overcome mine, then shall our lives be at thy disposal. Dare thou?"

"A battle of gods would certainly be a strange thing; but how are they to fight?"

"If the God I serve shall send down fire from heaven and destroy thy god yonder, so that your Manitou be consumed to ashes, will you spare us, and become a Christian?"

THE UNIVERSITY OF TORONTO.

"I will, if I see the fire come and burn the sacred totem of the Objibwas yonder. But there must be no white man's tricks. It must be fire from yonder cloudless sky," replied the chief.

"I have no fire near me, chief, but my God in answer to my call will send His fire to consume your idol, and if I prevent it not will also destroy thee and thy warriors."

"That I will better believe, old Joss-a-keed [medicine man], when I see the sacred totem burning, and not sooner. I heed not woman's words."

"Do you accept these terms, chief?"

"I do!" replied the chief, confidently.

"Warriors of the Objibwas, you are witnesses to this. Will you swear by your totem to faithfully do as you have heard promised by your chief?" asked the priest, turning to the warriors.

"We all do!" replied the Objibwas.

"Then to this, chief, you also add pardon for your daughter?"

"Yes; show us your great medicine, you old witch doctor."

"And permission for the black fathers and the white traders to preach and trade with your nation is by you to be freely granted?"

"I do! Let the fire from your Great Spirit come and save you, for our knives are thirsty for blood," cried Waboegonas, impatiently.

"In the name of Heaven, what do you propose doing, father? Cannot you see the murderers are mocking you?" asked DuLuth, excitedly.

"It is in the name of Heaven I act, my son, and may Heaven forgive the sin, if sin there be, in what I am about to do; but the end fully justifies the means we use. Now, chief, draw near and behold; there is no imposition practised. Oh for the all-powerful faith in God held by Elijah on Carmel!"

The chief drew closer to the image with evident reluctance, and near by him stood the priest. The warriors in a huddled group looked on with awed interest, while DuLuth, leaning upon the war-club, watched with anxiety what was to happen, of which he knew as little as did the savages. The monotonous death-song of the girl still continued, and the sun's disk had nearly reached the shade of the hemlock.

"In the name of Jehovah, I command fire to come down and destroy this heathen idol!" shouted the priest in Chippewa, at the same time extending the crucifix over the mass of feathers, grasses, and bark, already intensely heated by the sun's vertical rays. A bright, fluttering spot seemed to dance for a moment on the breast of the idol and finally remain perfectly still. In a few seconds more the chief started back amazed at beholding a thin column of blue vapor ascending, which almost immediately burst into a bright flame.

Astounded, the Indians beheld the strange phenomenon, which, owing to the inflammable nature of the material of which the idol was composed, became in a few seconds more a mass of fierce flames, and with a shout, "The white man's God has won!" all — with the chief included — fell prostrate to the earth and hid their faces in amazed terror.

So thoroughly surprised was DuLuth at witnessing this seemingly wonderful interposition of Heaven in their behalf, that he too fell upon his knees and strove to recall the long-forgotten prayers of his youth.

A BRANCH OF THE ST. LAWRENCE.

It only required a few moments to reduce the idol to a charred billet of smoking wood, and the deed was done!

"Arise, chief, and behold the power of my God," cried the priest, his countenance beaming with exultation. Trembling in every limb and thoroughly conquered, the chief arose, and gazed affrighted at the smoking cinder that had been his invincible god.

"Will the mighty black medicine spare Waboegonas?" he timidly asked, thoroughly subdued.

"Yes, chief, provided you submit to be here baptized a Christian, no harm shall reach you. But you and your warriors must carry out the agreement entered into."

"We will, great Joss-a-keed; thou canst do what may please thee best, only bring no more fire from the Great Spirit," pleaded Waboegonas.

It was a strange sight to behold these wild savages, thoroughly tamed by superstitious fear, kneeling around the priest, with their weapons deposited at his feet. The Jesuit looked like one transfigured, as he stood telling the story of Christianity in fluent Chippewa, till at last, gathering water in his hands from the brook, he administered the rite of baptism to each, beginning with the chief, all submitting in passive subjugation.

It was a wonderful triumph for the Cross over the scalping-knife!

Poor Wanena, momentarily expecting the death-blow from the cruel war-club of her father, had sat crouching, with her head enveloped in her mantle, crooning her song of death. She was perfectly oblivious of all else transpiring, till the terrified shout from the Indians caused her to look up. It was an awful sight which met her view. The totem was one mass of ashes, through which glowed the horrible visage of the idol. For the first and last time in the life of Wanena she fell into a deep swoon, and so remained till DuLuth raised her up, when with grief he took it for granted she was dead.

As for him, a thousand conflicting emotions were coursing through his mind. His astonishment was fully as great as that of the savages, and so remained till he could whisper to the Jesuit in French: "Tell me, father, did the Almighty actually send fire from heaven in answer to your prayers?"

"Alas! for my faith, my son, it was not so; but the seeming miracle had its origin in very simple and natural causes. This little burning-glass, which I affixed to the crucifix and gathered a focus of the sun's rays by it directly upon the idol, was the instrumentality in God's hands in saving us; but the end justified the means used."

"Well, father, in view of the result obtained, we will not stop to discuss or criticise the questionable theology; but our thanks are due to Heaven that you were permitted to keep the glass when I had lost my pistols and rifle."

"Which teaches us, my son, that it is not by might and power, but by God's spirit, men are saved, both in this and the world to come. But see yonder to the Indian maid. Can she be sleeping?"

DuLuth, as related, found poor Wanena in an unconscious condition,

A little water, however, sufficed to restore her, when she clung in frantic fear to DuLuth, who found new emotions surging in his bosom as the pretty maiden nestled in his arms. Soothing her with kind, endearing words, he led her in fear and trembling to the presence of her dread father, and said: "Waboegonas, now that all is peace between us, I have a favor to ask. Let this little hand I hold belong to me, if its beautiful owner will consent. What say you, Wanena,—can you become the white trader's bride?"

"Wanena has risked her life for the chief she loves, and joy would fill her heart to be taken to his lodge," said the happy girl, nestling still closer to the trader.

"What says the great chief to this?" asked DuLuth.

"That my best-beloved daughter is yours, white chief, especially as you promise to make her your wife. The mother who bore me gave her life for a false lover,—my father,--and thus left me as a curse to all pale-faces. Wanena has the spirit of my mother, and will be a true wife to you. I am rich in lands and furs. Ten thousand warriors will reply when Waboegonas shouts his war-whoop, and his daughter will not go to the lodge of the white chief with empty hands. Take her, chief, and may her fate be happier than that of her mother—or of mine. I have spoken."

"Chief, doubtless you have suffered, but all things come to an end; so with your suffering and revenge. In my mating lawfully with your daughter a new era opens up for you and your people, and I and the good father here will do all we may to elevate and instruct the Objibwas."

"Son, said I not, 'Stand still and behold the glory of God'? Are not these hands still wet with the water of holy baptism?"

"True, father; and now let the holy sacrament of marriage follow upon the heels of the other. Make this maid my lawful wife."

"Gladly, my son, gladly; but first let me here receive her by baptism into the bosom of Mother Church;" and kneeling by the little brook in the despoiled sanctuary of the heathen, the first Objibwa woman received Christian baptism, after which the words were spoken which made her the loving wife of Greysolon DuLuth. The Indians, now assured that no fire would consume them, looked upon all this with much interest, and in the case of Waboegonas it was wonderful how the look of his countenance had softened and humanized. The change effected in him was real.

"If the white chief and black father are ready, we must cross quickly to Pawating," said the chief. "Otonogas is there with many warriors, and the battle may even now be fought."

"Merciful Heaven!" cried the priest, "and we lingering here! Let us at once seek to stop the slaughter. Away, chief, and prove thy new faith by thy works of mercy."

The two war canoes which had borne the men who came to slay but stayed to pray, sufficed to bear the extra passengers; and driven by stalwart arms the light barks flew over the lake till they arrived at Sault Ste. Marie. They were none too soon, as Otonogas had his men ready to attack the Chippewas that very night. The latter were just as eager for the fray, and a few hours later would have witnessed a perfect slaughter.

AN ISLAND IN THE LAKE OF THE WOODS.

But the arrival of Marquette, DuLuth, and the great Objibwa chief placed matters in an entirely different attitude. Waboegonas had but few words to say, though they were to the point. There would be no war; the missionaries and white traders were to enter and dwell where they pleased among the Objibwas; the worship of the Manitou was to be in the future dispensed with, and the God of the black father was to take his place henceforth in Indian theology.

It was a time of surprises all around. None was greater than that of the *coureurs de bois* when DuLuth introduced his Indian bride, who was received with all the honors.

The work of Père Marquette was very much aided and simplified by the story told far and near of the scene on Holy Island. His preaching was received with tenfold more favor, and the rivalry of the Joss-a-keeds, or medicine men, of the tribes, received a serious set-back. Churches were established from Mackinac to Duluth, and far into the interior, while the name of the beloved missionary was to the Indians ever the synonym for all true, good, and brave, till three years later, aged but thirty-eight years, he died.

Greysolon DuLuth is a character in history; and here it need only be said that he lived long and happy with his devoted, heroic Indian wife, who bore him brave sons and fair daughters. His name is perpetuated in that of the beautiful city at the head of Lake Superior, where can still be found those who boast descent from him and his beautiful bride.

CHAPTER VII.

A THOUSAND MILES TO THE MOUNTAINS.

HE Rocky Mountains are now one thousand miles away, over a level of green prairies, or steppes, that rise so gradually that the ascent is not noticed; over the Buffalo plains, where only the bones of the buffalo are left to remind one of the wild empire of gigantic animals; over seas of snow in winter and seas of bloom in summer, the home of the fox, the coyote, the prairie-dog, the nesting-places of the grouse and the prairie-hen.

The names of the places and railroad towns along the way themselves describe the journey, — as Meadows, Poplar Point, High Bluff, Portage la Prairie (on the Assiniboine River).

The towns, or railroad stations, occur at intervals of less than ten miles; as a rule they contain from about one hundred to one thousand inhabitants. Brandon, the great grain-market, at an altitude of some eleven hundred feet, has forty-five hundred inhabitants, or more. The town is less than ten years old, and yet it is already beautiful.

Near Fleming, the province of Assiniboia is entered, — a name as full of music as that of the river from which it is formed. Here and there are ponds, and colonies of water-fowl. At Broadview the Cree Indians begin to surround the stopping train. The prairie now rises rapidly until Qu'Appelle is reached, at an altitude of two thousand feet, some seventeen hundred and fifty miles from Montreal.

Regina, the capital of Assiniboia, has a population of more than two thousand. Near the railroad station is the governor's residence, and the headquarters of the Northwestern mounted police. At every stopping of the train picturesque cavaliers and blanketed Indians appear. The latter have polished buffalo-horns to sell. At some of the stations are bright flower-gardens in summer, and chained bears.

A PRAIRIE STATION.

Moosejaw, a busy market-town, has a curious name. The Indians call it The-creek-where-the-white-man-mended-the-cart-with-a-moose-jaw-bone.

The name contains the early history of the town. The white settlers abridged the name to Moosejaw, which unpoetic name the town seems destined to bear.

Next come the Old Wives' Lakes, alkaline, with no outlet, and surrounded by the wallows of the once long processions of buffaloes. At Medicine Hat, so called because it was the head of medical sup-

CITY HALL, WINNIPEG.

plies for the Indians in early days, Cree Indians and mounted police are again objects of interest. At Calgary, 2264 miles from Montreal, the Rocky Mountains come into view. Calgary is the first step on the immediate way to the regions of the sky.

Calgary is beautiful. Hills surround it, and white peaks look down upon it. Here Indians mingle so freely with the people that time seems to have been set back a hundred years. We are in the land of the red men. Ranches and great herds are here, foot-hills and terraces, and the green waters of the Bow River.

We are now at an altitude of more than four thousand feet. Suddenly the high mountain-walls appear in purple, silver, and gold. We are at the Gap. The snows are over us even in midsummer. The air grows keen; two peaks rise to the sky like the posts of giant-land; The whistle screams; we enter. We are now among the chimneys of the Carboniferous ages, going up, up, up, among the glaciers, and through the rents and ruins of stupendous heights whose history have long passed the memory of men. Castellated heights rise over broken walls; there is Wind Mountain, here the Three Sisters. Here are mountains on edge; there towers stately and solid rise from eternal bases; everywhere are dark forests, cascades, and clear-water streams.

Look into the distance among the clouds. A great mountain is hurrying to meet us, so it seems. It is miles away, but it approaches and hangs its crystal fountains over us. How it divides the sky! How majestic it marches through the blue air! It is Cascade Mountain.

Where? In the Rocky Mountain Park, or, as it is now known, the Canadian National Park, or Banff, or Banff Hot Springs. Banff is the Lucerne of the American Alps; it will one day be the American Baden-Baden as well. Here is the future pleasure-ground and sanitarium of Canada, of England, of the new cities rising and enlarging on Puget Sound. Banff is a plateau amid granite-like towers that rise like unconfused Babels, and of stairways to the sky. Heaven and earth there meet, and over the emerald waters of the Bow one seems to drift in the regions of the sky.

The Cascade Mountain is some ten thousand feet high. It has met us. The train slows. A lovely village is near us. Under the green forests of Sulphur Mountain carriages sweep down from large

RAFTING: BREAKING A GLUT.

hotels. Mounted police again appear. Well-to-do-looking people are waiting at the station. There is animation and bright looks everywhere. Yet all seems strange, as though we were out of the world. We are in the high altitudes now. Mountains foam with cascades, glaciers glisten, the Bow runs clear with glacier water. One feels light and happy, as though a great pressure had been lifted. The sky is a living splendor. We are at Banff.

There was one little animal that greatly amused our travellers at two points on the way; it was the coyote. Foxes were often seen in the morning hours, running away from the coming train. Prairie-dogs were met everywhere on the plains. They were too well accustomed to living near the track to be frightened. The coyote, or little wolf, most interested the passengers, and a story was related by an American traveller which well illustrates the habits of this cunning animal. We give it here in the story-telling form of the newspaper or magazine, with some expansion for the sake of greater interest.

"WOLVES! WOLVES!"

OR, THE ROGUISH LITTLE COYOTE.

"'C-o-y-o-t-e.' Audley, what does that spell?"
"Coyote," I said. "I think it is a Mexican word."
"And what is a coyote, Audley?"
"A kind of wolf, I think; is it not?"
"A wolf, a wolf!" Aunt North adjusted her spectacles, and then exclaimed again, "A wolf? Audley, what do you think I am reading?"
"I do not know, Aunt; a letter?"
"A letter from Elmer. Listen. 'One night the cunning coyotes carried away our pies, stole them out of our closet through the open window, and we found the empty plates among the sage-bushes.'"

Elmer lived in New Mexico. He was Aunt North's nephew. His father and mother died in his boyhood, and Aunt North had given him a home and an education. She had offered the boy a home from the principles of duty and charity. But Elmer had a quick wit, a loving nature, and very attractive manners, and she came to love him. She seemed to think of him all the time. At last, he was the world to her. Her affection spoiled him. She sent him to college, and liberally supplied him with money. His money and his generous, affectionate nature made him very popular among the students; his easy social life led to dissipation; he was expelled from the college, and he returned to Aunt North in disgrace.

"Elmer," said the good lady, "you have done wrong, but I stand in your dead mother's place, and will forgive you. No mother ever turned against her son."

Aunt North was a maiden lady. She was rich, according to town estimate. Her father and grandfather had "traded at sea," to use the local designation of an old-time commercial life. She had inherited a good estate, kept it, and increased it. She had had but one weakness in a long life, — it was for Elmer. Her affection for him became so strong that she seemed blind to his faults. The tempter was always wholly to blame in her eyes when Elmer did wrong. When she said to him, on his disgrace, "I will forgive you," he had replied, "You are like a mother, Aunt," and had kissed her.

"Like a mother." The words were golden to Aunt North, and they turned into actual gold to Elmer. Aunt North "set him up in business," for these pretty words and the kiss, people said. He failed in something less than a year. But Aunt North only said, "The poor boy is very unfortunate, and I stand in his mother's stead, and pity him." Among his misfortunes there came another to him; he fell in love with a young woman of a pretty face, but without good sense, — "not facalized," the neighbors said, — and one day this unpromising couple disappeared from the place, the former taking with him his creditors' money. Where the handsome couple had gone no one knew, and no one but Aunt North and Elmer's creditors cared to know.

Aunt North paid his debts. She "stood in his mother's stead."

"I cannot give up Elmer," she said. "'Charity suffereth long and is kind, endureth all things, hopeth all things, thinketh no evil.'" Aunt North liked to quote this Scripture. "I was not strict enough with the motherless boy, but I meant well; I shall never give him up. We help people by believing in them and hoping good of them. I shall still love, believe, and hope. He has a heart, after all. I shall live to see a change in him; I feel it in my bones." Aunt North, like other good people of her town, believed "her bones" to be prophetic.

By "a heart" people thought that Aunt North merely designated that poetic superficial affection that expresses itself in tender words and pleasing familiarities. She was a lonely woman; no one had told her that any one loved her but Elmer; no lips had kissed her cheek but Elmer's; no companionship had ever been like Elmer's; for years Elmer's development and education had been all her thought and life.

After his disappearance she seemed to brood upon his memory, and the happy years they had passed together. The townspeople called him a "scapegrace," and blamed her for her fond attachment to him, and she came to care nothing for society in which her heart's idol was only condemned.

THE THOUSAND ISLANDS.

Where had he gone? Would he ever write to her? Did he remember her with love?

Years passed, when one day there came to her a letter from New Mexico. It was from Elmer. He was living on a ranch in the Organ Mountains. He begged her forgiveness for the "youthful mistakes" that he had made, and filled a page with loving memories which he felt reasonably sure his fond aunt would fill out and indorse like a check. Aunt North read the letter a hundred times, and always ended it with, "My own dear boy, I always believed in him."

One day she read it to Judge Holden, who had the care of her estate.

"Miss North," said the judge, "let me advise you. Do not answer that letter at all. There will come another soon, asking for money. Wait and see. You will not answer it, will you?"

Aunt North was silent. The prophecy of her "bones" was very active just now in her mind.

"Not till I get another," she at last said hopefully. "I'll wait until I hear from Elmer again."

"You will hear from him again soon enough," said the judge. "That letter is only a feeler. He knows how; don't you ever be befooled by such a scatter-brains as he again. Now, I warn you. I know women; and women are women! When they lose their hearts they lose their heads."

"Oh, judge, we used to be so happy once; and—"

"And what? I should think it was 'and'!"

"And 'charity,' you know."

"No, Miss North, you stick to Audley here; he's got some moral principle and common sense. So Elmer's found something to do in New Mexico; let him do it. Don't you go to sending him money; keep your money for Audley. He'll know how to take care of it."

During the last year Aunt had become an invalid. Her disease was a peculiar kind of rheumatism, that had affected and stiffened her joints; "acidity of the blood," one of her many doctors had termed it. She had been obliged to use a crutch, or thought that she had, from the first development of the disease; of late she had used two crutches, and hardly took a step without a halt and a sigh.

So she sat in her arm-chair day by day, and her mind seemed to be far away among the Organ Mountains, and the coyotes also seemed to be very active in her imagination.

"You said, Audley, that a coyote was a wolf?"

"Yes, the American jackal."

"A jackal!" Her cap-border rose like wings. "Oh, Audley, I've read about them in the missionary magazines. They rob the dead."

Here was an evolved view to the terrible coyote.

"How would you like to live in New Mexico, Audley, among the wolves and the jackals?"

"I should hate to have them eat up my pies," said I.

"Pies!" exclaimed my aunt. "Oh, Audley, you have none of those finer sentiments that Elmer used to have!"

Another letter came from Elmer. It described a sunrise in the Organ Mountains. It was a glowing letter, full of poetic thoughts and images. The sun was described as rising behind enormous pillars of earth, that lifted themselves to the heavens like organ-pipes. The air was a "crystal sea," and in these "gardens of the gods" and "resplendent atmospheres" "all diseases of mind and body, in most cases, utterly disappeared."

Aunt North's imagination kindled. If she could only go to this land of magical healings and enchantments, her old days of health and happiness might return to her.

She read the letter to Judge Holden.

"Harden your heart, harden your heart, and don't lose your head," said the judge. "He knows what he's about. People die in the Organ Mountains. I never heard of a Mexican greaser that lived forever."

Elmer's next letter described a moonrise in the Organ Mountains. It affected Aunt as Byron on Lake Leman might have enchanted a school-girl. She read the Aladdin-like description aloud to me. Toward the close of the letter her voice faltered, and she ceased reading. Her eyes filled with tears.

"I always knew it," she said.

"What?" I asked.

"That Elmer loved me. Listen!"

She read, her hands trembling with emotion: "'A little girl has been born to us; I shall name her Mary North, for you, dear Aunt.'"

She put the letter over her face and cried like a little child. Then her tears ceased; a light of hope came into her beautiful face.

"Audley, I used to be so happy!"

"Yes; well?"

"Do you not think, Audley, that you and I could go to the Organ Mountains, if we engaged a palace car all to ourselves?"

"But you are a crip— You cannot walk, Aunt."

"Yes, I know; but we would have a car all to ourselves, Audley."

SOUTH SASKATCHEWAN RIVER, MEDICINE HAT, ASSINIBOIA.

"But think what it would cost, Aunt."

"Yes, I know; but I have spent little money on myself since Elmer went away. I am not poor, Audley, — not very poor. The trip might cure me; my bones seem to say so. The air of New Mexico is wonderful, Elmer says. Don't mention to any one what I have said. Judge Holden would want a 'gardeen' appointed over me if he knew that I dreamed of such a journey."

There gradually came a far-away look into Aunt's face. Her life became a dream. Her "bones" were full of prophecy.

"Next month is Thanksgiving, Audley."

"Yes."

"I wish that we could go and visit Elmer, and see his little girl, and give him a surprise; that would be something to be thankful for. I have always thought that Thanksgiving Day should be one of family reconciliations. If I were a governor, Audley, I would put that in my Proclamation; I would ask every family to make the day one of reconciliation. That would be something to be thankful for."

"I wish that you were able to go, Aunt."

"Audley, when the mind is able, the body commonly is able. I am going to write to the agent of the Southern Pacific about it. Elmer was once as a son to me; we must be reconciled."

One morning Aunt came into the room on her crutches, looking very happy, holding a letter in her hand.

"Audley," she said, "I am going South, and I wish you to go with me. I think the journey will do me good. I may find some new doctor there, too."

"Where, Aunt, are you going?"

"Well, to New Orleans, and farther, if I am able. It is all arranged."

"When are you to start, Aunt?"

"We will start the week before Thanksgiving week. The dates are all arranged. We are to have a special car as far as El Paso, — you and my maid and I."

"El Paso? El Paso is not — is not anywhere near New Orleans, Aunt."

"Tut, tut! Oh, no; but I know where I am going. It will be a splendid trip for you, and it will get me out of the ruts of life. I feel that a change would do me good; I feel it in my bones."

I was a lad of fifteen years. This would be my first long journey. I hardly knew where I was going, but I knew I was going to El Paso, and the very name had the charm of romance. I had also heard Aunt speak of the railroad "connection with the Atchison, Topeka, and Santa Fé route," which also sounded very grand. Santa Fé, the oldest town in America, — would I see that, and the Organos Mountains, "earth's great silent organ," as Elmer described them, "behind whose golden pipes rise the sun, and whose silver pipes the moon," and the coyotes, whatever they might be? Aunt seemed to have forgotten the coyotes, the "wolves that ate pies."

Aunt left the town on her crutches, amid the remonstrances of all her friends. Every one believed that the journey would somehow end in a visit to Elmer, and every one thought that her heart was better than her head.

Away to Buffalo, to Cincinnati, to Chattanooga, and then away again from the great shadow of Lookout Mountain to the regions of the cotton-fields; past Birmingham at night, with its furnaces blazing against the black sky; over the long bridge of Lake Pontchartrain, and into the old French city of New Orleans! How delightful it all was to Aunt, and what a geography lesson to me! I seemed to live a week in a single day.

Aunt did not stop in New Orleans at all; she did not leave the car. In an hour after our arrival we were flying away toward the green fields of Texas, past live-oaks trailing with moss, and old plantations and quaint negro cabins.

It was a long ride from New Orleans to El Paso,

A GOOD HARVEST.

but we arrived at the latter place one listless sunny afternoon, and found it full of fine hotels, to one of which we were taken. The town was alive with Mexican people, and the next morning I took the horse-car and crossed the Rio Grande, and visited the old church in El Paso del Norte, in Mexico.

It was a region of brown mountains of all kinds of queer shapes, that glimmered in the clear air and bright sun, without any vegetation, not so much as a tree. The charm of the place seemed to lie in the brightness of the air, the splendor of the sunlight, and the barren grandeur of the castle-like mountains. It seemed to me much as Elmer had described the region, a "castle land of the giants."

Aunt rested but a single day; she seemed impelled to go on. We found ourselves on a palace-car again, this time on the Atchison, Topeka, and Santa Fé Railroad, and the wonder of the brown mountains with their fantastic shapes grew. A day's ride brought us to a quaint town, seeming more Spanish than American, and here in a good hotel, half windows and balconies, our long railroad journey came to an end, and Aunt began to make inquiries about "one Elmer North." The people at the hotel knew him. He lived about five miles from the place, and I engaged a mule-team to take us there the next day, at Aunt's direction.

We were among the Organ Mountains. Everything seemed colossal and strange. The world was pictured in my mind like a vast cathedral, and the mountains around me were its grand organ, silent indeed, but grand.

We sat on the upper balcony of the hotel that night, and saw the harvest moon rise. I never had dreamed of anything so scenic and beautiful. We saw her appearing, like a silver world behind the stupendous pillars of brown earth, as in a dream. The splendor was inconceivable as she emerged into the clear air above them. The world seemed changed into some mighty temple, into which the goddess of night was descending like Dian, for the moon appeared not to rise, but to fall. The town was still, the lights few. We went to rest early.

The next morning, after some assistance, Aunt was seated in the mule-team. I thought it a hard seat for her with her lameness, which latter I noticed seemed less troublesome; but she showed great resolution, and the people of the hotel and the driver were very kind to her. The morning air was clear and exhilarating. She left the little maid and her baggage at the hotel to await further orders. I went with her, and was soon lost to the grand scenery that filled the atmosphere around me, in watching the cunning little prairie-dogs, as they appeared and disappeared on every hand.

"You are sure that Mr. North is at home," said Aunt to the driver, with an expression of anxiety in her face.

"Yes, I think so; he may have gone to the protracted meetin', up to Santa Fé, — his wife's turned Methody, — but I guess not. They have a young child, only a few months old, — a little girl. I guess you'll find 'em there, but I can't be certain. A woman can't stay at home forever in these mountains, you know; it makes 'em go crazy. They'll be at home to-night, anyway. Are you any particular relation of theirs?"

"Yes, I'm his aunt."

"He'll be proper glad to see ye, I reckon Where did you come from?"

"From — near Boston."

"Ah, did you? So far away from everybody, too. I've hearn tell of the place. It was where they fit the Revolutionary War. A very old place, I reckon."

The sun brightened. The mountains seemed to burn. The atmosphere became a calm, living splendor.

"That's North's place over yonder," said the driver.

A long white house appeared amid an island of low green trees and a gray border of vineyards.

We presently met a tall, lank settler on horseback.

"Norths at home?" asked the driver, abruptly.

"No, I guess not. He's gone with his wife to the protracted meetin'."

"His men are at home?"

"No, gone to the cattle-show."

"Sho! you don't say so. I've brought down some company. They'll all be at home to-night, won't they?"

"Oh, yes, yes, be at home to-night. Let his company stay until they come home. 'T will give 'em a chance to look around a little."

Aunt looked troubled.

We soon arrived at the clean white adobe house. The driver got down and opened the door.

"All right, lady; I'll help you down and get you in. It's all right. North and his folks will be home before long, and proper glad to see ye."

Aunt was helped down with trembling limbs, and with a most distressed face.

We went into the house. It was a simple place, but very neat. Aunt sat down, laying her crutches on the floor. I paid the driver, and the team rolled away in a glimmering cloud of dust.

"I don't feel quite right to be left here, a stranger, in this way," said Aunt. "Let's keep the door shut, Audley; suppose a pack of those wolves — coyotes — should come, and the folks all away?"

The day passed in dead silence, — a long blaze of sunlight. Aunt watched through a little window for the return of Elmer, but no human being appeared. There was plenty of food in the house, and we felt free to eat what we needed.

At last the great red sun went down between the pillar-like mountains. Aunt began to look very anxious, and I shared her fears. The moon came up as the sun went down. The mountains stood like great shadows against an ocean-like sky. The mountains seemed to grow in size, and the silence of everything was oppressive. Hours passed; the evening was late. We listened

PORTAGING A CANOE IN THE WOODS OF CANADA.

almost breathlessly for any sound. Moonlight, awful shadows, and silence! At last we heard a far-away cry.

"Hark! What's that?" said Aunt.

It was answered by another sharp cry. Then it seemed to be answered by a hundred cries.

"Wolves! wolves!" said Aunt. "The mountains are full of wolves. Don't you hear them?"

She began to tremble.

"Fasten the windows," said she. "I'm going to have a trembling-fit."

The poor woman shook all over. I began to shake in nervous sympathy.

She then rose up, and walked to and fro the long, connecting rooms, wringing her hands. I did not notice at the time that she did not use her crutches; I was too much frightened to think of that strange event.

"Audley, do you know the way back to the town?"

"Yes."

"Are you sure?"

"Yes."

"Could you run there?"

"Yes."

"*They* may not be at home to-night, and we might be eaten up by coyotes before morning. I have read of such things. The mountains are full of them."

"'T is five miles to the town," said I.

"But 't is only about half that distance to that last lot of houses that we passed."

"About two miles, Aunt."

"Audley, let's go."

"But you cannot run, Aunt."

"Why not? Yes, I can. It is the will that runs, don't you know? I can run as fast as you can. I used to run when I was a girl. *Why* can't I run?"

"I'll go out and see if the road is clear and safe."

"I'll go too."

The road lay level in the full moon. The air was like a silver sea.

"Audley, what shall we do? I'll start if you will."

Just then there pierced the air the most terrific, spiteful cry, or bark, that ever fell on my ears. It was, or seemed, answered in the distance, and then the same sharp cry seemed to change into a hundred, as though one wolf had suddenly become multiplied into a hundred wolves.

"Yep, yep, yep, yep!" and we looked around in wildest terror, and were about to re-enter the house, when we saw an object with a little head on the top of an adjoining shed.

"They're climbing the house," said Aunt, "a hundred of them. We must run. Just hear them! We cannot go back now. Run!"

"Yep, yep, yep, yep!" I never heard such a peculiar, spiteful sound. I verily thought that a pack of wolves was climbing the house, and would be likely to leap down upon us if we returned. I ran; Aunt followed, holding me by the hand. She faltered once, and said something about "crutches;" but there came another piercing cry from the vicinity of the house, which seemed, as before, to change into a hundred voices, and she started forward again with renewed energy.

The noise seemed to be answered from every hill.

"They think they've got us," said she; "a hundred of them, or nearer a thousand. Sounds as though they were biting one another's heads off. They do sometimes, I've read,—just eat one another up."

After this startling recollection we flew. Lights soon appeared ahead, and then came up a great mule-team full of people. It stopped.

"Hello, strangers! what is the matter?" said a man in a very pleasant voice.

"Wolves! wolves!" said Aunt, panting.

"Wolves! wolves!" echoed I.

"No, I guess not, good woman. Where did you come from?"

"Boston."

"Boston! Did n't run all the way, did you? Are you on a visit?"

"I don't know how I ever got here, but I came to visit Elmer North."

"Then you have not far to go. I 'm Elmer North."

"Oh, Elmer, Elmer! Let me get up there. The wolves are after us, — a whole pack of them."

Aunt mounted the team like a school-girl, and sat down, saying, "Oh, I am so glad that I am safe!"

"This is n't Aunt Mary, is it?" said the handsome man.

There was a tiny cry. "This is very astonishing," he added. "*That*'s little Mary. Aunt, what were you running for?"

"Wolves! wolves!" Aunt uttered the words with awful emphasis.

"Wolves! There are no wolves here. This is a safe country. I never saw a wolf in my life."

There filled the air another piercing cry, that, as before, seemed to change into a hundred. "Yep, yep, yep, yep!"

"There, don't you hear them, — a whole pack of them, at your house, too? They *electrified* me."

EARLY TRAVELLING ON THE PLAINS.

"Wolves! That pesky little coyote! He wouldn't hurt you no more than a cat. He's sort of company for us. We don't harm him. We've made him tame by leaving food for him out in the yard. You must have lost your head, Aunt; but never mind."

"There are a hundred of them. You must have lost your ears, Elmer; but never mind."

"Oh, Aunt, you don't understand; one little fellow makes all those noises. Why, Aunt Mary, how did you get here? I was never so surprised in my life."

"I came to spend Thanksgiving with you. I've a kind of theory, Elmer, that Thanksgiving Day should not only be one of reunion, but of family reconciliation. Don't you think so?"

"Yes, and you are welcome, Aunt Mary; you are welcome. See, here is my wife. But I thought you were —"

The team shortly stopped before the long white house. A pretty little animal ran out of the open door, and passed like a gray streak in the moonlight over the brown dust.

"There goes your wolf, Aunt Mary, — the whole hundred of them. One little coyote has many voices, and these voices as many echoes. You left the door open, and he's been up to some thieving, I'll be bound. Here, Aunt, you get down and take little Mary, and we'll go in and have some supper, if that coyote hasn't eaten it up already."

Aunt took little Mary and carried her into the house.

"What are these crutches for?" asked Elmer, as soon as a light had been procured.

Aunt looked at them, and, like the "little woman" in the nursery rhyme, began to cry: "A miracle! A miracle has been wrought! Oh, I am so thankful! I knew it would be so! I felt it in my bones. I used to be lame, but New Mexico is very electrifying; you said 't would be so, you know."

Thanksgiving Day we sat down to a table savory with game from the Organ Mountains. The doors and windows were open; there was a gentle coolness and a glimmering brightness in the air, as though there was being sifted down from the sun-hazes a shower of gold.

"It is a beautiful day," said Aunt, after the meal. "We ought to recount our blessings. We are all well; we ought to be thankful for *that*."

"And your heart has been as true as a mother's to me," said Elmer. "I did wrong in my young life, but I will be a true son to you now, and as long as I live; and my motive is not money or any personal advantage."

"I knew it would be so." Aunt here, as usual, proceeded to speak of her prophetic bones. "I have my boy's heart again; let us be thankful for *that*. I was right, Audley. Thanksgiving Days should be forgiving days. We owe it to our own blessings to make them so. To rise above self and make others happy is the true Thanksgiving. I wish I were a governor, but I don't expect that I ever shall be."

"And little Mary here," said Elmer's wife; "let us be thankful for *her*."

"And there goes that miserable little coyote with his hundred tongues and no one knows how many echoes," said Aunt, with a jump. "He did me more good than all the doctors I ever had. Let us be thankful for *that*."

CHAPTER VIII.

STORIES OF THE CANADIAN RIVER SONGS.

HERE was a young French Canadian on the train, who was called Jean. He had been a raftsman on the Ottawa; he had easy manners, a generous heart, and good-nature, and could sing happily the boat-songs of the St. Lawrence and the Canadian rivers. Several of the songs which he sang on the train have pleasing histories, and some accounts of them are given in a French work called "Chansons Populaires," which we find dedicated to the Princess Louise and Marquis of Lorne. The collector is Ernest Gagnon. Of course the two most popular airs to Canadian ears were "La Claire Fontaine" and "Vive la Canadienne," which Jean rendered with that sympathetic action which belongs peculiarly to the French *habitants* of the province of Quebec. We give a translated history of these folk-songs, with a verse or two.

LA CLAIRE FONTAINE.

From the little child of seven years to the old man with white hair everybody in Canada knows and sings "La Claire Fontaine." One is not a Canadian otherwise. The melody of this song is very elementary, and offers little of interest to the musician. Nevertheless, because of its great popularity it is often taken for the theme of airs of dance and even of concert music. In Normandy they sing a song of which the words are nearly the same as those of our "Claire Fontaine," but the air is wholly different.

> " À la claire fontaine
> M'en allant promener,
> J'ai trouvé l'eau si belle
> Que je m'y suis baigné.
> Lui y a longtemps que je t'aime,
> Jamais je ne t'oublierai."

It is a very simple love-song; a young lover loses his sweetheart by caprice, and wishes the old happy days of their courtship were brought back again. The refrain is quite suggestive, sad and spiritual:

> " Long time have I loved thee,
> I will never forget thee."

This song, sung by an American in the mechanical American way, would mean little, but put into sympathetic action by a French Canadian would be full of emotional suggestion; there would be recognized a soul in it, all the more beautiful because suggested in an evasive manner. Jean was asked to sing it again and again, and a warm-hearted French Canadian seldom refuses to grant a friend any favor.

"VIVE LA CANADIENNE."

The melody of this song, as well as that of "La Claire Fontaine," holds the place of the national air, until something better turns up. It is needless to say that the words of "Vive la Canadienne" are of comparatively recent composition, and did not come to us from France; but I must say that the first stanza of this song is the only one which is generally known: —

> " Vive la Canadienne,
> Vole, mon cœur, vole,
> Vive la Canadienne,
> Et ses jolis yeux doux
> Et ses jolis yeux doux, doux, doux,
> Et ses jolis yeux doux."

THE NIPIGON.

"VIVE LA CANADIENNE."

Jean sang the "Song of the Three Rivers" several times; but the most acceptable song of all to the company as a whole was "En Roulant, ma Boule," a provincial song of France, that always delights the ear whenever and wherever heard. It is a mere collection of nonsense rhymes, and may be lengthened at will by the rowers on the sunset rivers and streams. The song relates that a king's son had a silver gun and went out to shoot a white duck for the down; and the rest of the story may be supplied at will, provided that the words "En roulant, ma boule, roulant," are repeated to measure the strokes of the oars.

Tom Moore's version of the popular Canadian boat-song of the Ottawa was sung by Jean and several of the other emigrants who knew it well. In fact, there were few on the car who had not heard

> "Row, brothers, row; the stream runs fast,
> The Rapids are near, and the daylight's past."

Jean sang the gay paddle-song of the Red River of the North, which strangely enough is a tale of tropical orange-trees. It must be pleasant for the Red River voyager to dream of the tropics with —

> "A heart to love,
> So gay, gay, gay."

PIERRE, THE FRENCH CANADIAN SINGER.

THE BURNING OF THE POWDER-CANDLE.

I can see the old chest now in my mind as I used to glance at it hastily, very hastily indeed, in my boyhood. It stood there, scarred and dusty, among the ancestral rubbish of the tool-room. The fact that I only cast telescopic glances at it was due to my early spiritual education, and to a very alarming remark that was once made to me by Jerry the clam-digger: "Don't go there, Sonny; there is where Pierre the French boy saw the Devil; don't go near the tool-room." I needed no further instruction in regard to the matter. Had the tool-room contained a less startling legend, I might have been tempted to some intrusion among the superannuated farming implements; but no Rhode Island boy who ever listened to the chimney-corner legends of the ubiquitous individual mentioned by Jerry would have ventured on any spot that *he* was supposed to visit. In the fine old days of the Charter and Berkeleyan philosophy, when tar-water was supposed to be the remedy for all the ills of

AN EMIGRANT TRAIN CROSSING THE PLAINS.

life, the spiritual world seems to have been very near to Rhode Island. The old Puritans of the Plymouth Colony seem only to have had visions of grim ghosts and graveyard people, and the early Boston folks were accustomed to see yet more awful scenes; but Rhode Island, thanks to hopeful Bishop Berkeley and Roger Williams, had a more merciful ghost-world, and a brighter spiritual atmosphere, and it came to be regarded as a disgrace for a Rhode Island man to meet the Evil One anywhere, and we trust it is so still, now that the old Charter has long passed the period of its great usefulness. In fact, it is related that when the Evil One last appeared on the green plantations of the blue Narragansett Bay, it was to a stately Baptist dame, whom he wished to terrify from attending evening meetings. She was humiliated to have met him, and at first did not speak a word, but went on her way indignantly. He at last announced officially who he was. "Then you are a poor critter indeed, and you ought to be ashamed of yourself," replied she promptly; and since then, we may imagine, good angels only have haunted the ways to the conference-room and the Quaker meeting.

Who was Pierre the French boy? I would ask Aunt Experience Smart, the whilom village teacher, when we next went hen's-nesting in the old barn. I would know the meaning of the awful legend so darkly outlined by Jerry the clam-digger.

The morning after making the resolution to seek for occult knowledge was a beautiful one indeed. The sun came broad and golden through curtains of damask, and rolled in flames up the dewy sky. The great elms dried, and the locusts chorussed in their green tents, and the world seemed all life and light and vivid splendor. Cool winds rippled over the seas of corn, and the ospreys hung in air on motionless pens, screaming with content. There was a tremendous cackle in the barn, announcing great events, and Aunt Experience listened with a serene hopefulness at the probable large increase of her revenues.

"Come, Sonny," said she, putting on her calash, the most marvellous bonnet ever invented, — "Come, Sonny, let us go to the barn and gather up the eggs."

She pushed the roses away from the door, and I let down the bars for her, and we turned into the orchard, followed the path to the barn. The orchard was full of pencilled sunlight and cool shadows. We could hear the mowers rifling their scythes near by in the meadows, and breathe the air of the new-cut hay.

The barn doors were open. How hospitable are the doors of an old Rhode Island barn! When all other doors were closed against some poor wanderer of humanity, he would be told he might go and "sleep in the barn;"

and there he would bury his sorrows in profound slumber among the sweet harvest of the meadows.

The swallows were skimming the air, and their young were twittering in the plastered nests among the beams. Now and then a mother-swallow would dart into the peak under the roof, when all the air above would turn into ripples the silvery notes of the young broods awaiting to be fed. The mows were half full of clover, and the air was odorous everywhere. We stopped on the cool barn floor to breathe the air and look away to the sea-meadows and the white sails of the violet sea.

"This is a beautiful world, Sonny," said Aunt Experience. "Don't never leave the farm, Sonny. Blessed are they who are born on the farm and know enough to stay there. *All* of the good Lord's gifts come to the farm."

She crooked her arm over her calash, and gazed into the over-sea of sunlight that glimmered everywhere, a picture of contentment for a Hogarth.

Her day-dream was interrupted. There was another cackle. An astonished hen had left her nest under the ruffled impression of invaded rights; the tax-gatherers had come to Jerusalem. The great hubbub was in the tool-room, among the cobwebs.

"Go, look, Sonny," said Aunt Experience. "Stole her nest in the old sea-chest, likely as not. That's where I used to keep my Rhininjun [Rye and Indian] meal."

I opened the door very cautiously. No dark object appeared, — only the industrious hen. I held the leather latch-string in my hand for prudence and security, and then I ventured to remark, —

"Aunt Experience, who was Pierre the French boy?"

"Pierre — yes, Pierre; he was the farm hand that frightened old Deacon Woodpecker out of his palsy. What made you ask, Sonny?"

"Did he ever see the — see anything strange in this room?"

"Oh, la no, Sonny; it was old Methuselum. Who has been telling you that story? Run along and get the eggs."

"But who was Methuselum, Aunt?"

"Methuselum? Why, he was old Methuselum; don't you know?"

Here was indeed a mysterious order of events. Pierre the French boy had met the dark wanderer of the evil atmospheres in this cobwebbed room, or else old Methuselum, — I wondered if it were the patriarch Methuselah, — and he had frightened old Deacon Woodpecker out of his palsy. My imagination began to grow and glow, and a dark apprehension came over me, even there amid the meadows of lucid sunlight, under the protection of Aunt Experience's calash.

REPULSING AN ATTACK ON AN EMIGRANT TRAIN.

"But where did Pierre the French boy see old Methuselum?" I persisted.

"Right there by the chest. He had horns on, and Pierre had just woke up in the chest and lifted the cover, and —"

A shadow darkened a broad patch of sunlight outside. Hens flew in every direction. Aunt Experience rushed to the barn door, and shook her apron with a spasmodic "Shoo, shoo!" A hawk had swooped down, and we presently heard a chicken peeping in the sky.

"I declare, it does make my heart ache to see a poor chicken carried off *so*," said she. "I wish I had a gun! I don't believe in killin', but I would kill that there hawk, I declare I would."

It was a mere matter of the imagination. We fancy that Aunt Experience had never used a gun, or any weapon other than a Rhode Island buttonwood whip.

Here the excitement abated, and she broke off a broad burdock-leaf growing near the open door and began to fan herself.

"*Who* had horns?" I continued.

"Oh, don't ask me anything more about Pierre! If you will be a good boy, I will give you a powder-candle next Christmas, and I will tell you the whole story while it is burning, the same as I did the story of the 'Wee, wee pig,' last year. Pierre thought that he saw the Evil Spirit, but it was only old Methuselum. It is a story for a winter night. Let's gather up the eggs and go field raspberrying."

Here was indeed something to look forward to, — a powder-candle, and a story that would make clear all these darkly mysterious events associated with the tool-room and the old carved sea-chest.

My readers may have never heard of the old powder-candle of Rhode Island days. It is, indeed, a departed light, but few Christmas inventions ever created greater interest and amusement. The Rhode Island Baptists did not celebrate Christmas in their churches, nor the Quakers; yet nearly all the old farmers' families burned a powder-candle on Christmas Eve. The custom had been brought from some provincial towns in England, and it spread in Rhode Island in the following strange way. Each farmer used to kill each fall the beef for his own use; and the good dames of his richly stored household used to melt the tallow in an enormous pot, and dip into it candle-wicks over and over, until the wicks grew to be candles. The candle-dipping day was an event in the thrifty household. Into one of these wicks a goosequill filled with powder was tied, to follow an old provincial custom. This wick became a powder-candle. When burned, it would explode as the flame reached the quill; and the watching of the burning of the candle by the young people of the family and their invited friends furnished one of the most dramatic events of the year. As it had been the old English custom to burn the powder-candle on Christmas Eve, the rich Episcopal families of Newport and elsewhere burned their powder-candles on the same date of the twelve-day festival, and Baptists and Quakers conformed to the custom.

The burning of the powder-candle on Christmas Eve was often accompanied by the telling of some marvellous story, the climax of which was to be reached just as the candle exploded. Many of the rich families had obtained their wealth by trading on the African coast, and among the story-tellers were the Guinea negroes, who would relate adventures with the native forest giants, and with snakes "a thousand feet long." All the family and household listened to these tales out-imagining Cervantes, Smollett, Fielding, and Scott, from the grand-dame in her high cap and crossed kerchief, to the turnspit and pickaninny. The negro fiddler was sure to be found at the more aristocratic gatherings, and roasted Rhode Island greenings and cider were served after the great shout that followed the explosion of the candle, which for a time turned the room into smoke and darkness, and made the timid cringe with real or pretended nervous fear. It was the enjoyment of a modified form of this curious custom to which I had already been invited by Aunt Experience, who always fulfilled her liberal promises. Then I should know who Pierre was, and Methuselum, and how Deacon Woodpecker's palsy was cured, and the real truth of the awful event which Jerry the clam-digger had hinted had taken place in the tool-room in the barn. How I waited for the autumn trees to turn, the chestnut-burrs to open, and the snows to fall!

It came at last, that eventful December, and in the mean time I had avoided with a mediæval horror the tool-room and the old barn chest. I had even refused to help pile up the pumpkins and squashes in the tool-room. How could I know whether the inhabitant of the haunted air was at home or not, or when he might appear? I think it would have turned me idiotic to have a glimpse of *him*, and I had no wish whatever to meet Methuselum, even if he were the patriarch, as a part of his name seemed to suggest.

Snow fell; the candles were dipped and dried, and with the candles, the powder-candle with a big quill of rock powder. I was allowed to invite my friends to see the burning and listen to the mysterious tale of the old barn chest.

Aunt Experience was a natural story-teller, one of the story-books of old. Almost every family had one natural story-teller, as every old castle in

England once had its natural minstrel. They were living books, these old entertainers, and their faces furnished the illustrations. They acted their stories, as well as told them, and exercised a sort of magnetic influence over their hearers. The Guinea negroes were geniuses in producing nervous results while relating such stories.

I never shall forget Aunt Experience's last year's Christmas story on the occasion of the powder-candle. It was an English story, and a very curious evolution of the Hebrew story known as "A Kid, a Kid which my father bought with two pieces of money; a Kid, a Kid." The story was an allegorical history of the Jews, and the most orthodox people might relate that on Christmas Eve.

Not all the stories of the Orient, or of Grimm, Andersen, or Fielding, ever so charmed me as this Christmas tale of the "Wee, wee pig," told while the powder-candle was burning its thrilling tallow. I will produce a specimen of it, as among the curiosities of the story-telling art. In order to read it correctly, or tell it, the words "wee, wee" had to be uttered in a little complaining squeal, like the cry of a young pig, and no one who has not heard the peculiar cry could tell the story effectively, or appreciate its queer and comic influence. It began in this wise: —

"Once upon a time there was a wee, wee old woman who lived in a wee cottage in Cockermouth, England. This wee, wee old woman was one day sweeping her house with a wee, wee broom, when she found a wee, wee sixpence. The wee, wee old woman took the wee, wee sixpence, and bought a wee pig, and started to drive the wee, wee pig to her wee, wee home. She came to a wee bridge over a wee, wee river, when the wee, wee pig stopped, and refused to move. Then the wee, wee old woman said to a wee, wee stick, 'Oh, stick, do beat wee, wee pig; wee, wee pig won't go over the bridge, and I sha'n't get home to-night.'"

It would fill pages to relate the trials of this wee, wee old woman, which grew and grew, and were ended at last by a little gnat which bit a bear on the inside of his nose, when the following astonishing series of events happened. The bear, stinging with pain, began "to kill the dog, the dog began to kill the cat, the cat began to kill the rat, the rat began to gnaw the rope, the rope began to hang the butcher, the butcher began to kill the ox, the ox began to drink the water, the water began to quench the fire, the fire began to burn the stick, the stick began to beat the pig, and the wee pig began to run over the bridge." Just here the powder-candle went off with a blackening explosion; all shrieked, and ran about in the darkness as if in the greatest terror, after which followed a charming merry-making, and the

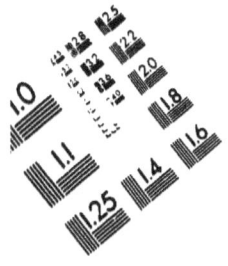
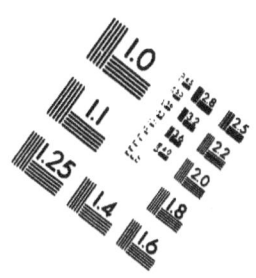

**IMAGE EVALUATION
TEST TARGET (MT-3)**

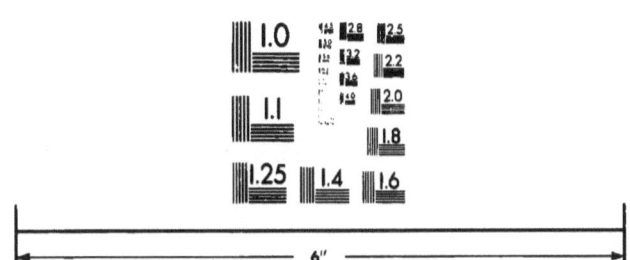

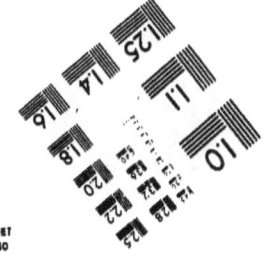

Photographic
Sciences
Corporation

23 WEST MAIN STREET
WEBSTER, N.Y. 14580
(716) 872-4503

"wee, wee old woman," and, "the wee, wee pig," and the guests, negroes and all, brought the scenes of the night to a happy conclusion with a jingle of sleigh-bells. They are gone, all gone, those happy days, and the snowy marbles reflect the starlight on the forgotten graves of the actors on the old Rhode Island hills.

Our dinner on the evening before the burning of the candle was especially sumptuous. Turkeys, Yorkshire puddings, apple dumplings with potato crusts, all kinds of dishes made of pumpkin, roast pig, rye pancakes and gingerbread, Rhode Island johnny-cakes and apple-sauce, suet pudding, berry cakes, boiled pudding, apples, nuts, and cider, — what a board it was! I have never seen the like in any modern hotel in Boston or New York.

The long-awaited evening fell with a crisp, frosty air, and a jingle of bells. They came, the old Rhode Island names, — the Potters, the Almys, the Buffons, the Barneses, the Chases. The candles were lighted, and the great kitchen was filled with children, with lovers in the dark corners of the parlor, and old men with buckles on their shoes before the great roaring sitting-room fire.

Aunt Experience came down from her room in huge cap, laces, and brown satin dress. The young people seemed awed by her stately presence as she sat down in her high-backed chair. She lighted the powder-candle, and proceeded to relate the story of "Ginevra," in Rogers's "Italy." She then seized the silver snuffers, glanced slowly and mysteriously around, and said, —

"There is a carved sea-chest in the barn that has a very grave history; but it did not prove to be a tomb, as you shall hear. Listen."

The room became very still, and the powder-candle burned slowly and silently. She gave the burnt wick one pinch with the silver snuffers, and continued: —

"The old people all remember Pierre Rigot, the Canada boy who used to sing such beautiful songs at the huskings, and whose only fault was that he would drink too much, — poor Pierre!"

Aunt paused, and cast her eyes about the room.

"He came to us friendless and poor, and we gave him a home, and the young people liked him on account of his amiable ways, his handsome face, and pleasant, mellow voice. I will first tell you how he was the means of curing Deacon Woodpecker of the palsy, and then I will relate a strange event that happened in the tool-room of the barn.

"I ought first to tell you what I had learned of Pierre's history. He had a father and mother living at Hochelaga, Canada, and the memory of his mother ('My poor mother!' he called her) was always very dear to him. He said that his father 'drank hard,' and used to abuse him, and that was why he had come to the States to look for work. He had been brought up a Catholic, though he gladly attended meeting with me, and came to love the old Quaker preachers.

"How sweetly he used to sing in French the old Canadian songs! I recall them now, and his bright, dark eyes and pleasant smile. His heart was always full of sympathy; he felt for every one in pain, and when he sang, it seemed as if his soul was speaking.

"There was one song of his I shall never forget, and I will quote a part of it to you in French, for perhaps I shall have occasion to speak of it again. His soul used to seem to take delight in it, — a sort of poetic and spiritual delight that made his young face beautiful. Where he learned it I cannot tell. The music was full of emotion.

> 'Le matin, quand je me réveille.
> Je vois mon Jésu venir.
> Il est beau à merveille,
> C'est lui qui me réveille.
>   C'est Jésu!
>   C'est Jésu!
>   Mon aimable Jésu!
>
> 'Je le vois, mon Jésu, je le vois
> Porter sa brillante croix
> Là haut sur cette montagne,
> Sa mère l'accompagne.
>   C'est Jésu!
>   C'est Jésu!
>   Mon aimable Jésu!
>
> 'Ses pieds, ses mains, sont clouées,
> Et son chef est couronné
> Des grosses épines blanches;
> Grand Dieu! quelle souffrance!
>   C'est Jésu!
>   C'est Jésu!
>   Mon aimable Jésu!'"

The candle sputtered at times, but it would require at least a half-hour for the flame to reach the powder-quill, and the great company filling the rooms and doors were all eyes and ears, and stood in interrogative attitudes.

"Well, about the deacon's palsy."

"There was a ferocious bull on the place, called Brindle. Pierre had the charge of him, and kept him perfectly under control. I never saw any animal paw the earth and bellow like Brindle, and the whole town seemed afraid of him. He used to chase the people who came berrying in our pastures, and I never saw fat people and lame people and short people so astonishingly nimble and active as when old Brindle took after them. I have often heard terrible screams on the hot summer days, followed by bellows that might have shaken the hills, and have sent Pierre to see that no harm was done to the flying berry-pickers.

"Pierre used to bathe in the pasture brook under the great elm every Sunday morning in summer before dressing for meeting. The bathing-place is exposed to the bridge, and I used to provide for him a white bathing-suit of under-clothing and have it ready when he asked for it.

"One Sunday morning in June he asked for his bathing-suit, and I handed him a red flannel covering, and he hurried away. The bell began to ring for meeting, and he did not return.

"Just then I saw good old Deacon Woodpecker and his little wife coming along the way very slowly. The deacon was hobbling on a crutch, and his wife was leading him by the arm. The thrushes were singing, and the orioles were swinging among the sun flood in the elms. I stepped out of the door under the morning-glories.

"'This is a beautiful morning, Miss Smart,' said the deacon, with a very melancholy look.

"'Yes, glorious,' said I. 'How do you do?'

"'Miserable, miserable. I can only just hobble along, as you see, and I never expect to take another step in this world without pain. My pilgrimage is almost done, and a weary journey it will be to the end. I have been c'enmost an hour coming half a mile. I shake so, and then I have the spring halt so, and the pain catches me here, and here, and here, and everywhere, — oh, oh, oh!' and he uttered a dismal groan, and added, 'I could not go a step faster if it were to save the town. Some folks thinks I am spleeny, but I am not! If you were to tell me the house was on fire, I could not bring a bucket of water. 'T is oh! and oh! and oh! with me, and will be until I die.'

"He hobbled on, a perfect tableau of wretchedness and hopelessness. He presently turned, and said, 'Would you mind letting down the pasture bars for me? The way will be shorter across lots. All my ways of life must be short now.'

"I let down the bars, and the deacon passed over them, with the assistance of his little Quaker-like wife. I saw them go up the hill, among the sweet-ferns and wild roses, and went to my room to prepare for meeting. I had hardly undone my hair before I heard a bellow. I was sure it was Brindle. I recalled the deacon in the pasture, and my heart beat; but I remembered that Pierre was there, and the thought brought relief.

"I hastened to the door, when the most astonishing scene that I ever saw met my eyes. Brindle was appearing above the hill, his tail erect, tearing up the earth with his feet, and bellowing; and Pierre, arrayed in red, like a Mephistopheles, his wet clothes sticking to his form, was on the animal's neck, holding on to his horns. At every plunge that the animal made, the boy's red form was thrown into the air, but he clung to the horns still. What could it mean?

"The deacon had stopped. Brindle saw him, and putting down his head and giving a snort and bellow as of pain, he rushed with the force of a hurricane toward the afflicted man. I saw his little wife bravely shake her parasol. Then I saw the poor deacon drop his crutch and begin to brush his face in a very unaccountable manner; and then (could I believe my eyes?) I saw him start and *run*, — run like a boy toward the great rock in the pasture, leaving his poor little wife in the open field. Up the road he went like a badger, followed by the bull, and screaming, 'Help! help! Miss Smart, Miss Smart, run, run! O Lord! O Lord!'

"Something had maddened the bull, and was still maddening him. What could it mean? I asked over and over. Presently I saw the deacon wheel around and around on the rock a half-dozen times, and swing his arms like a windmill, and then he leaped off the rock, and in the face of the roaring animal he ran like a wild boy toward the pasture bars, crying, 'Help! help! O Lord! O Lord!'

"The people going to meeting stopped, and armed themselves with clubs and sticks, and went into the pasture to rescue the little Quaker-like deaconess, who had fallen down in a limp little heap, and thought that the supreme crisis of the world had indeed come.

"Pierre leaped from Brindle's horns. His eyes glowed with excitement.

"'Boy,' said I, 'what does this mean?'

"'I cannot help it,' said he. 'Brindle did not know me in *red* clothes, and he dove after me. I lifted myself up on the branches of a tree, and *there* was a hornet's nest. It was awful. Then I dropped down on Brindle's back, and oh, oh, oh! I am all stung up!' He began to rub his wounds, and I could see that he spoke the truth.

"The people gathered to hear the thrilling recital, but half a dozen hornets, which had come to verify this strange tale, soon dispersed them, and set them flying with oh's of terror. The valiant band rescued the deaconess, and long before the rescue the deacon had gained the steps of his own home, crying, 'O Lord! O Lord! Have I come to this?'

"Talk of miracle cures! He was not lame again for years; but alas! his influence as a deacon was ever after greatly impaired. (Let me snuff the candle again.)

"Pierre inherited a love of liquor; he learned to drink at the huskings, and this became the poor boy's weakness. He was invited to all the merry-makings to sing the French Canadian songs, but he usually came home light-headed, and I at last forbade him to accept all invitations. I hated to do so, for we all loved Pierre. For a time he obeyed me.

"Years passed. Pierre took to his old ways, and I could not restrain him. At the huskings, on Thanksgivings, and at Christmases, Pierre was sure to get intoxicated. He was always penitent after these humiliating days, and often promised reformation, but his will-power seemed unequal to his resolution. I almost dreaded the coming of the merry-makings and holidays for his sake. (Let me snuff the candle; it burns well now.)

"The village Squire's name was Jeffrey. He was an odd character, and did many things unbecoming the debt that he owed to a dignified profession; but I one day carried the burden of poor Pierre's infirmities to him, and asked him his advice.

"'Can he be reformed?' asked I.

"'Of course he can,' said he. 'Any man can reform if he have a sufficient motive. The slattern is not a slattern when she has a beau; tell any man that you will give him one thousand dollars to keep from his besetting vice for a month, and he can do it. A man in love rises above all his temptations, and a sudden opportunity to make money will for the time make the weakest character as virtuous in his acts as is the strongest. A frightened man always loses his temptations.'

"'But what would you do in the case of Pierre?'

"'When you find him drunk again, send for me.'

"There was a Guinea negro who lived with the lawyer, very old, named Methuselah, but commonly called Methuselum. One day, before Christmas, Squire Jeffrey and Methuselum were riding by and saw Pierre under the orchard wall stupidly drunk. The lawyer stopped the carriage and fastened the horse, and the two took up the stertorous body of the poor boy and carried it into the barn. It was near night, the short red twilight of the white winter day. (I must snuff the candle again.)

A SUCCESSFUL ASSAULT ON A PARTY OF PIONEERS.

"I saw what Squire Jeffrey was doing, and I drew over me my thick shawl and went to the barn. The Squire had gone into the tool-room, and was taking the rubbish out of the old broken sea-chest.

"'What are you going to do, Squire?'

"'Reform Pierre. I have always said that any person can be reformed by a sufficient motive. The revival preachers all understand that. Wesley did — Whitefield.'

"I protested. I have no faith in tricks of any kind, and fear is not the most powerful and permanent motive.

"He laid an old horse-blanket in the chest.

"'Methuselum,' said he, 'help me lift the boy into the chest.'

"They did so, and wrapped him in the blanket, and the Squire closed the lid, putting a cob under it so as to leave a sufficient place for breathing.

"'Now, Methuselum,' said he, 'I want you to watch by the chest, and strictly follow my directions.'

"'Yes, sah.' I can hear his broad tone now.

"'First, let me fix you.'

"'Yes, sah. Do as you say, Massa.'

"The Squire took down the beef's hide and horns which hung in the room, and put it over Methuselum, so that the horns might project from the negro's head, and the hoofs be conspicuous.

"'There,' said he, placing a broken chair near the chest a few feet away, 'you sit down here, and when the boy wakes up, you stare at him, and grin at him, *so*, and so, and SO! He does not know you, and when he begins to ask questions, you tell him that you are Lucifer, and that he is in Tophet.'

"'Yes, sah. Dat I will; all them things, sure.'

"'I will hide and do the rest.'

"'Oh, Squire,' said I, 'this does n't seem right. You will never reform poor Pierre in any such way as this. Fear is not a sufficient motive for the reformation of any one. There is only one power in all the world that will conquer evil habits, and that is love. Pierre has a heart; reach that, and you may change him.'

"'Bring me a candle for Methuselum,' said the Squire, 'and some of that medical phosphorus from the house.'

"I did so. Phosphorus had begun to be a popular medicine at this time.

"The candle was lighted, and set down near Methuselum. The phosphorus was rubbed over the palms of the negro's hands.

"'When he begins to wake,' said the Squire, 'rub your hands over your face. Remember, you are Lucifer. Do as I have told you. You go away, Miss Smart, and I will wake him.'

"It was quite dark now. The shaded candle shed a dim light about the room, and old Methuselum, with his black face and luminous hands, great mouth and cow's feet, was indeed a fearful-looking object. To complete the awful figure, the Squire put a cone-like eel-basket on the top of his head, and rubbed phosphorus over it, so that it looked like a fool's cap of fireless light.

"'Now,' he said, 'I am going to wake Pierre.'

"He pounded upon the chest. I stepped into one dark corner of the room, and the Squire into another.'

"There was a stertorous breathing in the chest, but no response.

"The Squire raised the lid of the chest and shook the boy, then closed it again on the cob.

"A half-hour passed in waiting, with several attempts to awaken the boy, when a movement was heard in the chest, and a pitiful wail, 'Where am I?'

"Then the lid of the chest began to be slowly raised in the shadow, very slowly. It dropped down again, and we heard a groan of terror. Then all was still.

"The lid was slowly raised again. The poor boy's eyes ventured to look again on the awful object watching over him in the shadows. I could see his hand tremble as he held up the lid.

"'You — sur,' said Methuselum, plastering his face with the phosphorus.

"'You — sur,' repeated Methuselum.

"Pierre dropped the lid in terror. We could hear him praying in a dazed and bewildered way. I wished to rush forward and break the delusion, for I have no sympathy with deceptions of any kind.

"The lid was cautiously raised again. Methuselum, all aglow with phosphorus, now met the bursting eyes of the boy. The negro, in the strange light, with his horns, hat, hoofs, and open mouth, presented the most terrifying object that I ever saw.

"'You — sur?'

"Say, 'Down, Caleff; what would you have?' mumbled the Squire.

"'Down, Caleff; what would you have?' said Methuselum, like a spectre of darkness and fire, his white teeth grinning as if gloating over the ruin of human souls.

"'Where am I?'

"The negro, following his master's instructions, played the cruel part well, and represented himself as the Spirit of Evil, as he indeed looked in the thick

PREPARING A HOME IN THE WEST.

and uncertain shadows. The Squire seemed greatly amused, but I had too much pity and sympathy for the boy to care for anything but his rescue from such a perilous fright.

"Pierre fell back again, overcome for a moment by these exciting shadow scenes. What beings surrounded him? He was uncertain, in the low light and his clouded brain. At last we heard a movement in the chest again, followed by the *chink* of an empty bottle, possibly in his pocket. The sound evidently awakened his old appetite. We heard him mutter, 'It is no use.' Temptation was on him again, even amid all these fearful uncertainties. Temptation, without love, without hope. Heaven pity the man to whom the evil hour comes in this way!

"The lid of the chest began to lift again, slowly, slowly. A white hand rose out of it in the grewsome candle-light, and in it was a bottle.

"He gazed on Methuselum.

"'Say — come here,' he said tremblingly. 'I want to go to sleep — to sleep forever. May my poor old mother never know! She loved me, and I would have died for her. Come here. Can you, — can you tell me how I can get this bottle filled once more?'

"I saw the bottle waving to and fro, glittering. I could endure the scene no longer, but rushed forward to the chest.

"'Oh, Pierre, Pierre!' I said, 'have you come to this? Can it be possible that your soul is enslaved by drink like that? Oh, Pierre!'"

"Squire Jeffrey was furious.

"'Miss Experience,' said he, 'you may see in *him* an utterly hopeless soul. No power on earth can ever break the habits that hold him. He is as much enchained by evil as though his fate was already fixed. Boy, get out of that chest!'

"He seized Pierre and shook him."

Aunt Experience gave a glance at the candle. She saw it was burning near the powder-quill, and moved away from it. "He shook him *so*," she continued, laying her hands on one after another of the boys, so as to direct attention away from the candle, that the explosion might come unexpected, and be the greater surprise. "And old Methuselum rose up *so*." Aunt was acting now. She moved her arms about as though to represent the confusion of the tool-room, and to make the mental atmosphere as nervous as possible.

Flash!

There was a sulphurous explosion, followed by a chorus of shrieks. The powder-candle had gone off. The rooms were filled with powder-smoke, and poor Pierre was for the time forgotten. Laughter and cries, jokes, kisses, and all kinds of antics followed, and when the air cleared, apples and coffee were brought out, and the boys and girls were provided with a candy-pull. The black fiddlers played the Virginia Reel, and Money Musk, and Fisher's Hornpipe, and the Devil's Dream, and the merry-making lasted until the hands of the old English clock pointed to midnight. Then voices chorussed "Merry Christmas," and all went home under the crystal stars of the frosty morning.

The excitement that followed the explosion of the powder-candle, and the candy-pull and merry-making, had led us all for the time to forget the fate of poor Pierre. As soon as the last sleigh-bells had died away in the snowy roads, the French boy's incomplete history recurred to me. I returned to Aunt Experience as she stood before the dying embers of the great logs and said, —

"Did the Squire's experiment reform Pierre?"

"No," said she, "but another experience did."

"Tell me," said I.

"I will to-morrow night," she said. "It is too late now."

The same question on the morrow seemed to have come to the minds of a number of the guests, for the next evening several people called, and each asked Aunt Experience the same question, — "What became of Pierre?"

The Christmas night came with a cloud of snow. The winds whistled about the corners of the house and down the great chimneys, and we were glad that the interrupted story of the merry evening before was to be continued; for with all his weaknesses there was something in the history of Pierre that had won our hearts.

"Poor Pierre," continued Aunt Experience, "was n't reformed by his experience in the old carved sea-chest. Deception and terror do not change one's nature. Only love does that, — a sense of love, human and Divine. The Squire's theory was right, although he was so swift to lose confidence in it after his unfruitful experiment.

"The quickening power came to Pierre at last like a good angel, and fulfilled all his better desires, and enabled him to live his better and his true self; for our better selves are our ideals.

"One day there came to the boy a letter from Montreal. It told him that his father was dead, and said that the dream of his old mother's heart was that he would let her come to him.

"He brought the letter to me.

"'My poor old mother!' he said. 'I would do anything for her; my heart bleeds. Miss Experience, if you will let me bring her here, I will never drink

RAT PORTAGE, LAKE OF THE WOODS.

a drop of liquor again as long as I live,— indeed, I will not. I love my mother. I will do anything for one I love; I would die for such a one, Miss Experience. You think me weak and bad, and have given me up to my failings; but there are some people that I love better than myself.'

"'But, Pierre, the fright of the old barn chest did not give you any will-power, or correct your ways. How can I be sure that the care of your mother would?'

"'That was a cold, heartless trick and deception,' said Pierre.

"'But suppose I were to allow you to bring your old mother here, and you were to fill her last days with double sorrow by drinking again?'

"'No, before God, Miss Experience, that shall never be! Unless some one tell her, she shall never know that I ever drank at all. I love my mother; and oh, it would make me so happy to make her happy in her old age. She had such a hard life with father. I have seen her go hungry for days; and I have seen him strike her, I have. I am sorry I have inherited his weakness, but, Miss Experience, I have prayed and struggled for deliverance a hundred times, and when I woke up in the old barn chest I thought that God must be dead. Give me a chance to follow my better heart now, and you shall never see me drunk again.'

"'But where would you live, Pierre?'

"'Oh, let me hire two rooms of you in the old house under the hill; you say that you would tear it down, only that you were cradled there. We would be so happy, and it would make you happy in your prayers to think you had reformed me. Would n't you like to be happy with your prayers? I think that would be the greatest happiness on earth.'

"I hesitated.

"'Miss Experience, I have struggled; my soul has struggled in the night. I wish I were a spirit, for spirits can have their desires, and we poor creatures cannot. Oh, I wish you could see my true heart! You would know that I am *not* bad there.'

"I sat in silence. How beautiful he looked,— his dark eyes and his fine form! The silence became painful.

"He at last looked up to me and said, repeating a part of the Pauline apostrophe: '"Charity believeth all things, hopeth all things, and thinketh no evil. It suffereth long and is kind." Miss Experience,' he added, with a sudden flow of spirits, 'let me sing you a song.'

"His anxiety passed away like an April cloud, and he sang in French the queer old ballad of 'Dans les Prisons de Nantes,' or how the jailer's daughter helped a handsome young prisoner to escape. The words themselves were a ripple of music, and the story had an ending which put one into the best heart.

> 'Dans les prisons de Nantes
> Lui y a-t-un prisonnier, gai, faluron, falurette,
> Lui y a-t-un prisonnier, gai, faluron, donde.
>
> 'Que personn' ne va voir
> Que la fill' du geôlier, gai, faluron, falurette,
> Que la fill' du geôlier, gai, faluron, donde.'

"He laughed when this song-story was over and the last 'falurette' had melted in air. His sympathetic manner engaged my heart in spite of its hardness, and I grew so human that I said, —

"'Well, Pierre, you may let her come.'

"'Oh, Miss Experience, you are so good! the world is all sunlight now, —

> "Quand il fut sur ces côtes
> Il se mit à chanter, gai, faluron, falurette,
> Il se mit à chanter, faluron, donde:
>
> "Que Dieu béniss' les filles,
> Surtout cell' geôlier, gai, faluron, falurette,
> Surtout cell' du geôlier, gai, faluron, donde.
>
> "Si je retourne à Nantes,
> Oui, je l'espouserai! gai, faluron, falurette,
> Oui, je l'espouserai! gai, faluron, donde."'

"One September day, when the golden-rods were fading, and the apples were mellowing, and the locusts piping in the still sunlight that was an ocean of golden lustre, the stage-coach came rattling down to the village, past the red orchards, yellow cornfields, and rowened meadows, and left a single passenger there.

"It was the old mother of Pierre.

"He went for her with a wheelbarrow, his face full of delight. The farm horses and wagons were all away. So, like the hero of the nursery rhyme, he brought her home in a wheelbarrow, but without any such disaster as that related in the old ditty.

"A little woman she was, decrepit, but with a very refined and sympathetic face, and manners all vivacity and grace. It seemed to make her perfectly happy only to look at Pierre.

"Pierre began to work on the farm with new fidelity. He had a care for everything. How faithful he was! Training-day came; he did not go to the parade, but remained at home with his old mother, and they had a little spread of peaches and cream and melons and election cake. Training-day used to be one of special temptation to Pierre.

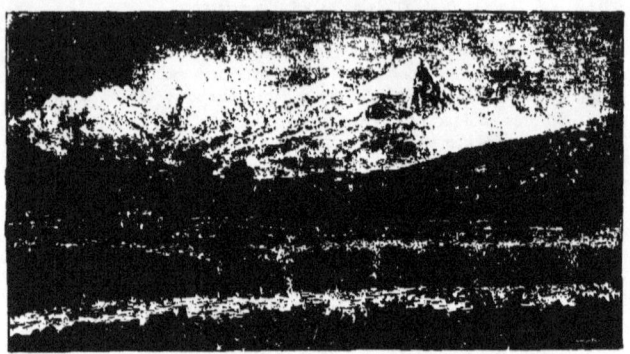

THE ROCKY MOUNTAINS FROM ELBOW RIVER.

"The huskings came. He went and sang ballads as of old, and delighted the young with the old French boatmen's melody, 'En Roulant ma Boule,' the paddle-song of the Ottawa. But when liquor was passed around, he always said '*Merci*, — I do not drink any more; mother, you know — excuses.' If one tempted him further, he would break into, —

 'Rouli, roulant, ma boule roulant,
 En roulant ma boule roulant,
 En roulant ma boule.'

and the tempter would lose his purpose in the pleasantry.

"Thanksgiving came with rustic merry-makings, and Christmas with bountiful dinners and musical nights, but none of the merry-makings brought a drop of liquor to the lips of Pierre. When I called on his mother on my way to the village, she once said, 'God bless you for being so good to Pierre; it takes but little to make life happy, if that little is love. A golden heart has Pierre, and I think it has been touched by Heaven, like an altar. A singing heart is the most beautiful altar in the world; you have made two hearts sing. Pierre and I share such thoughts as these between us. This is a beautiful world.'

A VIEW ON THE ELBOW RIVER.

"In the winter the old French-woman died. How Pierre wept as they laid her away under the snow! 'He will return to his old ways now,' said every one. But he did not. There came another sufficient motive, — sympathy.

"The spring brought the great epidemic of typhoid fever, that desolated the town. Pierre did not fear it at first, but as case after case proved fatal, it became difficult to obtain watchers to take care of the sick. The best watcher in the town was Pierre. Night after night the boy might be seen going to some sick-room, and for two months his nights were passed in the atmosphere of the pestilence. He was so feeling, gentle, and tender! He anticipated every want. Everybody spoke gratefully of him, even Squire Jeffrey.

"But one day, amid the early blooms of May, the report went round that Pierre had become exhausted, and was lying in the old house sick and alone.

Our own home was full of sickness and anxiety, but I sent the doctor to see Pierre, and he returned with the dread announcement, ' He has the fever.'

"There was no one to take care of him in the condition of affairs. I sent a farm hand to see him three times a day, and I visited him each evening and administered medicines. I have never met such a soul as his, and I shall never forget those evening visits.

"' Miss Experience,' he said, ' I am going to die. It makes me so happy to think that the Lord is willing to take me now; I might fall into my old ways again. Last night I had a dream, Miss Experience. I thought I saw a great cross uplifted in the western sky, and the cross was pearl. That was a good dream. This is the month of May, a good time to go away, — and I am going soon. But, oh, I pity the tempted!'

"He grew worse, and was delirious for weeks. He fancied that he was in the old barn chest. One day, in a sudden return of reason, he said to me, — .

"' Miss Experience, when I am gone, let the old Quaker minister come and say " Our Father." He need n't say anything more. Why should he for Pierre? God will take care of me. Miss Experience, Heaven loves me, and I have overcome the world.'

"One day the hired man came running with the message, ' Pierre is dying, and he wants to see Miss Experience.'

"I hurried away to the old house, and stopped to breathe, before I entered, under the blooming cherry-trees. It was a beautiful morning. The old orchards were loaded with flowers and humming with bees; every breeze scattered over the cool, green sod drifts of apple-blooms. The cherry-trees were white and the peach-trees red. Bluebirds were flitting in the woods, and orioles flaming among the sun-filled elms. Oh, it did seem dreadful that a young life should go out into mystery amid scenes like these!

"I entered the room. He lay there, amid the sickening odors of the fever, a breeze from the orchard blossoms now and then stealing over him. A humming-bird darted in at the open window and out again.

"His face lighted up with gratitude.

"' Oh, Miss Experience, I am glad you have come,' said he. ' It is a beautiful morning, and I am going away soon. Miss Experience.'

"' Well, Pierre.'

"' Did you ever think that new horizons come to you wherever you go; they are lifting, lifting, lifting, — those curtains of heaven.'

"' Yes, Pierre.'

"' I am dying, Miss Experience, and new horizons are lifting. I think that it will always be so, forever and ever. The same hand made both heavenly flowers and these. This is the month of May, and I am going away into God's great shining gardens. I shall be with mother to-night.'

"His spiritual eye seemed to receive light. He looked upward, and his soul seemed to glow through his thin white face, like a golden lamp in a vase of alabaster.

"'Miss Experience!'

"'Well, Pierre.'

"'The pearl cross that I saw,— I hope it was meant for all poor souls. I love everybody, Miss Experience.'

"'Well.'

"'Put over me a wooden cross. Put I. H. S. on it; that means more to me than you can see now. You will see more when the horizon lifts, Miss

ONE OF THE HUDSON BAY COMPANY'S STATIONS.

Experience, and you wait by the doors in the morning. And put on it,— put on it, "Pierre and his Mother."'

"The cool May breezes came in, and the room was full of the echoes of bird-song everywhere.

"His face changed. His eyes grew lustreless, and there followed a deep breathing, slower and slower. A perspiration spread over his face; then there was a tremor in his hands. The beautiful eyes became fixed. I wiped away the sweat, and kissed his forehead. His breathing became mechanical. His breath was cold, and I thought he was gone.

"But he seemed to return to the world again.

"'Miss Experience,' he said, as if waking from a dream, 'the horizon — the horizon is lifting. It is brighter beyond. I cannot see you, Miss Experience, but I can see. Everything is growing clear. I see the pearl cross lifting, lifting —'

"He felt for my hand. I took his. There was a flutter of breath, and his lips parted motionless, but the power to close them seemed to have gone forever. But they trembled again; the tide of life flowed back on the shining sand once more.

"'Miss Experience, you do pity me, don't you?'

"'Yes, Pierre.'

"'But I am happy here,' — his white hand fell on his heart.

'Je me réveille,
Je vois mon Jésu venir.

'When I awake,
My Saviour near I see,
Most wonderfully beautiful;
'T is he who wakens me:
C'est Jésu!
C'est Jésu!
Mon aimable Jésu!'

"He seemed lost in happy dreams. Then the old French mariners' melody that he had heard somewhere, and that had ever haunted his poetic mind, came back again, —

'Ses pieds, ses mains,' etc.

'His feet, his hands are pierced,
And to his forehead clings
A crown of thorns. Oh, think, my heart,
What dreadful sufferings!
C'est Jésu!'

"An angel's wing passed, — so it seemed to my fancy. The last flutter of the soul came.

"'Pierre!'

"The room was silent, the lips silent, the face silent.

"'Pierre!'

"The birds were singing in the orchards and woodland pastures; the flowers were blooming everywhere, and the breezes winging amid buds and balms.

"I closed his eyes, crossed his hands, and covered him with a sheet. The inward struggle was over, the outward, — where, oh, where, ye celestial horizons of God?"

CHAPTER IX.

BANFF.

MONG pyramids older than the Pyramids! Lift your eyes ten thousand feet. See Cascade Mountain flowing with crystals; note the solitary bird whose gray wing encircles the peak. On what an upheaval of rocky temples its eye looks down!

But the Bow River; will it compare with Lucerne and the clear waters of Uri? The Swiss lakes are purple, but the Bow is green. Both Lucerne and Banff are as wonderful for the clearness of their waters as for the height of their mountains.

But the Hot Springs of Banff; what are they? What is Sulphur Mountain? It is a mountain that pours hot sulphur-water, clear and gold-like, from its sides. Where is this water heated? Only theory can answer. How? Only theory can speak again. Far up the mountain it pours forth. What volcanic caverns and wells are below them? No eye has seen; no one can tell. People come to this volcano land and go, but know no more of what is beneath them than of what is in the stars above them. One stands by the yellow stones of the mid-mountain hot springs, and feels that the earth, like life, is a mystery.

No carved Lion of Lucerne is here; but what is the Pool of which one hears? Let us go and see. A house, a covered passage, lights, and a roof of stalactites; a great well, clear as glass, through which bubbles rise out of the earth. Look down, — fairy-land. Look up, — a dome of gems.

BANFF SPRINGS HOTEL, CANADIAN NATIONAL PARK.

How beautiful is Spray River, glacier fed! How glorious is the cascade of the emerald Bow River under the very balconies of the great hotel! One may hear the eternal music of the waterfall here,— the symphony of the glaciers, the chorus of the hills, but not at Lucerne.

A few miles ride, what peaks appear! The Inglismaldie, Peechee, more than ten thousand feet high. Yonder we may reach the Vermilion Lakes, or Devil's Head Lake with its fifteen miles of glacier splendors.

But we cling to the Bow. "And he shewed me a pure river of water of life, clear as crystal." The Bow is a water rainbow. The red or pink phlox covers its banks with flowers,— red, blue, emerald; the sun adds gold. Where are we? Shall we stay, or back to the common world again?

A bird flies swiftly over the broken wall of the sky. A gray cloud shows its head. It sails up, and darkens; there is a rush of cool winds through the gorges. The cloud puts out the sun. There is an electric gleam across it. Hark, it thunders! not as from a cloud overhead. The mountains thunder; gleam follows gleam. The cloud marches on; great shadows fall everywhere; it lightens again; the cloud bursts; there falls a deluge amid a thick darkness, illumined by fiery flashes. But a sky all roses breaks where the cloud first appeared.

On the retreating cloud is a rainbow — two — broken parts of many. How cool is the air! What a sense of rest and trust is in it!

The cloud is withdrawn at last and the stars are left. An hour or two passes. On the glaciers there rises a great circle of silver fire. The valley fills with a dim light, a live mysterious splendor. The moon is over the mountain and is rising among the stars. The Bow reflects the march of the Night Queen. There is silence everywhere, except the music of the waterfalls. Sleep comes easily in this rare air. We turn away from the luminous enchantment; we seek the seclusion of the great hotel, and are glad to rest the overpowered senses, and glide away in dreams to those fair lands where we left our hearts in the trust of others.

Beauty is not love, and to be perfectly happy one must see beauty through other eyes than his own.

Ban' has a single grand hotel and several small inns. A part of the town is occupied by the mounted police. These handsome officers would have a lonely time were it not for amusements. They are as a rule famous as story-tellers; they love music and in-door games and all kinds of curious diversions. They are men of gallant bearing and high intelligence. They provide many entertainments for tourists and guests at the hotel. Later on we will give you some account of amusements at Banff.

Our travellers stopped three days at Banff. One of these evenings was spent on the balconies of Banff Hotel in story-telling. The moon rose over the mountains, turning them into crystal palaces, and the cascade made music, while the travellers' narratives pleased the ear.

It was agreed that each guest on the balcony should relate the most interesting episode of travel within his recent experience. The first story was related by one of the Canadian mounted police.

THE LOG HOTEL.

Paul Yates was a lover of the Rocky Mountains. Year after year with a party of young friends he made pedestrian tours through the plateaus of British Columbia, among the stupendous chimneys of the Carboniferous ages, usually starting from Calgary, going through the Gap and down the winding valleys and cañons of the Bow and Wapta rivers to the Puget Sound.

Paul was a young man of good principles and habits, but of nervous temperament and a very active imagination. He saw everything that is sublime in Nature in the mountains, — the cloud shadows, the sunset fires on the glaciers, the colors of the glacier rivers and streams, the grizzly bear in the

MOUNT STEPHEN, NEAR THE SUMMIT OF THE ROCKIES.

clefts of broken volcanoes, and the gray eagle wheeling over all. I have seen tears fill his eyes as he gazed on the majestic mountain-walls of the Cascade and Gold ranges, on Mounts Hector and St. Stephen. He had a poetic mind, and that double sight which is the gift of a fine nature. These qualities were very delightful to literary people and artists, but seemed quite ridiculous to less susceptible folks.

"If Paul were to see a pussy cat in a fog," said one of his companions, "it would be a tiger."

"Say, Paul, you never saw a ghost in the Rockies, did you?" said I to him one day, chaffing, after he had been telling me about some wonderful cloud shadows on the Vermilion Lakes and glacial meadows.

"No; but I once had an experience in the Rockies that was more fearful to me than the seeing of a ghost, were there such a thing, could have been."

"What was it, -- a bear out blueberrying?"

"No; I might call it my other self."

"Well, I declare, Paul, I never quite understood you. So you have more than one self. Which are you now?"

"Myself all the time, now."

"There was a time, then, when you were not yourself, but some other self? Is that the way the matter stands? Your *other* self! I declare, Paul, that idea is too good to keep; I must tell the schoolboys about it. But when was it you were your other self, and how? Give me some account of it."

"You will not look upon the matter so lightly when I tell you my story, although the adventure has a comical side to it. Nothing in my life ever troubled me as that experience did. I should be afraid of the same experience now, had I not learned how great is the power of correct habits and moral self-control. I will tell you.

"I first went to Banff because I was out of health. I had a cough, was very nervous, and the doctor said that I had a chronic follicular disease, and that the best remedy would be a summer at the Hot Springs. Life in the mountains helps one physically, mentally, and morally, and the prescription was not a hard one for me to take.

"There was then an old inn near Banff which is not now used for a public-house. It was a great log-like structure, and had been a hunters' or prospecters' lodge in the year before the railroad. It was pleasantly situated among great firs, running streams, and intervales and plateau meadows.

"It was evening when I first reached Sulphur Mountain. The stars hung low like lamps among the great mountain shadows. The place seemed walled with mountains that touched the sky, and there was a solemn stillness everywhere. There was a piny odor in the air; everything seemed solitary amid such shadowy outlines.

MOUNT STEPHEN HOUSE.

"An old mountain horse took me to the lodge where a party of adventurous travellers were stopping. I ate my supper in a dark, strange dining-room of bare logs. I took my trunk, or rather leather portmanteau, to my room myself soon after supper. I was tired and excited, and I wished to be alone.

"The windows of my room looked out on Cascade Mountain. There stood the great pile of shadow, with a light silvery twinkling in the glaciers on the summit, under the golden light of the stars. I sat by the open window for an hour or more. I seemed to feel the grandeur of the surroundings which I could not distinctly see. I went to bed at last, my pulses throbbing, and dreaming, even before I fell asleep, of the glorious morning to come, when for the first time I should clearly see a sunrise in the mountains.

"In my portmanteau was a long, bordered night-gown, a present from my sister, who made for me a mountain outfit of underwear, and added the priestly looking night-robe. It was not a garment for a log-house on an Indian trail, and I was so weary, nervous, and excited that I did not unlock my trunk before retiring. I was alone; no courtesy was due to any one, and it gave me a sense of relief to lie down in a cool bed in my simple light underclothing.

"I was suddenly awakened, late in the night, by a cry as of agony in the adjoining room. 'Help! help! for Heaven's sake! come here, landlord! landlord!'

"My heart bounded, and I started up in bed. I listened with stifled breath. There was a movement in some of the rooms; people were awake, and evidently preparing to answer the call should it be repeated.

"I glanced out of the window. The moon had risen and was hanging over the plateau. The tall glaciers of the mountains glistened in the white light like a ghost. I had a painful impression that I had seen the same mountain in that sheeny robe before. It seemed to me like a ghost of a mountain, and it somehow suggested to me the wearing of a long white priestly robe. The mountain looked like a mantled god.

"Presently I heard a nervous step on the stairs, and I felt sure it was that of the landlord. The step approached the door of the adjoining room, and a loud rap rang through the hall.

"'Say, Professor, what is wanted?'

"'Heaven knows! Come in here. There's been a ghost here, or something; I don't know what.'

"'Professor, you have been dreaming. Nightmare!'

"'No, I have not; I saw it as plain as I see you now. There's been an apparition in here, or something, in a long white robe.'

"'How long ago?'

"'Half an hour, it may be. There is no mistake about it. I saw it; looked like a priest in a tableau, or — Oh, it was awful, sailing about; and its eyes were *sot* [not the best grammar for a professor].'

"'Why did you not call before?'

"'I could n't get my breath. Here, landlord, you just wait.' I 'm going down to sleep on the box lounge in the office until morning, and then I 'll *go*. I never saw a ghost before, and never believed that there was one. The moon shone in at the window, and you ought to have seen its eyes. I tell you it was awful.'

"I heard a real professor, whoever he may have been, moving rapidly about the adjoining room.

"'Landlord!' he exclaimed; 'say, landlord, I cannot find my watch.'

"'What kind of a watch was it?'

"'Small gold one; belonged to my wife. Her name is on it, "Mary Mott." I would n't lose that for anything. My purse is here, but my watch is gone, sure. What next, I wonder.'

"'Did you not bar the door?'

"'No, I forgot it. I never passed such a night as this before, and would n't spend another such hour for all the mountains in the universe.'

"I heard the door close, and the two men passed through the hall and down the stairs.

"In the morning I looked out upon the beautiful scene of Cascade Mountain in the clear steel-blue air. Near it rose the Devil's Head, skirted with green trees. The little plateau was a circle of mountains. I seemed to be in a fortress of giants, outside of which lay the world. The grand trees of the glacial meadows glistened. On one side of the place broken ledges arose like the walls of giant castles, on the other, cool green hills. At the head rose a cliff like a steeple, some ten thousand feet high. Banff is a great cathedral of Nature, and no other cathedral uplifts around it such granite towers.

"I went down to the log dining-room. I found it full of excited people, adventurers, prospectors, and several ladies, talking over the events of the night.

"'I will tell you just how it looked,' said the Professor, whose name I incidentally found to be 'Mott.' 'It had on a long white robe, with a yellow border, and a yellow pocket on one side. One never sees anything of the kind here.'

"My heart leaped again. This was a perfect description of my night-dress in my strapped portmanteau.

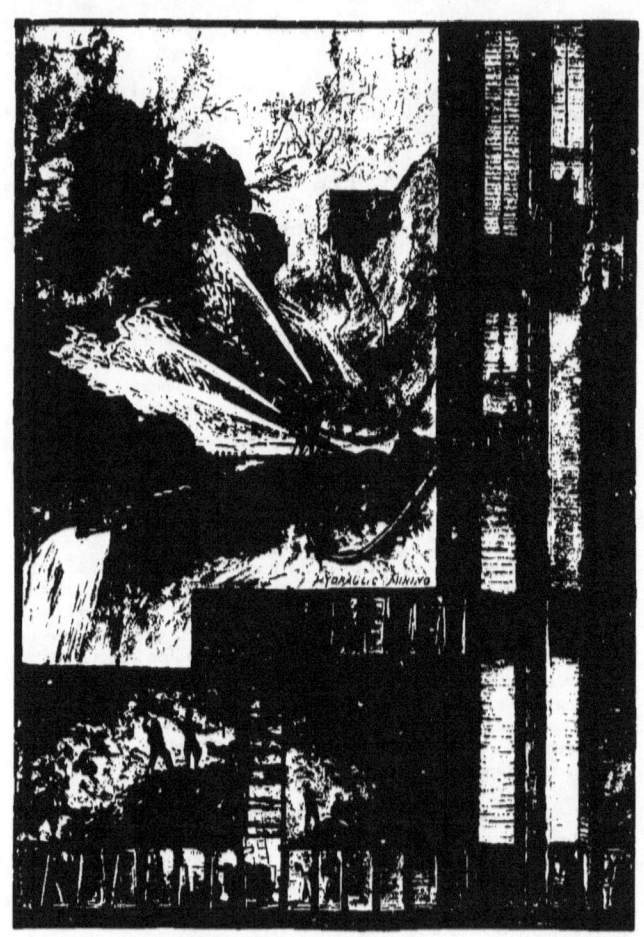

HYDRAULIC MINING IN THE ROCKIES.

"'But a ghost, Professor Mott, could not have taken away your watch,' said an incredulous boarder. 'Ghosts are done with time, you know.'

"'I should hope so, if they have eyes like *that*. But it would be a strange kind of a thief that would enter my room in a long robe with a yellow border, here in the mountains. No mortal man on earth ever had a night-dress like that one, unless he was crazy.'

"'But, Professor, a ghost would n't have a *pocket*, would it?'

"'I don't know whether ghosts wear pockets or not. One might if he came after a watch. The watch is gone; that is certain.'

"'But you do not think, Professor, that the watch has gone out of this world?'

"'Heaven only knows. I hope that it will never be brought back by the being that took it away, as much as I think of it, — at least, when I am in the room. The gold of the Indies would never tempt me to look upon those eyes again. *It* walked about just like machinery. I tell you it was *awful*.'

"The professor rose from his chair to illustrate how 'awful' the visitor was.

"'Then,' said he, 'I woke up; the moon was shining on Cascade Mountain, and there it stood just like a frozen dead man, *so*. Its eyes were fixed on the mountain, *so*. At last it lifted its hands up *so*, like a priest, its great sleeves waving *so*. Then it spoke in a hollow voice, just like a talking-machine. "Silver robes, silver robes," it said, just like *that*. "Silver robes for the mountain. Watch it, watch it, watch it!" I should think it did *watch* it. It stood there, I have no idea how long, — it seemed to me a life time; then it turned just like *that*, and marched out of the room with a noiseless tread, as though its feet were feathers.'

"I had little appetite for breakfast, — why, I could not tell; a nameless, mysterious fear crept over me.

"I went to my room, and unstrapped my portmanteau. On the top lay my night-dress, — a long white robe with a yellow border and pocket. I had taken it merely to please my sister. I took it out and held it up. There was something in the pocket. I put my hand into the pocket, and drew out a small gold watch. I examined the case. On the back was engraved in ornamental scrolls, 'Mary Mott.' I locked the door, and sank on the bed in terror, a cold sweat creeping over me.

"What had I been doing during the night, and what was I to do now? My conscience told me that it would be the manly thing to go directly to Professor Mott, and tell him what I had found. But every one would believe me to have been a thief, who had been frightened into confession by the events of the morning. No one in a strange public-house kept by a half-breed landlord would credit the story I would have to tell.

"I rose, put the night-dress in my trunk, and covering the watch with my hand, stepped into the hall. The Professor's door was open, and the room empty. On a wooden peg near the door hung a vest. I entered the room, stuffed the watch into the vest's watch-pocket, and hurried back to my own room and barred the door, and lay down upon the bed again, sick at heart and a terror to myself.

"A sense of relief gradually came to me, and I fell asleep. When I awoke, the Cascades seemed everywhere alive with waterfall music, the room was full of cool thin mountain air, and the crystal tops of the mountains were covered with sunshine.

"My mind was clear, and I began to think of what had so recently passed. I had been living another self, of which I had no memory; I had been another self. I had arisen in the night, unstrapped my portmanteau, put on my night-dress, gone into another room, returned from it with a watch, taken off my night-dress, put it into my travelling-bag, barred my door, and it may have been, gazed from the windows on the moon rising on the mountain; and yet I knew nothing of it all except by circumstantial evidence.

"I resolved not to sleep alone again. Could I find a room-mate in the hotel?

"The Professor did not leave, as he had intimated, in the morning. I made his acquaintance, and we went together to visit the Sulphur Pool, Devil's Head Lake, and the falls of Bow River.

"'Professor,' said I, on our return at noon, 'I was greatly alarmed last night. I wish I had some one to sleep in the same room with me.'

"'So do I,' said the professor. 'If I had, I would stay.'

"'I do not like to stay, myself, under the circumstances,' said I.

"'Could we not take a room together?'

"'I would be glad to do so,' said I.

"The Professor went to his room, and presently came down to dinner wearing the identical vest into whose pocket I had put the watch. He took a seat beside me at the table. I saw the outline of the watch in the pocket.

"After the meal was over, I asked, 'What time is it, Professor?'

"He put his hand on his watch-pocket, unconscious of his supposed loss, and a strange, wild, dazed look came into his face.

"'My watch is here — *here*,' he said. 'Now I understand it all. I did have the nightmare.'

"The Professor and I took a room together, and I immediately wrote to my father and told him all these strange occurrences, and sent the letter to Calgary for mailing. He consulted a physician, and returned answer by the mounted police. The physician said that such things often happened in youth, when the nerves were weakened and the mind was suddenly placed in a state of excitement: that its cure was habits of self-control; that its danger would pass away with returning health; and that it would not be likely to recur in after life. There has never been any recurrence, so far as I know, of this dual life.

"The Professor passed the month of August at Banff, and became quite intimate with me.

"The September days came. How beautiful they were in the mountains! I had used the waters of the springs freely. My health had returned. I had gained ten pounds in weight in some six weeks; my spirits rose with my health, and so I came to love the mountains and the mountain air.

"The day was fixed for me to return to Winnipeg, and one evening I opened my travelling-bag and began to repack it. I took out the bordered night-dress, which I had not worn, and threw it over a chair. Presently I held it up. While doing so I heard a step, and the Professor opened the door.

"'Hold!' he exclaimed; 'there it is again!'

"'What?' asked I

"'What? The very robe I saw in my nightmare.'

"'Oh, Professor, I was almost crazed that night. I was weak — was all alone in a strange room — and — and —'

"'What, boy?'

"'My other self walked about in my sleep.'

"The Professor sat down.

"'I can believe it all now,' he said, 'but I could not have believed it then. But there is a mystery about the watch. I felt in that very pocket that night, and it was not there.'

"My father had written to me to tell Professor Mott the true story. I now did so, and showed him my father's letters, and read to him what the physician had said. 'You will not *arrest* me, Professor?' I asked.

"'Arrest what, — your *other* self ? No; but it seems that both your selves used the same body, and only one that awful garment. When you get back to Winnipeg, put that habiliment away with your other self. I hope you will never have any use for either again.'

"I never have had. When the nerves are strong and the conscience clear, a person generally has but one self, and it is my purpose to live so as to secure these blessings. I have been able to strengthen myself by always doing what I believed to be true and honest. A strong will has given tone to my nerves, and my nerves to my body. A visit to my physician brought me this good advice, which I have tried to follow.

"'A person with a vivid imagination,' said the doctor, 'needs to cultivate a strong moral will and habits of self-control. The self-controlled man seldom walks in his sleep. His daily habit governs the night. It is so with many nervous diseases. If young people would learn to govern themselves when young, and to give up their own wills to the highest interests of the moral life, many forms of nervous diseases would be avoided. Habit becomes the governing power of life. Follow your better will and self, my boy, and you probably will never be troubled by the ghost of that other self again.'"

THE BRITISH CORPORAL'S STORY OF

A SONG IN TENNESSEE.

"I was travelling through America," said Corporal True, "to visit the battlefields of the War for the Union. I was on my way to Atlanta, Georgia, with a view to following, as nearly as possible, the old historical route of Sherman's army in its famous march to the sea.

"'Shall I see Lookout Mountain as I pass through Chattanooga?' I asked the conductor of a train from Washington to Jacksonville, Florida. 'Is it near the city?'

"'See it?' said the well-informed conductor, smiling. 'Pardon me, but if you have eyes you will not fail to see it. We pass *under* it. Lookout Mountain hangs over Chattanooga. Why do you not stop over a day or two, and visit the battlefields, and see the celebration?'

"It is not literally true that Lookout Mountain hangs over Chattanooga, though it seems to do so from a little distance; but it is quite true that the main line of its railways passes under the mountain and through its rocky base.

"It was the evening of the 3d of July. The sunset was blazing amid the pines of the Carolinas, and a soft light was gathering over the wood wiers and cottonfields. Late in the evening we would be in Chattanooga, near the battlefield of Chickamauga, the cemeteries where slumber two armies of dead soldiers side by side, and the scene of some of the most thrilling and poetic events of the war. The night was dark and still, full of cabin lights and fireflies. Blazing furnaces at length broke open the cloud of darkness, and the kindly conductor said, —

"'Yonder is Lookout Mountain.'

"I gazed from the car window, and although I could see no mountain, I saw a long row of lights twinkling in the sky, as though there were a habitable region in the air.

"'Hotels,' said he.

"'Is that the place of the Battle in the Sky?' I asked.

"'Pardon me, sir, but there never was any battle on Lookout Mountain,' he said, 'except in poetry. I am merely quoting General Grant's own words. The facts were these: In November, 1863, the Federal army occupied the city of Chattanooga, and the Confederate army the plateau on the mountain. On the 24th a cloud settled down upon the mountain, and a Federal force advanced under the cover of the cloud up the mountain-side, and the Confederates retreated before it. There was a great rattle of musketry, and it was telegraphed to Washington and the North that a battle was raging above the clouds. The fog-cloud was followed at night by an eclipse of the moon; the next morning the Union flag was seen flying in the early light from the highest point of the mountain. The Confederates had evacuated the mountain plateau, though few soldiers of either side had been killed or wounded.

CANOEING IN THE NORTHWEST.

There was great joy in Chattanooga over the capture of Lookout Mountain, and the skirmishes in the fog-cloud and darkness became magnified into a great battle, and though history disproves it, poetry will ever have it so. Sentiment would make it so, but it was not. You could not understand the situation unless you were to see the city and mountain under a fog-cloud. Perhaps you will.'

"The train stopped.

"'Carriage for the mountain,' said a negro driver.

"I was whirled through the darkness, over tortuous ways, for an hour, up toward the lights and the stars in the sky, so it seemed, and found rest at last in a good hotel, and wondered what the morning would reveal to me. I only knew that near me was Missionary Ridge, and somewhere below me in the glimmering darkness was Chattanooga, the Tennessee River, the battlefield of Chickamauga, the great national cemetery, and the monumented field of the Confederate dead.

"The night was still. The hotel stood near to the edge of a rocky precipice which I was told descended almost perpendicularly to the city to overlooked the valley of the Tennessee. I lay awake long, thinking of the past. It was here came the missionaries of the American Board to the Cherokees, and gave the name to the long, green, smoky mountain-wall, — Missionary Ridge. Here was the home of the Indian patriot, John Ross; here in these fastnesses of curving hills lived the Union men of Tennessee; here was the scene of the great war contests that once thrilled the nation as it stood listening to the click of the telegraph; here was Rosecrans's headquarters; here Thomas swept over the doubtful field; here was the place of the high-spirited achievements of Longstreet, Polk, and Bragg. I had never seen the place, but this view of it common newspaper history had made familiar to me.

"While I was thinking upon these things I heard a distant tinkle of music, and a harmony of sympathetic voices broke on the still air: —

> 'Rise, shine, and give God the glory, glory,
> For the year of jubilee;
> Oh, don't you hear dem bells a-ringing, ringing,
> For the year of jubilee!
> Rise, shine,' etc.

"The song came from some old negro servants in a dooryard, out-house, or cabin. It was native music, and it haunted me for days. I was awakened in the early morning by a cannon — a *feu de joie* — in the valley below. I was soon dressed, and threw open the window and stepped out on the cool balcony in the morning air. The scene was grand beyond description. Flags floating in the breeze filled it with patriotic sentiment. Over the mountain range, cool, shadowy, and dewy, was rising the unclouded sun. The smoky light made the great luminary fiery red. The air was refreshing. There was every promise of a clear day.

"Below lay the valley of the Tennessee, and the winding river with its old plantations and grain-encumbered farms. Under the mountain, or nestling close to its rocky side, lay Chattanooga, merely Ross's Landing fifty years ago, but a rich city to-day, full of growth, spirit, and enterprise, and destined to become at no late date one of the most beautiful and influential cities of the re-crowned South.

"There were flags everywhere. Patriotism had meant something here; and the fine buildings among the glimmering spires blossomed like hanging gardens with the national emblems. The soldiers' cemeteries — those great cities of the dead — lay full in view, and in answer to our inquiry a negro servant pointed into the kindling air, and said, 'Chickamauga!'

"'Chickamauga!' Yes, but the land was peace, and how lovely was the scene! The fires had been lowered in the furnaces of the great iron-works. The roads were full of odd vehicles, and people in holiday attire. There came a peal of bells. Was it possible that here, twenty-five years ago, human blood soaked the earth like water, and that around me in the many cemeteries of Tennessee were fifty thousand soldiers' graves?

"I spent the day in visiting Rock City, Lulu Lake, and the place of the once great army hospital erected by General Thomas, and afterward turned into a school.

"The mountain plateau was full of fantastic rock scenery, and recalled the Garden of the Gods, of Colorado. The air was cool, even under the bright, fierce sunlight. The groves of oak, pine, and laurel teemed with summer life and beauty. The great hotels were filled with guests early in the day, and in many places on the mountain the flag of thirty-eight stars rose above the trees in the calm of the sun-bright air.

"I chanced to make the acquaintance of a State senator of Tennessee, who had come to one of the great mountain hotels to pass the day in cool and quiet. Near sunset we went to a bluff overlooking the Chattanooga valley, which lay like a great garden below us, watered by the serpentine flow of the Tennessee, the air blooming in the long distance with flags.

"'I shall never forget,' said the senator to me, 'the thrilling scene that occurred in Chattanooga in September, 1881. It had been agreed to hold during Chattanooga week of that year a reunion of both the army of the Cumberland and the Confederate army.

"'So great is the spirit of good-will and peace in Tennessee among all classes of people, that a plan had been arranged by which on the principal day of the celebration the American flag should be raised over Cameron Hill, the place of the principal cemeteries, by both Federal and Confederate officers at the same time, each of the respective corps pulling the cords together. As the flag of thirty-eight stars should ascend, the artillery was to peal forth, and the bands were to play both Union and Confederate airs, and so inaugurate an era of eternal peace and good-will.

"'Chattanooga was all preparation for the grand event. Patriotic sentiment was awakened as I have seldom seen it anywhere but here. The city was gay with bunting. Excursions had been arranged over all the great highways of travel. It was to be a festival like that which is so common at patriotic periods in Germany and France.

"'At midnight on the ⁂ ⁂ before the inauguration of this grand Peace Festival the bells began to toll. People rushed into the streets. Clang, clang, clang! on the still, starry, midnight air. Clang, clang, clang! What did it mean? The telegraph had sent into the sleeping city a lightning flash,— that intelligence which made the world sad, — *Garfield is dead!*

"'Should the festival go on? Yes, but under another programme. The city filled with a wondering, awe-struck crowd. The flag-raising was appointed to take place as planned.

"'I never saw men's hearts so moved as they were that day as they stood on Cameron Hill, waiting for the lifting of that flag. Out of the city swept a long procession of Federal and ex-Confederate officers, with reversed arms and banners draped, the bands playing the dirges of the heroic dead. Near the flag-staff stood a beautiful catafalque, a coffin of flowers, with floral crosses and crowns, the work of the ladies of Chattanooga.

"'The marshals of the two armies met at the foot of the flag-staff and saluted; two officers grasped the halyards, and amid an awful silence the flag began to rise. Red, white, and blue? Yes, and *black*. The cannon thundered, the bands played the "Star-spangled Banner" and "Dixie."

"'Up, up into the cloudless sky of that September day ascended the flag with its stripe of black. Men clasped each other's hands; women wept; every heart thrilled with emotion. I never beheld such a scene.

"'Then the bands broke into a dirge. The flag began to descend slowly, waved to and fro in the dazzling sunlight by the mountain air, and rested at half-mast. Orations followed; and seldom has an orator had an easier duty than under the inspiration of those thrilling events. I have often thought that the sentiment of that day is the one the whole country should share: "With malice toward none, with charity for all;" and "that government of the people, by the people, for the people, shall not perish from the earth."'

"I rose next morning and looked out to see the city. It was gone. The sun was rising red over Missionary Ridge, but an ocean, or lake, or great lagoon appeared to lie beneath me. The waves of the strange sea seemed rolling on the orange light among islands and archipelagoes. Did the city still lie beneath it?

A HOME IN THE NORTHWEST.

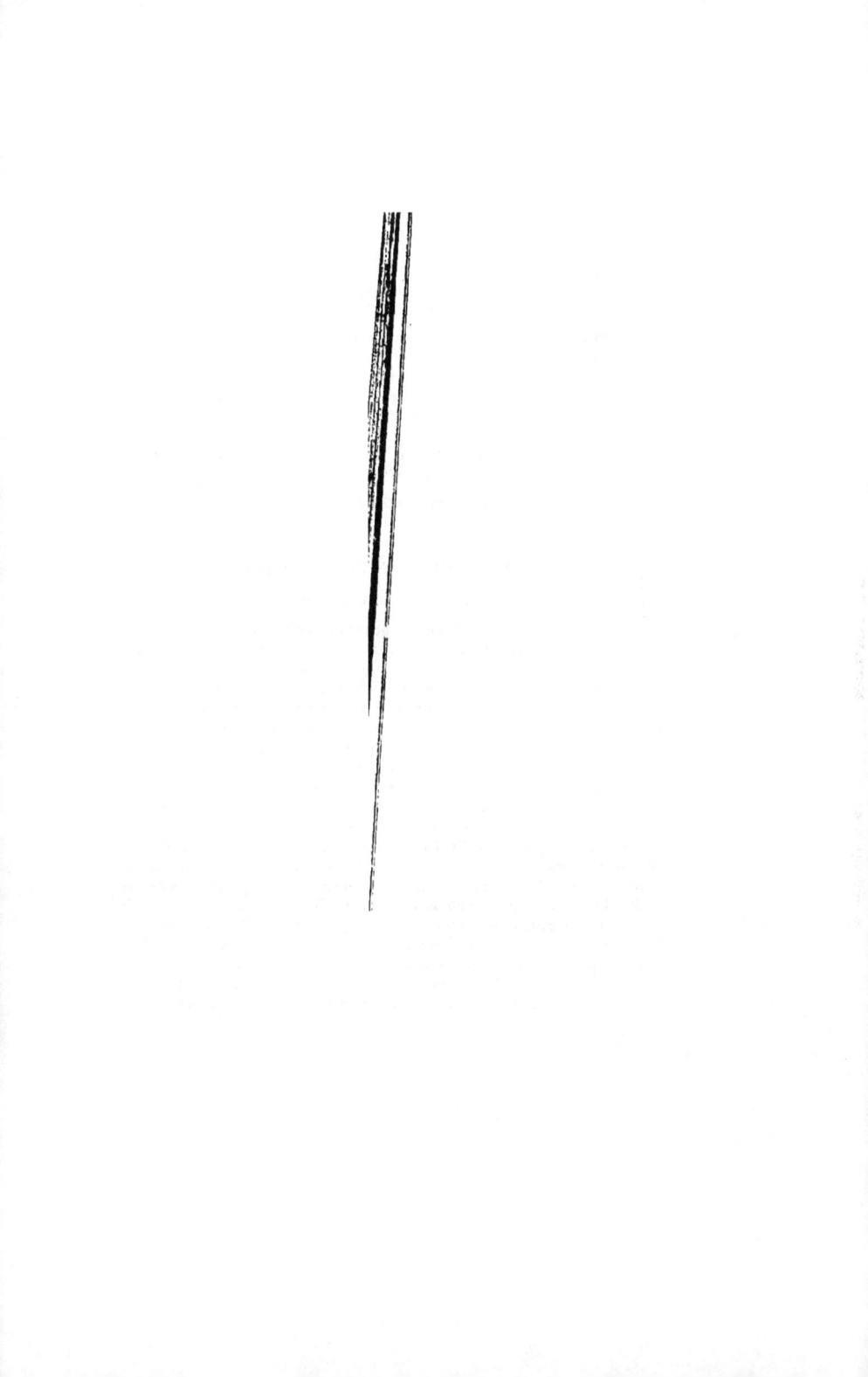

"Out of the mysterious regions of the fog below came a voice, joyous and melodious, —

'Rise, shine, and give God the glory, glory,
For the year of jubilee.'

"Slowly the great fog sea began to rise and dissipate, and the outline of the spired city to appear. Then I understood the poets' Battle in the Clouds, which I had not comprehended before. If the poets are historically wrong, they are in spirit right, when they mingle the cloud with the mountain in the great events of November 24, 1863. It was more than a battle; it was the change of front of America.

"As I left the mountain, I stopped to look up to the floating mists in the sunlight. Birds were singing. Suddenly came that joyous song again, —

'Rise, shine, and give God the glory, glory.'"

THE OLD YANKEE EMIGRANT'S STORY.

THE FOREST BLACKSMITH.

When I first heard old Ephraim, the pedler of watches, say, "Boys, I can tell you a story a great deal stranger than *that*, and you won't know any more when I've got through than when I began," my curiosity was greatly excited. By "that" he referred to the old story of Goffe the regicide, and the appearance of the so-called Angel of Deliverance at the attack on Hadley, Mass., during the Indian War. That was old Ephraim's favorite story. It embraced the incidents of the Judge's cave, the stone cellar at Guilford, the secret chamber at Hadley, and the appearance and vanishing of the white stranger during the old battle; no story heretofore had ever held me like that.

The itinerant story-tellers, such as lived in old colony times, are gone, like the minstrels of the days of the old English barons. A quaint class of people they were, these old New England story-tellers, — the pack-pedlers, the tin-pedlers, the tinkers, the wandering revival preachers, the huskers, and the fortune-tellers. The bread-cart man must be numbered among them; he carried the gossip of the town from house to house on Saturdays, usually with an old horse and red cart, and a jingle, jingle, jingle of bells. The old lady who earned her living by going visiting, and the travelling dressmaker, whose tongue was as pointed as her needles, belonged to the same class.

They are all gone; but I think that no better stories were ever told than those by the old-time entertainers as they sat before the great logs of the grand colonial fireplaces. They were often colored, it is true, by superstition, for the travelling tradesmen were a superstitious race, who feared the unseen more than the seen; but even the marvels of ghost-lore had a spiritual meaning, and illustrated goodness and peace, and the terror of evil, and there was the substance and philosophy of truth underlying them all.

It was the habit of most of these wandering story-tellers to remain over night at the farm-houses on their way. This habit enabled them not only to relate stories, but to collect them, and their best stories grew by repetition.

My youth was spent in an old colonial house at Warren, R. I., near Swansea, Mass., in view of Mount Hope, and amid the scenes of the early tragedies of the Indian War. The Baptist and Quaker founders of Rhode Island came to these plantations, and the exiles from Boston during the period of persecution and the witchcraft delusion. I have been a reader of stories for many years, but I still retain a vivid memory of the strong and subtle fascination of the old colonial fireside tale.

There was an old pedler by the name of Ephraim Pool, whose wonder-stories I distinctly recall. He lived in Guilford, Conn., and was accustomed to wander through the Connecticut River Valley in summer, and through Providence, and thence by Bristol Ferry to Newport, in winter. He was consequently at Hadley, Mass., during one part of the year, and at the old towns of the Mount Hope lands in winter, — two dramatic points in the old tragedies of the Indian War.

He sold watches and snuff-boxes, and cleaned and repaired clocks. He used to be called the Clock Doctor. He was an habitual snuff-taker, and used to pass the snuff-box often during the telling of a story.

I can see him now. "Here I am!" he used to say. "Come to set your clock all right again. The time will come when you won't see old Ephraim any more. Time will go on just the same after old Ephraim Pool has ceased to travel; yes, time will go on, but I don't believe clocks will ever go on half so well again. Have a pinch of snuff?"

To new listeners, the unexpected end of these customary introductory and very solemn words seemed very odd and comical. The snuff-box was old Ephraim's inseparable companion, and he punctuated with it all that he had to say. We used to light two candles instead of one when old Ephraim came, set a row of apples to roast before the fire on the great brick hearth, sit down on the red settle, and ask the genial and much-travelled snuff-taker for stories. The story that had the greatest interest for us was the attack of the Indians on Hadley, Mass., in the valley of the Connecticut, during King Philip's War, and the sudden appearance and disappearance of a so-called Angel of

Deliverance. The story in its historical relations is well known. It fascinated Sir Walter Scott, who tells it vividly in "Peveril of the Peak." It charmed Southey also, for it is highly poetic and spiritual in its suggestions, and the busy singer of Grasmere and Windermere had planned a long poem upon it, when his mind failed. It is at once one of the most thrilling and remarkable tales of American folk-lore. I well recall how old Ephraim used to tell it,— before the great fire, with his handkerchief spread over his knee.

"I am not so young as I was," he would begin; "my beard grows a little whiter, just a little, every year, and I set the clocks a little nearer the time,— the time for all of us. (Have a pinch of snuff?) Yes; well, as I was saying, I sha'n't be about here many more winters, so I shall have to please you this time, and I like to tell that old story right here, where the Indian War began. But, boys, I can tell you a story a great deal stranger than *that*, and you won't know any more when I've got through than when I began. But first let me tell you the story of old Hadley.

"Hadley, at the time of my story, was a little village in the woods. It was a Sabbath day in early fall when it all happened, and the people had gathered in the church. Old Nehemiah Solsgrace had just begun to pray, when a woman rushed into the church, with wild eyes and hair streaming, without bonnet or shawl, and shrieked, 'The Indians! the Indians!' just like *that*. (Have a pinch of snuff?) The prayer stopped, and all started up. In the silence there was heard a cry in the distance that would have pierced your soul. It was the war-whoop.

"The men seized their guns, for men went armed everywhere that doleful year, even to church. They rushed out-doors, and heard another wild cry, nearer now, and more fierce and defiant. What should they do?

"In the midst of the confusion appeared a wonder such as had never been known in New England before. There came stalking into the streets — from what place no one knew, but many believe from another world — a tall man like one of the old patriarchs. No one among the defenders, so far as known, had ever seen him before. His garments were of skins; he carried a sword which he flourished aloft (just like *this*); his hair was long and gray, his beard white and flowing, and he had the air of a leader of armies.

"He shouted, and his voice seemed to fill the village, — 'Behold in me the Captain of Israel. Follow me.' The people were awe-struck, but the men followed him. Out of the town went the white stranger, making a semicircle around the Indian warriors, unseen by them, and soon appeared behind the enemy, to their surprise and terror. The Indians, thinking they had a foe both before and behind them, fled in confusion.

"The white stranger returned to the village, followed by the men. 'Bring me a cup of water,' he said, 'and let us offer thanks for this great victory to God, who sent me to be the Angel of Deliverance.'

"All knelt down. He prayed in trumpet tones; it was a thanksgiving of such thrilling and lofty language as the people never had heard before. It ended with, 'Be still.' There was a deep silence, and when, one by one, they looked up, the white stranger was gone. (Have a pinch of snuff?)"

We usually spent an hour or more in asking questions to clear up this remarkable recital. Uncle Ephraim then would slowly tell us that the white stranger for many years was believed to be an Angel of Deliverance sent from another world; but he really was Major-General Goffe, one of the judges who had condemned to death Charles I., and who sought refuge in America, and was hidden in different places, once in a cave on the top of a hill near New Haven, once in a stone cellar at Guilford, and finally, for many years, in a secret chamber in Hadley, Mass., where he was when the Indians fell upon the place.

"But the other story?" we asked eagerly.

"It was something like this, only a great deal more strange," he said. "There were all kinds of strange things that happened and were expected to happen in old colony times, when people were fleeing from kings and parliaments and persecutions; but this took place not more than thirty years ago. I never tell the story of Goffe without thinking of the other, for there is a likeness between the two, as you shall see.

"I was a young man when it happened, but the scenes are all as vivid as daylight in my mind still. The old Mount Holyoke Female Seminary was a power then, under Mary Lyon, of blessed memory. I used to stop at several farm-houses in Holyoke. In one of my journeyings I was surprised to find not far from the village, in the woods, a new blacksmith-shop and a small cottage.

"'Who lives there?' I asked of a farmer by the way.

"'A stranger,' said he. 'They call him the Forest Blacksmith.'

"Seeing my curiosity, he continued, 'Name is Ainsley. Came here kind o' mysterious like. People don't know much about him. He isn't very handy.' The last remark was meant to imply a lack of experience or skill in his work.

"The shop was merely a covered frame and forge. The cottage was small, and seemed to consist of two rooms. In the doorway stood a woman with white hair, and a handkerchief crossed on her breast. Her face fixed itself on my mind like a picture; I can see it now. It was a quiet face, full of trouble.

GOFFE, THE REGICIDE AT HADLEY.

You may not understand that, but it was so. It was a beautiful face, that seemed to hide a weary, sad heart.

"The next summer, as I was coming up the valley, and travelling along the old Holyoke road, a storm overtook me one afternoon near the Forest Blacksmith's. The clouds darkened and settled down upon the mountains, and a heavy rain, mingled with hail, began to fall. I hurried along to the blacksmith's shop, found the man there, and sat down by the fireless forge.

"'You will allow me to rest until the storm is over?' said I to the man, who was not at work.

"'Certainly, friend, certainly. You are quite welcome; make yourself at home. It will all be over in an hour. Go into the house, if you like.'

"'The gentlemanly mildness of his tone and politeness of manner surprised me. It seemed strange amid such rude and simple belongings. I accepted his invitation, hoping to sell something to the woman, and went into the house.

"The woman with white hair received me very politely, but cautiously. She moved back and sat down in a great arm-chair, the only comfortable article of furniture in the room.

"The chair had a stuffed leather cushion. I noticed that she did not leave the chair during my stay, which lasted two hours. As I rose to go, I noticed again the heavy, stuffed leather cushion.

"Another year passed, and I came to the blacksmith's shop again one day, just at nightfall, early in September. The golden-rods were blooming about the door, and flocks of birds were gathering for migration. The low sun blazed behind the reddened trees, the sunbeams gleaming here and there among the branches and twigs. I hailed Blacksmith Ainsley, and asked him if he would keep me over night.

"'I wish I had better accommodations,' he said. 'I like to oblige a stranger, but I am not situated now as I wish I were. Ask wife.'

"I went to the door. The white-haired woman opened it with a questioning look, moved back to the same arm-chair, sat down, and offered me a rude seat. I repeated the question that I had asked the blacksmith.

"'Heaven forbid that I should not offer hospitality,' she said. 'But we have only two rooms, this and the other, and only two beds, here and yonder. Couldn't you go farther? It hurts me to say it; I never in my life turned away a stranger when I could help it.'

"'I will give you little trouble,' said I. 'I am very tired. Just let me lie down on the bed in the other room and give me a bit for breakfast, and I will pay you handsomely.'

"'It is not the pay about which I am thinking,' said she.

"'I knew that.' Her eye moistened, and her lip quivered.

"'Well, you may stay,' said she. 'It is not like me to say no.' She then became silent.

"The sun set. Shadows fell across the way. The old blacksmith came in and lighted a tallow candle. It was dry weather, and the blacksmith was speaking of the effects of the drought on the crops and cattle, when there was a sudden sound of horse's feet at the door.

"'Some one come to get shod,' said the blacksmith. The expression is not to be taken as it runs, but it was a common one.

"He opened the door. I can see him now. What a change came over him! His face turned pale, and an expression passed over it of utter helplessness and hopelessness, as though life had been stricken from his soul.

"His wife started up, and then she sank back into the chair again with an expression of intense anxiety and terror.

"The stranger came stalking in without any invitation. He was a man with a hard, determined face. He held his whip in his hand, and looked around.

"'What brings you here?' said the blacksmith.

"'I must pass the night here,' said the man. 'I have travelled far, and have business here. I wish you would care for my horse!'

"'But, stranger, I cannot accommodate you,' said the blacksmith. 'I have but one spare room, and that we have promised to this man who is sitting here.'

"'Can you give me a bit to eat?' he asked, turning to the woman. She did not move.

"'Get the stranger something,' she said to her husband. The man looked at her rudely.

"'Are you lame, that you do not rise and accommodate me yourself?'

"The old woman made no reply.

"'Here, husband, you are perhaps tired; sit down here and I will wait upon the stranger.' The blacksmith sat down in the arm-chair.

"'It would be better courtesy, I'm thinking, if you were to offer *me* that chair, tired as I am. Perhaps you do not know that I am an officer of the law,' said the man, brutally.

"The woman set the table. I could see that her hands trembled as she handled her dishes.

"'Supper is ready,' said she, at last.

"She passed to the arm-chair, which her husband offered her.

GLACIER HOUSE, SELKIRK MOUNTAINS.

"Do you not usually have grace before meat?' said he.

"'Yes,' said the old woman. 'Are you a godly man?' There was a hopeful tone in her voice.

"'I want you to say grace,' said the stranger to the blacksmith.

"The blacksmith rose. 'Kneel,' said the stranger, 'and you too,' turning to the woman. We all knelt down.

"The old blacksmith's voice began to offer thanks in a tremulous way, but it grew firm. Suddenly the light was blown out. The stranger started up, and walked about heavily in the dark. What did it mean?

"'I will get a light in a minute,' said the old man, and then went on to finish the prayer, showing in this a reverent sincerity that has always been a mystery to me. At length he rose from his knees, and stumbled about for a light.

"The old woman sank back into the chair. As she did so she uttered such a cry of distress, ending with the words, 'It is gone, William; it is gone!'

"'What?'

"When the lamp was lighted, the stranger had left the room. The chair was there, but the cushion was gone. The woman wailed helplessly, 'Oh! oh! after all these years!' She knelt down by the chair and cried like a child.

"'It is all over,' said the old man. 'Don't cry; there's another world, Amy.'

"I turned from this pitiable scene to look for my pack. It was where I had placed it. There were sobs from the woman, and intervals of silence, for an hour. I then went to bed, having first put my pack under the bedclothes at my feet. I was tired, but did not fall asleep until toward morning.

"When I awoke, it was broad day. The sun had risen, and the tinged leaves of the forest were glimmering in the light, warm wind. How beautiful everything looked through the little window! I rose, dressed, pulled my pack from the bed, and then went out to the other room. No one was there. The table still was set as on the evening before, with the food upon it. The great chair was there, without its cushion. There was no fire.

"I opened the outer door. The shop was empty; there was a dead silence everywhere, except the call of the jays in the walnut-trees.

"I started toward the village, but stopped to repair a clock and take breakfast at a farm-house. At the village I examined my pack, when another mystery appeared; I found that my watches were gone.

"I summoned a sheriff, and went back. The house was empty; everything remained as I had left it in the morning.

"The next year I came again to the place. It was deserted, as when I last saw it. No one knew who the occupants had been, or why or whither they had gone. I have asked myself a thousand times, What was in the leather cushion? Were the forest blacksmith and his old wife honest people? Who was the mysterious stranger? Why did he come?

"You know as well as I do, boys. (Now I will have another pinch of snuff.) People do not vanish now as they used to do; times have changed. As I told you 't would be, you don't know any more now than when I began."

MR. LETTE'S STORY OF TRAVEL.

THE "DEVIL AMONG THE TAILORS" AT THE PONCE.

Two years ago I went to Florida. I have long taken a great interest in the most rapidly developing part of America, and I went South to see Atlanta, Birmingham, and those parts of the Southern States that were growing most rapidly, and offered promising fields for emigration. I visited Tennessee, Alabama, and Georgia, then set forth for St. Augustine, Florida, going by the indirect way of Palatka.

I had seen St. Augustine ten years ago. I recollected it well, and set out from Palatka with the old vision in my mind. Out of a long region of shadowy palm crowns, sunny orange-groves, and swamp fields of glimmering palmetto the train swept into the open country by the sea, and crossed the St. Sebastian. What a wonderful change! There is no other like it anywhere. America seemed to vanish at the river. An Oriental city of airy towers, red-tiled roofs, and acres of palaces half buried in ancient trees rose before the eye. The Spanish tales of Washington Irving came to life again in memory. Were we looking out upon some conquered Moorish town in the Spain, of the conquistadors?

There was a light pull at my sleeve.

"And now we will go to the Children's Playroom in the Ponce, and see the 'Devil among the Tailors.'"

It was my little Florida cousin, a lad of twelve years. He pronounced "Ponce" as if it were a common English proper name.

My head had been the region of romance from the moment the turreted roofs and hanging gardens began to fill the eye. The palaces of coquina (shell marble) before me had arisen since I last saw St. Augustine, as under the wand of an enchanter.

"The Children's Playroom at the Ponce,"—what was that; and "the Devil among the Tailors"?

The train stopped at a long station. We stepped out into a tropical garden. The railway stations in England are famous for their flower gardens, but we never saw there any like this.

I stopped a moment to view the scene before me. The town lay under the quiet blue sky, green with fringes of orange-groves. The sky itself was wonderfully beautiful. It was as soft as that of Seville, delicately blue, as it were an arch over the luminous air. The balmy Gulf winds just stirred the gray Spanish mosses in the old live-oaks about the town; pinnacles everywhere kindled and blazed; open balconies and airy corridors,—all rising over acres upon acres of red-tiled roofs and trees eternally green. It was my first view of new St. Augustine.

"Have a 'bus for the Ponce?"

He, too, had Americanized the fine old Spanish word. It seemed like the throwing of a bottle of ink against a masterpiece of tone color. "A 'bus for the Ponce" and "the Devil among the Tailors," indeed!

My little cousin pulled me forward, and hurried me toward the town. At every step the wonder grew. A long line of carriages swept ahead of the foot passengers and travellers, and these were already being welcomed by the Spanish band. I was in the land of fancy again. America had at last produced a poem of Mosaic and native stone gems and sea marbles as romantic as the Taj, as lovely as the Alhambra; it was here.

"I am told that Flagler has spent six millions of money on his hotels, and is going to lay out four millions more. Do you think that he will ever get his money back?"

This was prosaic enough, and clipped the wings of my fancy. There was something really noble in the answer to the mysterious question which I had heard behind me.

"I think that Mr. Flagler feels a patriotic pride in what he is doing; that he is a true American gentleman, and does not consider the matter of gains or losses at all. What he has done is a historic credit to the whole country. A man who so spends his money is a benefactor."

The gentleman to whom the allusion was made is Mr. H. M. Flagler, the builder of the two principal palace hotels, the Ponce de Leon and the Alcazar.

The Spanish hotel palaces now confronted us, and we stood before the two lions' heads at the gateway to the Ponce de Leon, under the iron portcullis and its beautiful arch of tracery and airy colorings. Could this be America? We stopped to look around, amid the odors of rose gardens, the flash of fountains, and the music of mandolins. Courts, turrets, Moorish towers, loggias, and cool retreats, acres of red roofs, with art and beauty everywhere!

EARLY SETTLERS.

There was another pull at my sleeve.

"Let us go up to the Children's Playroom. I want to see the 'Devil among the Tailors.' We shall have time to see these things afterward."

"But what do you mean by the 'Devil among the Tailors'?"

"Oh, don't you know? It is a great game down here. Everybody goes to see it. You spin a steel top on a marble surface, and it goes whirring into a great dollhouse all full of little doors and rooms and compartments. In the little rooms the tailors are supposed to be at work, and the top bounces around each little room until it finds the door, and then it goes through and knocks over all the tailors, or most of them, and then it finds the door to the next little room, and goes spinning in and knocks over the tailors there, and so on and on; and he who can start the top so as to knock over the most tailors wins the game. Oh, it is all too funny for anything. The greatest people go to see it, — senators, governors, artists, singers. Come, and I will show you."

"But what do I care for a toy game amid all this magnificence?"

"Oh, there is too much of it! It makes me tired! I like to see something I can understand."

Oliver Goldsmith once attracted much attention on a London street until there came along a man with a hand-organ and a monkey. He was then left to pass on unnoticed. He thought the world very strange and changeable. The Ponce de Leon's gorgeous courts and rooms all seemed to lose their interest for young people after some genius introduced into the Children's Playroom at the top of the building the very, very funny game of the "Devil among the Tailors."

I allowed the persistent little hand to lead me on. We passed through the court, — who can describe it? — through the reception-room, all so bewildering as to be oppressive, amid music and flowers and tone colorings, over pavements of beautiful stone.

"The Playroom," said my little cousin to the elevator boy.

Up we went to a room in the rotunda, all beauty and balconies and outlooks on pile upon pile of historic art. I found myself amid a crowd that surrounded the seemingly magic toy.

Presently a small, bright-looking girl drew the string around the steel top through a hole in the board framework of a little platform of open-topped rooms, so as to give it force. It began to spin on the polished surface. It found its way into the first little room, or open compartment, and knocked over the tailor. It bounded around the room until it found the next little door, when it entered and continued its destructive work. It went on and on; it seemed as though it would never stop. What mysterious laws of motion kept it going?

The top entered all the rooms and knocked down nearly all the poor tailors.

There was a joyous shout. The number of the tailors overturned was marked upon a blackboard, when a boy came forward, a counterpart of little Lord Fauntleroy, and wished to try so to start the top as to topple over all the tailors.

It was fascinating; but what was I doing here in a children's playhouse, while I was on such historic ground?

There were the landing-place of the poetic old adalantado, Ponce de Leon; the scene of the Spaniards' Mission; the ruins of old Fort Caroline, of the

Huguenots; the bloody Matanza, green with eternal palms; gray Fort Marion, the place of the English sea-kings and the torture-house of the Spaniards; the decayed plantations of the Minorcans, and the shell lands of the Seminoles.

Here rose the pillar of stone with the arms of France; here Sir Francis Drake, who ploughed a sea furrow around the world, came pillaging the coast and returned thence for England with a ship of gold; here Mendenez reddened the land with noble blood; here Father Juniper preached, and Ribault and Laudonnière sang on the River of May, now the St. John's.

I broke away from the bewildering little game, and went down the bewitching palace stairs. I glanced at the famous dining-room and its panorama, where the exploits and dreams of old Ponce de Leon appear as if in a vision. Then I went out beyond all the great area of the mosque of old palaces to Fort Marion and the old sea-wall. The sky was flushed with the sunset, blue and amber and crimson. I had stood on the same place six years before.

I turned and looked back. Old St. Augustine was gone. The frost of 1886 had withered its ancient date-palm, and the fire of 1887 had swept from the Plaza the old cathedral and its cross of bells. Before me lay new St. Augustine, with taller date-palms and a grander cathedral, with new spires and towers, and acres of palace-like structures that had gathered to themselves the Spanish and Moorish art of a thousand years. It is the most beautiful and poetic city in America.

I had left my little cousin in the Playroom. I went back and found him there. He had been trying his hand at the wonderful top, much to the delight of a governor, an artist, and a poet.

"This reminds me of what Shakespeare — 'Puck' — says," said the governor to me.

"Do not repeat it," begged the artist. ("What fools these mortals be!")

"St. Augustine was always a place of tragedies," continued the governor, as one after another the poor tailors went over before the endlessly spinning top.

"Come, we will go to dinner," said I to my little Florida cousin; and amid the Spanish music of the band we went down to the dining-room of golden windows, and took our dinner amid the painted visions of the romantic old adalantado, Ponce de Leon.

THE GREAT GLACIER OF THE SELKIRKS.

ON THE GREAT GLACIER.

A half hour's walk from the Summit or Glacier House found our travellers on the stupendous mass of the Great Glacier. The Great Glacier, that looks so dark and broken from the railway,— what is it?

In reality it is a moving river of ice, grinding its way over the granite mountains,— a frozen Rio Grande, Colorado, or Columbia, travelling. Now it is shallow; now it measures a depth of two thousand feet. Great green forests and rocky cliffs border its slow eternal march.

When did this march begin? When was this mass, over which the eagles wheel, frozen? How old is this glittering ice-river?

No one can tell. The settler views it from the far-off valleys, and pauses in wonder. It lies in the sunset a pile of splendor, and the moon changes it into palaces of crystal in the high and voiceless air.

It pours down to the green valleys a thousand waterfalls. One hears these sun-loosened streams eternally singing. Every newly explored solitude bears witness to the musical glasses of the mountains.

The river travels over the wrecks of old volcanoes, and through rents that the ages have been crumbling. Was the great sea of ice once a sea of fire?

How many ages has the moon glimmered above it, and the night led over it the long procession of stars?

What eye first beheld it, and out of what mysterious migrations did the people who first saw it come?

What changes of fire and water and internal upheaval left it here to melt in the eternal sun, and be renewed again in the nights of the long arrays of winters?

Below it silently moves the glorious Columbia, which one has well called the Achilles of rivers. Sky-born indeed it is; we stand at its birthplace and try to dream how it falls through gorges and cañons, gathering force, until, a calm and placid flood, it mingles its waters with the far-off Pacific. Another stream has its beginning beside it, and rolls down to the north and becomes a river, and pours its flood into Hudson Bay.

Glorious and mysterious is the Great Glacier under the stars! It is the most beautiful mirror of heaven in the New World. Stand in one of its great caverns which beasts and eagles shun, and look outward and upward to the lamps of night. One seems more than mortal then; the lights of the homes of more than mortal beings seem to glimmer about him, and he wonders if he shall know more of the great city of the universe when his soul shall be free.

What to him are the selfish aims of life here? What is wealth; what fame; what the glittering halls that feed the animal appetite?

The soul can find no relief but in adoration. It thirsts for spiritual knowledge.

Life seems but a passing day in the calendar of the ages. A few springs light the hills, and a few autumns wither the leaves, and *immortalitas adest*, — eternity is at hand. Great resolutions crowd upon the soul, — to rise above sin, to be high-minded and spiritual, to serve humanity, to do the grand deeds of heroic endeavor with humility and awe. All dream such dreams on these mountain stairs. The old conceptions of life all change here.

As when one listens to a symphony, he becomes aware of great aspirations of soul to which he before was a stranger! One only knows how grand he is in his inner life when he has an experience like this. Immortality may have been a doubt at Calgary, but it is a certainty here. Only an immortal soul could so glow, expand, and feel its wings. Could such an inspiration continue, what godlike beings men would be!

But see that party of dark forms hurrying down the glacier toward the twinkling lights of the Glacier House! The spirits of speculation flock around them again. Ambition returns, — appetite, selfishness. On the Glacier thoughts were eagles cleaving celestial air; now they are buzzards again.

In the morning the train goes screaming away among the Selkirks. The tourists now seem like a different order of beings. But each one has had a view of soul possibilities that none probably ever had before. These views will return again in dreams, in solitudes, in churches, and by the caskets of the dead. Life will always be lifted by them; it is indeed a glorious thing to have stood at night on the Great Glacier of the Rocky Mountains, and to see one's self as the angels see life, and to have felt the movement of the little planet amid the ages gone and the ages to come, and to have wondered if conscious life is an endless progression, and to have felt that it indeed was so.

THE OLYMPIAN MOUNTAINS.

CHAPTER X.

IN THE AMERICAN SWITZERLAND.

HE five hundred miles ride through the clouds and great volcanic systems of the Rockies from Banff Hot Springs to Vancouver is the grandest that can be made in North America or in Europe. The train sweeps into a forested valley toward the Vermilion Lakes, and the glance backward is a thrilling vision. The road is upward. Presently a great ice-river appears, yellow with age, and Hector is reached, and Mount Stephen, at an altitude of 5,296 feet, about as high as Mount Lafayette, in the White Hills of New Hampshire. The station is at the summit of the Rockies. The scenery here is colossal and terrible. One feels his littleness and the lightness of his temporal concerns here if anywhere. Mount Stephen rises to a height of some eight thousand feet from the valley, — as high as the Greek Olympus. On its shoulder is an emerald glacier some eight hundred feet in thickness, which is slowly travelling toward the vertical cliff. We now follow the Wapta (Kicking Horse) Cañons.

The Wapta is like a Niagara broken loose, and finding its long way through mountains, dashing and foaming, and seemingly flowing backward as it rushes against tens of thousands of rocks and stones. Its apparent backward waves is not the cause of its being called the Kicking Horse. A mule, according to the tradition, refused to move forward or backward on the high pass over the cañon. He stopped in this most perilous place, and kicked and kicked. Hence the gorge became known as the place where the horse or mule stopped and kicked, or Kicking Horse Cañon, and the wonderful cascade river of the high Rockies took the unpoetic name. The Wapta is the true name, but that does not do justice to the wild, mad, glacial stream.

"Come this way," cries one of the passengers on the train. "Oh, such a cascade! but it is gone."

"Come this way, all," cries another. "Such a waterfall I never saw! We have passed it now."

"Here! here!" cry others. Tourists run from one side of the car to another. Some weep, some laugh, some are overwhelmed, and desire nothing so much as silence. The railway and river plunge together under towering cliffs. The Columbia River is reached and crossed, and we are in view of the supremely lovely Selkirks, which seem to be the feminine mountains in all this warring giant land.

YALE, ON THE FRASER RIVER.

The grandeur culminates at the Glacier House. The train stops before the Great Glacier, which is some thirty-eight miles square, and said to be greater than any in Switzerland. It rises like a roof of a grand cathedral, and over it towers the granite pyramid of Sir Donald, a shaft fit for the monument of a John Hampden

OTTERTAIL RANGE, ROCKY MOUNTAINS, B. C.

or a Gladstone, *a mile and a half high*. Think of a train ringing its bell between such a glacier and monumental pinnacle. Was there ever seen such a pass or monolith? Did ever a railroad car rest in such a place? The walls here touch the sky; tourists' heads hang on the back of their necks. He has not seen how grand Nature can be, who has not stood in this place. The Great Glacier is only about a mile away from the hotel. Beautiful is the name and more beautiful are the waters of the Illecilliwaet. It is a pea-green stream, fed by glaciers, and seems to bear to the world joy from the crystal palaces in the atmospheres of the sun. It calls for poets, for artists, for composers. It is poetry and art and music.

On, on goes the train, over violet and emerald rivers, under cities of castles that no man inhabits, through long snow-sheds, under dark cliffs and luminous glaciers, the scene shifting at every turn, — on, on, ever on. When will the wonders cease?

The mountains grow lower. There is a new peace in the air. The heavens are expanding and coming back again. The rivers grow wider. Houses multiply, and farms, and churches. There is a gleam of a violet harbor. How restful it seems! There are ships and steamboats and the English flag. We are gliding into a city again. The train goes slowly. The conductor hurries through the cars and cries, "Vancouver!"

VANCOUVER.

There are three cities on the Pacific slope of British Columbia that are indeed beautiful in their situation and surroundings. They are Vancouver, New Westminster, and Victoria. A city of wonderful growth is Vancouver. It seems destined to become the London of Canada. In 1886 it was a forest, and such a forest! The trees were giants. Let one stand before the high stumps of the two trees that form the natural gate-posts of the great Vancouver Park, and he will wonder at the battle between the pioneers and the trees, and that man ever was able to make so rapid a conquest. There was a stump in New Westminster that it cost some forty dollars to remove; there is a hollow stump of a giant tree near Fraser River, in which it is said that two horses and a yoke of oxen could be stabled; and we are told of old evergreen lords of the forest that tower above three hundred feet high. The dooryards of the expanding city of Vancouver are full of stumps that are large enough for tables.

CARIBOO ROAD BRIDGE OVER THE FRASER RIVER.

Mountain walled is Vancouver, with the blue Puget Sound rolling like a winding river amid the great forests at the foot of the long elevations. The climate is the Chinook, or almost continuous April weather. The census? No one can fix it any more than one could count an old herd of the plains that gathered force on its march. The city is levelling the great trees in the dark forest valleys, and is building, building; the tap of the hammer is heard like the drill of an army. The poor emigrant knows that a continual fire will waste anything, and so about the high stumps of the immense tree she

HOTEL VANCOUVER, VANCOUVER, BRITISH COLUMBIA.

keeps the flame in continual activity. The great woods smoke; the new settlements smoke; the hills smoke.

Here is Canada's future port of China and Japan. Here is the port of the great coal-mines. Here is the market of one of the most wonderful farming districts. A mighty sweep of history is intended for Vancouver.

The Cascade Mountains smile upon her, — the snow-lined and shining Olympus; behind her rolls the glorious Gulf of Georgia; out of her streets sweeps the gigantic water-road of the Fraser;

ON THE HOMATHCO RIVER, BRITISH COLUMBIA.

and Mount Baker looks over all like a beneficent father, crystal crowned, and mantled in eternal snow.

New Westminster, from the hills overlooking the Fraser, is a twin city of progress and beauty. There can hardly be a more thrifty community in the world than here.

Victoria is a little England, in climate, in people, in quiet homes protected by inherited wealth, and in parks of wonderful beauty. Here the traditional fine " old English gentleman " would find himself quite at home and at ease. It looks serenely out on the Juan de Fuca, and is guarded by mountain walls that fill the air. Thence go ships to the many ports of the world, — to Asia and South America. Americans who stop at the quiet hotels are filled with delight at the beauty of the mountains, the sea, and the air; they are reluctant to leave the noble parks, and the cathedral-like aisles of the woods. The English people all love the little Liverpool that was, and the great Liverpool that is to be.

THE JAPAN CURRENT.

Look upon your map of ocean currents in your physical geography, and you will find a stream of water running between the coasts of China and Japan and the Puget Sound. It is called the Japan Current. It is four thousand miles long. Its water is warm, and it warms the shores of the Pacific from Mexican California to Alaska. Over this stream ships sail rapidly, and usually in calm water, and over it a great body of the commerce between England, America, and Asia is likely to come and go.

Look again on the map of the world, and see how long is the present distance between the English ports and those of China and Japan. England carries her goods to eastern Asia over an ocean route of some twelve thousand miles. The ocean route from the ports of the Puget Sound is only about four thousand miles, and British Columbia and Washington and Oregon will soon be able to produce for the Asiatic market many of the goods and supplies now manufactured in England.

And how great is that market likely to become! The population of China is some three hundred and sixty millions. Japan is growing in intelligence, and is calling upon the world for all the arts of progress.

. The great Northwest Territory is full of productions that eastern Asia needs and must have, and it is the law of trade to seek the shortest routes. The boast of Vancouver that she will rival Montreal, and of Seattle and Tacoma that they will one day be the New Yorks of the Pacific, is not without a basis of reasonable suggestion. The State of Washington is to act no common part in the future of the United States. She is likely one day to lead the great Republic.

Over this warm ocean current between Asia and the Puget Sound what processions of ships may go during the centuries to come! What trade-transforming steamers! what argosies of wealth that will bring back golden fleeces! what navies! what pleasure craft! It is this water-belt that is likely to bind the oldest and newest civilizations, and bring them into one common brotherhood. Here the West will meet the East, and will teach the East the same truths that the East gave to mankind thousands of years ago. So nations rise and decay, and progress passes from one land to another; but truth lives and seeks its best interpreters, and they who receive it become powerful and wise, and their acts encircle the earth!

STORY OF THE NAMING OF PLACES ON PUGET SOUND.

The years 1891 and 1892 should witness some patriotic celebrations in British Columbia, Washington, and Oregon, besides those that relate to the Columbian discovery. Four new stars have lately appeared on the American flag, and the brightest of these is Washington. It was in the years 1791 and 1792 that Puget Sound, Mount Baker, and Mount Ranier (Tacoma) received their names; and these years may well be made to commemorate the worth, magnitude, and glory of the great voyage of Vancouver and his lieutenants to the Northern Seas.

It was on the 15th of December, 1790, that Capt. George Vancouver received his commission as commander of His Majesty's sloop the "Discovery;" and since the days of Drake, and the old sea-kings of Elizabethan age, few

TRADING-SHIPS ON THE NORTHWEST COAST.

vessels have set forth from any port that opened the way to such grand historical achievements. The discovery of the Northwestern Empire must now rank among the great events of the world. Here the rich port cities of the Pacific are to rise and grow. Already England finds her swift commercial highway from Liverpool to Hong-Kong over the Canadian plains and mountains, and out of the sunset ports of Puget Sound. The violet waters of this Mediterranean of the West are already white with sails, and crowding with the floating cities of giant steamers. Look upon the map and note the warm ocean current that runs from Japan along the shores of Alaska, and down to the coast of Northern California. The shores of this warm ocean-river are to be a new world. The great ports of iron, coal, lumber, and precious ores, of hops, fruit, and a hundred agricultural industries, of the teas of China and the silks of Japan, are to be in the Puget Sound. Here is to rise the *other* New York and the *other* Boston.

The discovery and naming of the Puget Sound, its grand mountains, bays, and rivers, have been made great events of history by the emigration that is flowing to these April regions from all enlightened lands. We copy from the journals of George Vancouver his own account of these beginnings of the wonderful history. Vancouver seems to have had a heart formed for friendship, and he named many of the places of the sublimely picturesque region that he visited under the blue spring sky and in the burning noons and long crimson morning and evening twilights of the June days of 1792, for the honor of his faithful officers and his best-loved friends. Among the officers on the "Discovery" we find the names of Lieut. Peter Puget, Lieut. Joseph Baker, and Joseph Whidbey, names that are eternally fixed in the geography of the northern empire. The following notes and extracts are little histories of remarkable interest and value. They closely follow Vancouver's own narrative.

Following the coast northward from Cape Mendocino, on Tuesday, April 24, 1792, Vancouver sighted an extremity of the mainland projecting from the high, rocky coast a considerable way into the sea. This he distinguished by the name of Cape Orford, in honor of his friend, the Earl (George) of that title.

Sunday, the 29th, he discovered the first sail he had seen for eight months; she proved to be the ship "Columbia," Captain Gray, of Boston, the same who had been reported to have penetrated the Strait of Juan de Fuca, but who had really only penetrated it for fifty miles. On the same day the snow-covered summit of Mount Olympus was seen. Later in the day Cape Flattery was rounded, and the Strait entered.

Continuing their progress until nightfall of the 30th, they anchored for the night under a long sandy point of land projecting from the cliffs into the sea. This point, from its resemblance to Dungeness in the British Channel, Vancouver called New Dungeness.

During the afternoon Vancouver's third lieutenant had discovered a very high, conspicuous, craggy mountain, towering above the clouds, and covered with snow as low down as they allowed it to be visible. From their anchorage it rose very conspicuously, and in compliment to the lieutenant it was called Mount Baker.

On Wednesday, May 2, 1792, a harbor was reached which, says Vancouver, could not have been placed more happily for the protection of the port from winds and enemies, had it been designed by the most able engineer. This he named, after his ship, Port Discovery. A few days were now spent in making the necessary repairs to sails, etc., and the serenity of the climate and of the season was extremely favorable to the execution of their several duties.

Monday morning, the 7th, the "Discovery's" yawl and launch, and the "Chatham's" cutter, properly armed and supplied with stores, started out to extend their researches into the new country.

The result was the discovery of a pleasanter, safer, and more capacious harbor than Port Discovery; to this port he gave the name of Port Townshend, in honor of the noble Marquis of that name.

Marrow-Stone Point was the name given to a high, steep cliff which seemed to be principally composed of that stone.

A round, snowy mountain which bore N. 42° E. from here he named Mount Rainier, after his friend Rear-Admiral Rainier.

The expedition was continued; but the weather changed materially, and while thus detained in an inlet several oak-trees were found in the vicinity. In consequence of this valuable discovery, the place obtained the name of Oak Cove. Leaving the cove, a high, perpendicular, bluff point which divided the inlet into two branches was called Foulweather Bluff, because of the change of weather. The western arm was followed.

Saturday, May 12, they directed their course back to Port Discovery, now seventy miles distant.

Friday, the 18th, both ships set sail to explore farther the two branches of the inlet, beginning at Foulweather Bluff, the "Discovery" taking the eastern, and the "Chatham" the other. The result was the complete exploration of Puget Sound, so called because of Lieut. Peter Puget's exertions.

In the mean time Port Orchard and Vashon's Island had been discovered and so named, the one after Mr. Orchard, a gentleman on board, the other after Captain Vashon of the navy, a friend of Vancouver.

VANCOUVER NAMING THE PLACES ON PUGET SOUND

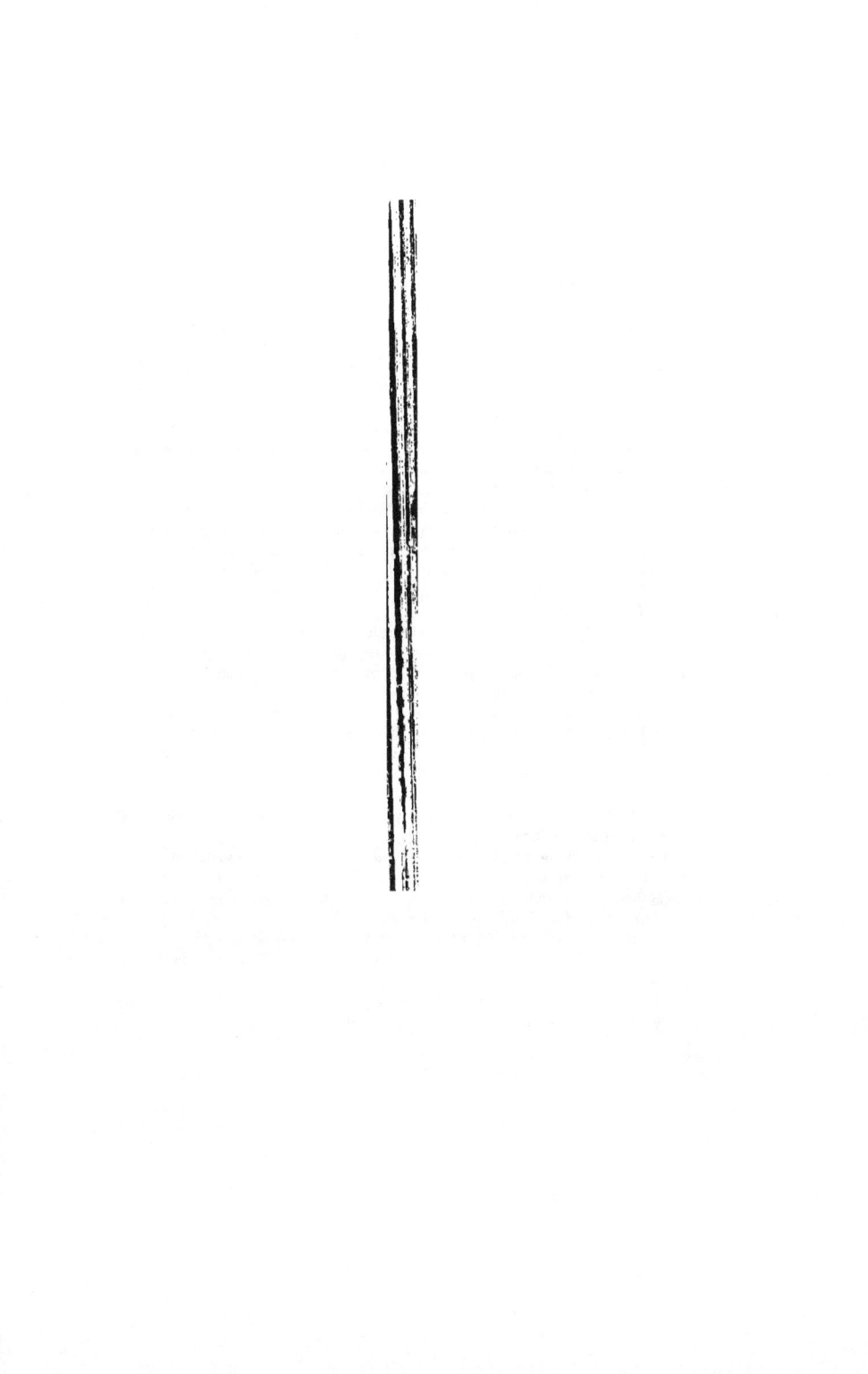

Restoration Point (lat. 47° 30', long. 237° 46') received its name May 30, 1792.

Saturday, June 2, an excellent harbor was discovered, and named Penn's Cove, in honor of a particular friend.

A fortnight had been dedicated to the examination of the large inlet, the southern extremity of which had been called Puget Sound, and Saturday, June 2, it was duly distinguished by the name of Admiralty Inlet. The country in the vicinity of this branch of the sea was the finest they had yet met with, notwithstanding the pleasing appearance of many others.

Sunday, the 3d, all hands were given a day of needed rest, and Monday being the anniversary of His Majesty's birth, Vancouver went on shore and formally took possession of all the countries north of 39° 20' north latitude, that he had explored, in the name of, and for, His Britannic Majesty, his heirs and successors. The entire interior sea he "honored with the name of the Gulph of Georgia, and the continent binding the said gulph and extending southward to the 45th degree of north latitude, with that of New Georgia. This branch of Admiralty Inlet obtained the name of Possession Sound; its western arm, after Vice-Admiral Sir Alan Gardner, was called Port Gardner, and its smaller or eastern one Port Susan."

Proceeding up Admiralty Inlet, its north point (lat. 48° 16', long. 237° 31') was called Point Partridge, and its west point (lat. 48° 10', long. 237° 31'), after his esteemed friend, Capt. George Wilson, of the navy, he distinguished by the name of Point Wilson (June 6).

Sunday, June 10, it was discovered that the eastern shore of the gulf, from lat. 48° 27' to the north point of entrance into Possession Sound, in lat. 47° 53', was an island, in its broadest part about ten miles across. In consequence of Mr. Whidbey's circumnavigation it was named Whidbey's Island.

June 13, a point in lat. 49° 19', long. 237° 6', was named Point Grey, in compliment to his friend Capt. George Grey, of the navy.

The vessels continued their route northward, occasionally despatching boats on surveying expeditions, on one of which Mr. Johnstone, master of the "Chatham," discovered a passage to the sea: this, July 13, in his honor, received the name of Johnstone's Straits.

In the early part of August they reached and passed through the inlet which Mr. S. Wedgborough in August,' 1786, had named Queen Charlotte's Sound.

On the way every inlet, point, and island received a name, either suggested by circumstances or given in honor of an esteemed friend.

STORY OF JUAN DE FUCA.

But there is another celebration of an event that may well claim the attention of our Pacific friends, — the discovery of the Straits of Juan de Fuca by the Greek pilot of that name, in 1592.

Who was Juan de Fuca? Was there indeed ever such a man, or are his supposed discoveries the dream of fiction?

These questions have been discussed over and over by Spain, England, and America, for the last two hundred years.

Alexander S. Taylor, in an article in Hutching's California Magazine entitled "Memorials of Juan de Fuca," sets the question at rest by publishing the following letter from Michael Leck, English Consul to Venice, 1596: —

"When I was at Venice, in April, 1596, haply arrived there an old man, about sixty years of age, called commonly Juan de Fuca, but named properly Apostolos Valerianus, of nation a Greek, born in Cephalonia, of profession a mariner and an ancient pilot of ships. This man being come lately out of Spain, arrived first at Leghorn, and went thence to Florence, where he found one John Douglas, an Englishman, a famous mariner, ready, coming for Venice, to be pilot for a Venetian ship for England, in whose company they came both together to Venice. And John Douglas being acquainted with me before, he gave me knowledge of this Greek pilot, and brought him to my speech, and in long talks and conference between us, in presence of John Douglas, this Greek pilot declared, in the Italian and Spanish languages, thus much in effect as followeth: First, he said that he had been in the West Indies of Spain forty years, and had sailed to and from many thereof, in the service of the Spaniards. Also he said that he was in the Spanish ship which, in returning from the Islands Phillippinas, toward Nova Spania, was robbed and taken at the Cape California by Captain Candish [Cavendish], Englishman, whereby he lost sixty thousand ducats of his own goods. Also he said that he was pilot of three small ships which the Viceroy of Mexico sent from Mexico, armed with one hundred men, under a captain, Spaniards, to discover the Straits of Anian, along the coast of the South Sea, and to fortify in that strait, to resist the passage and proceedings of the English nation, which were feared to pass through those straits into the South Sea; and by reason of a mutiny which happened among

THE "ROOKERY" ON THE NORTHWEST COAST.

the soldiers for the misconduct of their captain, that voyage was overthrown, and the ship returned from California to Nova Spania, without anything done in that voyage; and that after their return the captain was at Mexico punished by justice.

"Also he said that shortly after the said voyage was so ill ended, the said Viceroy of Mexico sent him out again in 1592, with a small caraval and a pinnace, armed with mariners only, to follow the said voyage for the discovery of the Straits of Annian, and the passage thereof into the sea which they call the North Sea, all along the coast of Nova Spania, and California, and the Indies, now called North America (all which voyage he signified to me in a great map, and a sea card of my own which I laid before him) until he came to the latitude of 47 degrees; and that there finding that the land trended north and northeast, with a broad inlet of sea, between 47 and 48 degrees of latitude, he entered thereinto, sailing therein more than twenty days, and finding that land trending still sometime northwest and northeast and north, and also east and southeastward, and very much broader sea than was at the said entrance, and that he passed by divers islands in that sailing, and that at the entrance of this said strait there is on the northwest coast thereof a great headland or island, with an exceeding high pinnacle or spired rock, like a pillar, thereupon.

"Also he said that he went on land in divers places, and that he saw some people on land clad in beasts' skins; and that the land is very fruitful, and rich of gold, silver, pearls, and other things, like Nova Spania. And also he said that he being entered thus far into the said strait, and being come into the North Sea already, and finding the sea wide enough everywhere, and to be about thirty or forty leagues wide in the mouth of the straits where he entered, he thought he had now well discharged his office; and not being armed to resist the force of the savage people that might happen, he therefore set sail, and returned homewards again towards Nova Spania, where he arrived at Acapulco, anno 1592, hoping to be rewarded by the Viceroy for this service done in the said voyage. Also he said that after coming to Mexico he was greatly welcomed by the Viceroy, and had promises of great reward; but that, having sued there two years and obtained nothing to his content, the Viceroy told him that he should be rewarded in Spain, of the King himself, very greatly, and willed him therefore to go to Spain, which voyage he did perform. Also he said that when he was come into Spain, he was welcomed there at the King's Court; but after a long suit there, also, he could not get any reward there to his content, and therefore at length he stole away out of Spain, and came into Italy, to go home again and live among his own kindred and countrymen, he being very old. Also he said that he thought the cause of his ill reward had of the Spaniards to be for that they did understand very well that the English Nation had now given over all their voyages for discovery of the northwest passage: wherefore they need not fear them any more to come that way into the South Sea, and therefore they needed not his service therein any more. Also he said that understanding that the noble mind of the Queen of England [Queen Elizabeth] and of her wars against the Spaniards, and hoping that her Majesty would do him justice for his goods lost by Captain Candish, he would be content to go into England and serve Her Majesty in that voyage for the discovery perfectly of the northwest passage into the South Sea, if she would furnish him with only one ship of forty tons burden, and a pinnace, and that he would perform it in thirty days' time from one end to the other of the strait; and he willed me to so write to England. And upon conference had twice with the said Greek pilot, I did write thereof accordingly to England unto the Right honorable the old Lord treasurer Cecil, and to Sir Walter Raleigh, and to Master Richard Hakluyt, that famous cosmographer, certifying them hereof. And I prayed them to disburse one hundred pounds to bring the said Greek pilot into England with myself, for that my own purse would not stretch so wide at that time. And I had answer that this action was well liked and greatly desired in England; but the money was not ready, and therefore this action died at that time, though the said Greek pilot perchance liveth still in his own country, in Cephalonia, towards which place he went within a fortnight after this conference had at Venice."

CHAPTER XI.

ARTHUR BURNS'S RANCH.

N arriving at Vancouver, our tourists' first purpose was to visit Arthur Burns. So back they went into the region of the beautiful Cascade Mountains, over the blue Gulf of Georgia. Helena went with them, and the visiting party consisted of Mr. Lette, Charlie, and Helena.

The landing nearest to the ranch was a low shore under high bluffs, or bluffs that seemed high with their giant firs. Some of these trees were as tall as Bunker Hill Monument. There was but one house at the place, a log hotel, which was also a post-office. The hotel was chiefly patronized by lumbermen and fishermen.

The bluffs were matted with vines, and were full of *red* whortleberries, — a delicious fruit. Wild morning-glories flowered

A SETTLER'S HUT.

in the cool, dewy shadows, and strange birds flew hither and thither wherever a footstep went. The air here was cool and vigorous, and there was a solitary silence everywhere.

The steamer pulled away from the landing, to return again at nightfall. The party took a corduroy road; it was indeed a *corde du roi* road, and fit for a king, if grand arcades of ancient trees make a kingly way. It was constructed of logs laid side by side, and inclined so that lumber could be slid down to the Gulf.

Up this silent way the party hurried, only stopping now and then to pick some blackberries or red whortleberries, or to drink from some clear water-spring. The trees grew taller and the shadows and silence deeper. At times, through some opening, a silver glacier appeared far away in the Cascades, and glistened in the sun.

A FRONTIER HOUSE.

They came to a waterfall and rested. The stream flowed downward, and from afar one could hear its music in the distant arcades of firs. At this waterfall the way to the ranch became a trail.

How lovely, solemn, and majestic the way seemed! The sunlight covered the interwoven pine tops like a tent. Crows flew cawing away — and jays.

They at last came upon a little black bear, which scampered off in the greatest alarm. These bears are quite harmless unless attacked, and are more afraid of a settler than the settler is of them.

Suddenly they found themselves at a little Swedish log cabin in a clearing. The settlers came out to meet them, and brought them water and berries. They were evidently honest people, of good hearts and fair intelligence. They had cleared a large garden by burning.

Soon they came to other clearings and cabins. The people here were hard at work burning land for gardens and grain. Then they passed a lake or pond out of which flew a flock of ducks, and which is covered with wild geese in the fall. Then they saw some deer, which are very numerous, then an old Indian squaw who appeared very

THE GREAT BLUFF, THOMPSON RIVER.

friendly; and at last they stood before a little cabin of logs and splints, and beheld a handsome young man in scanty clothing standing in the door.

"This is the place," said Mr. Lette, "and there he is."

The young man at first did not recognize the party.

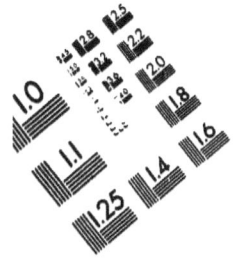
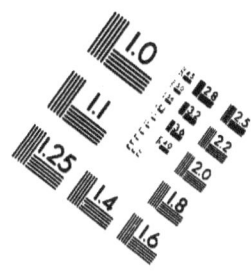

IMAGE EVALUATION
TEST TARGET (MT-3)

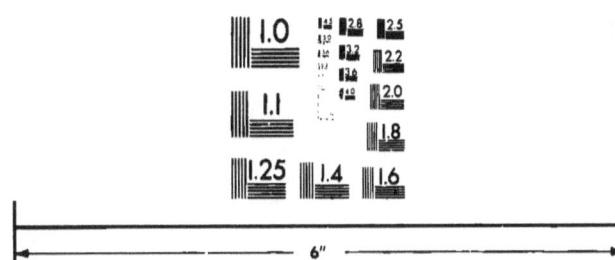

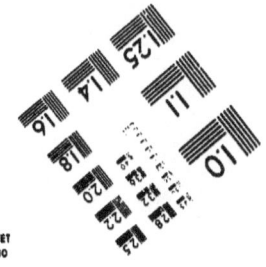

Photographic
Sciences
Corporation

23 WEST MAIN STREET
WEBSTER, N.Y. 14580
(716) 872-4503

"Hurrah for the Hôtel de Batteau!" said Mr. Lette.

Arthur leaped over the ground to meet them. "Hurrah it is!" said he. "That's just what I have called my place,— the Hôtel de Batteau. There it is, one room. You are good to come to see me. I shall never forget this. Come in. This is Wilhelmine."

A fresh, honest-looking Swedish girl, with blue eyes and broad face, came to the door. She spoke English imperfectly. The furniture consisted of a small sheet-iron stove, and some boxes that Wilhelmine had covered with cushions, and a bed made of pine logs and pine needles and blankets. There was no glass window, only a wooden slide. The cupboard of the Hôtel de Batteau contained three plates, and as many cups and saucers, a pitcher, some bowls and spoons, and some knives and forks.

Wilhelmine was cooking some salmon for dinner.

Our guests looked around. They were evidently of the opinion that they would not be expected to dine at the Hôtel de Batteau.

"We have only a couple of hours to stay," said Mr. Lette. "Tell us all about your life."

"Yes," said Charlie. "Are you happy here?"

"I am," answered Arthur. "Ask Wilhelmine."

"Very — beautiful — health — enough to eat — *everything*," said the bride of the Hôtel de Batteau, Wilhelmine.

"But, Arthur," said Charlie, "how do you expect to live? Your money must be already spent."

"I am going to work in the lumber-mill a few miles from here on the Gulf for a year, and spend what I earn on my place," said Arthur.

"Won't Wilhelmine be lonely?"

"She is going to work in New Westminster a part of the time, and spend what she earns in furnishing a house which we hope to build in the fall. Winter does not come until late here, and is short, and consists of a season of rainy nights. So I am told."

"But do you have to bring your provisions up here on your back?" asked Charlie.

"Yes, what we have. The woods are full of game, so that we shall not require to buy any meat. Fish is plentiful, so we will not need to buy any. We can obtain wheat flour from a ranch on a

THE PEACE RIVER.

little prairie a few miles from here; and so I think we can live if we have health."

"But are you not very lonely?"

"No; we live in the future. It is our happiness to look forward, to plan and hope. The imagination is the same here as in London, and most people derive their happiness from their imagination. We love each other; we expect to work, and to have a fine ranch some day, and we own ourselves, which is more than half the people of London do; and we are very happy."

"How will you clear your land?"

"A part of it is prairie land. This I shall put into grain when I am able. The wooded part is very rich soil. I shall burn a place for a garden and a prune-orchard. The province will run a road through this section soon, and we shall have a school-house. The Swedish settlers are a religious people, so we will build a log church, and Wilhelmine has a good voice, and will sing in the choir. We will have a large ranch for poor people some day, and all our own. I am glad I came. I feel that I have something to live for now. I expect hardship, but I also expect independence in the end, — a home of my own; and I shall be happy in the growth of the country. Yes, my good friends, I am glad I came, and I thank you for all your helps. I wish I could offer you a good dinner at the Hôtel de Batteau, but I cannot. Come here again in ten years, and I will give you one that will surpass any in the Charing Cross Hotel or the London club-houses. Let me bring you some water from the brook. The brook reminds me of the story of the old Hôtel de Batteau."

A CARIBOO WAGON-ROAD.

Arthur brought some water from the running brook.

"This came down from the snows of the Cascades," said he. "See how *honest* and sparkling it looks! Try it!"

"Health!" said Mr. Lette.
"Health!" said Charlie.
"Health!" said the Montana girl. "I am sure that you will succeed."

Arthur was asked what he had for amusements.

"A man should take his enjoyments in his work," said Arthur. "But in the evening, when Wilhelmine and I have talked over the events of the day, I get her to sing to me."

"Will you not sing a song to us?" asked Helena of the happy bride.

"If you wish it, I will try," said Wilhelmine. "Let us go out of doors."

They went out through the door of the little cabin, and sat down on the long log of Douglas fir. The cool shadows of the tent-like tree-tops fell across the log, and afar gleamed the crystal crown of the Cascades in the sun.

Wilhelmine had a beautiful voice, pure and clear, and she sang a popular Swedish love-song,—one that Christine Nilsson once sang to delighted ears in Boston Music Hall,—"When I was sweet seventeen."

How strange it seemed,—this airy, rippling song of the land of Gustavus Adolphus, in the American wilderness! A good song wins the heart; and our tourists went away, to carry in their memory the tenderest good wishes for brave Wilhelmine.

On the return to Vancouver the boat passed through a little fleet of long canoes filled with Indian families. These Indians were coming down from the North to pick hops in the Pugallup valley. Few things in America are more truly poetic and romantic than the hop-picking festival, for a gay festival it really is in this beautiful valley of Puget Sound. The glorious season, the gleaming mountains, the picturesque hop-farms, the Indians from many tribes, the night songs and dances, the plays, the torches, the gayety and good-humor, the full moon, the great excursions, all combine to make the season wonderfully ideal and romantic.

It was twilight as the boat dipped down the Gulf, — one of the long northern twilights of the inland waters, calm as a sea of peace, and splendid as a vision of celestial glory. The gold-crimson light

AMONG THE ISLANDS OF THE GULF OF GEORGIA.

burned through the tall firs like the sunset in the oriel windows of old cathedrals. The Indians sang, and long flocks of birds like gray clouds floated amid the white-blue light of the sky that bordered the red sea-fires of the west.

"I should think," said Charlie to Mr. Lette, "that emigrants would come here and find the country and climate all that had been represented, but yet not be able to gain employment, and so suffer and become discouraged. A man cannot live on grand scenery."

"I think," said Mr. Lette, "that the emigrant ought to have some five hundred dollars, with which to begin life in this new country. But the lumber-camps, the coal-mines, the small mining interests everywhere, the necessity for building and improvement on the part of capitalists, offer a large field for profitable labor; and if a person comes here with a spirit like Arthur's, with a resolution of success, and willingness to work, the chances are as a hundred to one that he will become a successful man."

THE CHINOOKER.

In British Columbia and Washington the people have one common name, the Chinookers. The mellow climate here is the gift of the Chinook winds. Everything old and noble bears the same nickname, — a five-hundred-years-old tree, a grave Indian, and in one instance it was applied to a very troublesome bear.

An English mining-camp in the Selkirks had been twice alarmed by the appearance on its border of a too familiar bruin. To this camp came an English speculator and some sportsmen. The speculator heard the report of the visits of the bear, and thought it might be an interesting investigation to return them. This bear had received the name of the old Chinooker.

One evening before a late supper the speculator, being weary of the monotony of the camp, said that he was going out for a walk.

"Where be you going, massa?" asked a negro cook.

"To call on the old Chinooker."

"Don't bring him home with you, massa," said the negro, who had hardly dared sleep for a week for fear of the bear.

The Englishman was gone until the dark shadows fell, and the camp-fire lit up the valley. The sportsmen were resting, and the negro was idly busy in keeping the coffee warm.

"Where is our gouty friend?" asked one of the sportsmen.

"Gone to call on the bear."

"Finds his new friend entertaining," said the other. "Milo [to the negro], blow the horn."

Milo blew a blast that shook the hills. There was no response.

The stars began to come out.

"Blow again, Milo," said the sportsman.

Milo blew the piercing horn again.

There was a stirring of underbrush at the fringe of the clearing. The hunters started up and seized their guns. The negro awaited with curious eyes the development of the mystery.

Suddenly the fat speculator's form appeared, flying toward the camp like a boy. In a moment after, the bear appeared. The two seemed to be running a race.

"Fire, fire!" cried the negro; "the bear am after him! Kill him, quick! There's no need of his catching *bofh of us!*"

By "bofh of us" Milo meant the doughty knight of the mines and his precious self. He knew the value of the cook who made the coffee.

The speculator ran. His hat was gone, and his short legs made up in activity what they lacked in length. He was in a terrible state of excitement until he came surely under the cover of the guns; then his face assumed a most delighted expression.

"You blew horn for me," said he. "That was right. Me and the bar's coming."

But poor bruin had a very inhospitable welcome, and found a place in Milo's dinner-pot for several days afterward. The negro never recovered from his fright on that evening, but was anxious to go "down So if" again; and the speculator himself made no more evening calls in the territories of an old Chinooker.

VANCOUVER ISLAND.

The Island of Vancouver seems destined to become a very important factor in the future, as one or more of the great ports to Asia, more especially to China and Japan, will be here. England will find from this island a short ferriage to Asia, as America finds her short ferriage to England and Europe by the way of Quebec, the St. Lawrence, and the Straits of Belle Isle or Cape Race. The ships with tea for Canada will follow the Japanese Current, as will the ships of fabrics from Japan. The Island of Vancouver is about to wed the islands of the Flowery Sea.

Bounded on the west by the Pacific Ocean and on the east by the Straits of Georgia, warmed in winter by the Chinook winds and

"ME AND THE BAR 'S COMING"

currents, having a climate of almost continuous springtime, overlooked by lofty mountains, and connecting by sheltered water-ways with the ports of Alaska, Vancouver has probably an eventful and historic part to enact in the re-mapping of the world, and such as is likely to surpass that already enacted by the maritime provinces.

A VINEYARD IN BRITISH COLUMBIA.

The cities here are likely to become larger and more important than Montreal or Quebec. In case of international differences it would probably become a place of fortresses and navies. It is an island which England and the Dominion of Canada will some day regard with especial pride. It is two hundred and seventy miles in length, and some forty miles in breadth, and has an area of about sixteen thousand square miles.

The outline of the island is especially picturesque. Here the buttress-like walls of Mount Arrowsmith descend for thousands of feet almost abruptly to the shore. The shores have fiord-like arms and sheltered harbors. Afar are seen the glaciers of the Olympian Mountains, in the State of Washington.

Here the atmospheres are bright and the summers cool, and the mind is always impressed with the grandeur of mountains and seas.

Victoria is the beautiful capital. It stands at the southeast extremity of the island, and has a very picturesque and intricate harbor. It is a free port.

The city is famous for its scenery, parks, elegant suburbs, and conservative English society. It is wholly unlike the progressive city of Vancouver.

English families of wealth and social position like it, and many such make it their provincial place of residence. It exerts a fascination over lovers of romance, poetry and art, and elegant seclusion. Vancouver says to the world, "Come!" delighting in growth and expansion. Victoria is more given to the traditions of the past. She is like an English seaport city.

INDIAN SALMON CACHE.

The trees of Vancouver are giants. Some of the Douglas firs are three hundred feet in height, and the stumps are large enough for houses, for which purpose holl

INDIAN GRAVES.

ones have been used. The Indians here are a very interesting people. The traveller is struck with their salmon caches along the shores, and with effigies that mark their houses and graves. These salmon caches are a kind of basket hung in trees or placed upon the high branches. Their purpose is to secure the fish from animals and birds, and to keep it sweet in the clear, pure air.

The carvings of the Vancouver Indians are quite skilful. They ornament the houses, and are used as a kind of family record. Many families have peculiar carvings which answer the purpose of a coat-of-arms.

The graves at a distance remind one of a house with the family grouped outside. The utensils used by the warriors are buried with them or placed on the outside of their tombs.

Vancouver was discovered by Juan de Fuca in 1592. Captain Cook visited it in 1778, and Vancouver in 1792. It was taken into the charge of the Hudson Bay Company in 1849, and became a part of the Dominion of Canada in 1871. It has made a most wonderful development during the last twenty years.

Wonderful also is the town of Nanaimo, the port of the coal-trade. Here, or near to the town, are some of the richest coal-mines on the continent. Many of the miners are Scotch, and the habits and customs of Scotland prevail here.

Near Victoria is the beautiful and calm harbor of Esquimalt, the winter station of Pacific vessels. The mountain scenery through the water-ways here is very inspiring. The officers of the English navy are as a rule very contented and happy here, in a climate where roses and laurestinus may be found in the gardens on the shore on Christmas Day.

Strange scenes may be found on Vancouver, like the Buffalo Dance of the Indians. In this dance the revellers wear buffalo heads for masques. But stranger than the Buffalo Dance, or the Wapiti's horns, or Potlatch masques, found in the stores in Victoria, are colonies of seals that come and go, and seem almost human in their loves and jealousies. It is said that St. Paul's Island has an annual population of over three hundred million seals.

Mr. Elliott, who furnished to the United States government an account of the mode of the capture of the seals on the islands of the Vancouver group, says: —

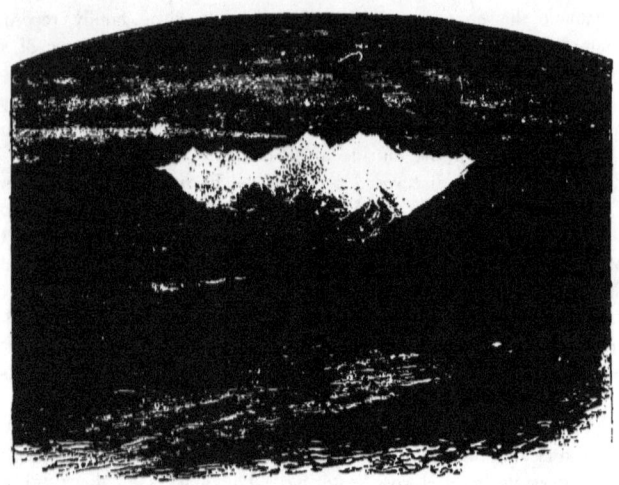

VIEW FROM ESQUIMALT.

"The full-grown male is from 6½ to 7¼ feet long, and weighs four hundred pounds. The old bulls will maintain their chosen position on the shore among the countless herds. A constantly sustained fight between newcomers and the first arrivals goes on incessantly. A well-understood principle seems to exist among them, that each shall remain on a special spot, usually about eight feet square, provided that at the start, and from the first coming until the advent of the females, he is strong enough to hold the ground against all comers, as the crowding of the fresh arrivals often causes the removal of those who, though equally able-bodied at first, have become weak by constant fighting. They are finally driven by fresher animals higher up in the rookery, and sometimes off altogether. Many of the bulls exhibit wonderful strength and desperate courage. I remarked one veteran who was the first to take up his position early in May, and that position, as usual, directly at the water line. This seal had fought at least forty or fifty desperate battles, and fought off his assailants every time, and when the fighting season was over I saw him still there, covered with scars and frightfully gashed, raw, festering, and bloody, one eye gouged out, but lording it bravely over his harem, who were all huddled together around him.

"The young seal is from the moment of his birth until he is a month or six weeks old unable to swim. If he is seized by the nape of the neck and pitched out a rod into the water from shore, his bullet-like head will drop instantly below the surface, and his attenuated posterior extremities flap impotently on it; suffocation is a question of only a few minutes, — the stupid little creature not knowing how to raise his immersed head. After the age of a month or six weeks their instinct drives them down to the margin of the surf, where the ebb and flow of the waves covers and uncovers the rocky beaches. They first smell and then touch the moist pools, and flounder in the upper wash of the surf. After this beginning they make slow and clumsy progress in learning the knack of swimming. For a week or two they thrash the water as little dogs do, with their fore feet, making no attempt whatever to use the hinder ones. Look at that pup launched for the first time beyond his depth; see how he struggles, — his mouth wide open and eyes staring. He turns to the beach; the receding swell which had taken him out returns and leaves him high and dry. For a few minutes he seems so weary that he weakly crawls up out beyond the swift-returning wash, and coils himself up for a recuperative nap. He sleeps perhaps half an hour, then awakes 'as bright as a dollar,' and to his swimming lesson he goes again. Once boldly swimming, the pup fairly revels in his new happiness.

"The fur seals after leaving the islands in the autumn and early winter do not visit land again until their return in the spring or early summer to the same 'rookery' grounds. They leave the islands in independent squads; apparently all turn by common consent toward the south, disappearing toward the horizon, and are soon lost in the expanse, where they spread themselves over the entire North Pacific as far south as the forty-eighth and even forty-seventh parallels of north latitude. Over the immense area between Oregon and Japan doubtless many extensive submarine fishing shoals and banks are known to them; at least it is definitely understood

that Behring's Sea does not contain them long when they depart from
the breeding-places. While it is remembered that they sleep soundly and
with the greatest comfort on the surface of the water, and that even when
on land in summer they frequently put off from the beaches to take a
bath and a quiet snooze just beyond the surf, we can readily agree that
it is no inconvenience whatever, when their coats have been renewed, to
stay the balance of the time in their most congenial element, the deep.

"The seals are driven slowly to the slaughter. Men get between them
and the water, and the poor beasts turn, hop, and scramble up over the

SEAL-DRIVING.

land. The natives then leisurely walk in
the flank and rear of the drove thus secured, directing and driving it to
the killing-grounds. An old bull seal, fat and unwieldy, cannot travel
with the younger ones, though it can go as fast as a man can run for one
hundred yards, but then fails utterly, and falls to the ground entirely exhausted,
hot, and gasping for breath."

The aboriginal inhabitants of Vancouver hardly interest the traveller more than the Celestials. Directly across the Pacific lies China, with three hundred and sixty million inhabitants, as we have stated; and England has made it easy for treaties with this great empire by protecting the Chinese in her American colonies. A happy, clean-looking, well-dressed people they are, as one finds them in Vancouver and Victoria. At Vancouver they have built a church, where they have preaching in their own tongue. Very grateful are they to the American and English teachers who instruct them. In one instance a lady by the name of Monk who had instructed them moved away from Vancouver to Montreal. Her work had been conscientious and sympathetic, and they wished to bring her back again. They raised the money to do so, and made her a present on her return. They are eager scholars, bright, quick, and active.

THE WAPITI.

The Swedish population of the new country, both in the provinces and States, sustains the traditional history of the men of the North. One finds the Swedish farmer everywhere. He is an American as soon as he lands. True to his history and the traditions of his race, he yet comes to America to be an American. He loves religion and liberty. The new country is like a Paradise to him.

The Roman Catholics have fine churches and institutions everywhere. One is surprised at the costliness and solidity of their buildings. Nowhere has the Methodist Church finer buildings than in Canada, and the Methodist Church in Vancouver would do credit to any city.

In these new cities the noble structure of the schoolhouse lifts its towers among the steeples. Education here is to do her noblest work. The provinces and States of the Northwest are all rich in school-funds and provisions for education. California is making herself famous for the building of great colleges and institutions of learning. The great telescope of the world is there. One University starts with a building and endowment fund of some twenty million dollars. The same educational spirit prevails in the empire on the Puget Sound. Harvard College will one day be small in architectural comparison with the educational structures that will arise on the

ON THE COAST OF BRITISH COLUMBIA.

northern shores of the Pacific, if the dreams and plans of the rich founders of the new cities are realized.

Mount Baker is the glory of the North. It is seen almost everywhere in the upper Puget Sound country, gleaming like a dome over the water-ways. Wherever one climbs a hill, the white-mantled mountain greets him like a bishop of the skies. Serene in the metallic blue of the wide heavens, its dome burns in the meridian hours, and turns into roses in the melting skies of the sunset. Distance lends it poetry, but nearness in moonlight makes it wonderfully beautiful, like the Taj, or the Capitol at Washington, — if such small structures may suggest a comparison.

There is a solitary grandeur in the high mountains that overlook the Fraser, the Columbia, and Puget Sound. Most of these frozen

SEYMOUR NARROWS, CANADIAN PACIFIC COAST.

domes are twice as high as Mount Washington in the East, and they once blazed with fire as they now glimmer in everlasting ice. They were chimneys of gigantic furnaces that have long ceased to burn. One dreams of the past on beholding them, and imagines the time when the heavens rained fire. Giant forests are now rooted in soil that once was ashes. There are traditions that Mount Hood and Mount St. Helen's have been seen to glow and blaze in the night like ghosts of the age of Carbon, but we do not know that these tales are true. An attempt has been made to illumine Mount Hood and Tacoma on the evenings of Independence days, and to produce the effect of artificial volcanoes; but the scheme has proved grander than its success. The illumination of these moun-

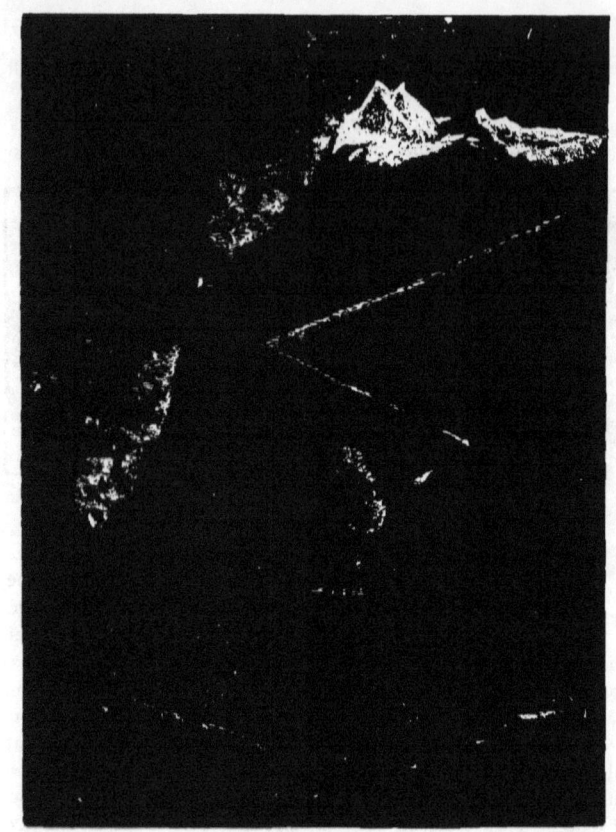

ROADWAY IN BRITISH COLUMBIA.

tains at night by means of electricity may become a feature of future national holidays.

The Marquis of Lorne says that British Columbia is by far the most beautiful of the Canadian provinces. It certainly is the most beautiful province in North America; but it shares its wonderful beauty and resources with Washington, which surely is the most beautiful of all the Union of American States.

CHAPTER XII.

THE NEW STAR ON THE FLAG.

ASHINGTON is the land of young men. It is the young mind that is developing her, governing her, and guiding her. New York may be proud of her commerce, Pennsylvania of her mines of iron and coal, Illinois of the mountains of grain that fill her elevators, Maine of her timbered forests, Nevada of her silver, California of her gold, and Massachusetts of her noble schools; but Washington is rich in all of these, or in the promise and expectation of them all. In this new Florida of the Japan rivers and airs that we call "Chinook" is Nature's masterpiece of America. It is bounded on the south by the imperial Columbia, the most beautiful of all American rivers, and is walled on the north by mountains that surpass the Alps; along its western forests rolls the Pacific, and from the sky everywhere crystal mountains look down like domes in the heaven, on forests and plains of eternal verdure, soon to be changed into summer seas of billowy grain.

SEATTLE THE WONDERFUL.

Beautiful is Elliott Bay with its purple waters, its deep harbors, and its majestic bluffs. Mount Tacoma (Rainier) seems to hang over it like a silver tent of some vanished god; the mountain seems to glisten everywhere, though so far away. It haunts the heavens. One turns toward it always, for in the changing light it is never twice the same.

SUNSET ON THE PACIFIC COAST.

One sees a hundred Tacomas in a single day, — a mountain of roses in the morning, of gold at noon, of sapphire at evening, and of silver under the falling curtains of night.

The Olympic Range as seen from blue Elliott Bay is also beautiful, though not as beautiful as Mount Tacoma. Is there anything in North America as beautiful as that? The Olympic Mountains are a sky-wall, with towers and pinnacles frosted with everlasting snow. The sun sinks down behind them and they are on fire.

There was no city of Seattle a few years ago, only a lumber-mill and a few houses in the midst of an apparent wilderness. Marvellous changes, however, are often wrought in these Western pioneer forests, and Seattle was destined to be a splendid example of what push and endurance can do toward building a city in a day.

Suddenly Seattle became a port. The Canadian Pacific ran into Vancouver, and the Northern Pacific into Tacoma, and steamers plied between the two, and the mid-sound town, with its open road to the Pacific, began to build, and to multiply its inhabitants. Capitalists came, and it began to be whispered, "Here will be the New York of the Pacific, the rich port of Asia and the East. The story of the uncovered wealth of iron and coal and precious ores in the territory around Seattle flew abroad; people came hurrying; the great pine-trees fell before the axe and fire; houses seemed to start up everywhere; armies of hammers seemed to be marching over all the hills, and from Lake Union to Lake Washington the wonder grew.

A sunset at Seattle is a glory ever to be remembered, especially if seen f'om the hills. Glorious Rainier, as the people here still call Mount Tacoma, the crystal Olympic Mountains, the cool blue bay, the deeply shaded bluffs, the evergreen arcades of the primeval woods, the over-sea of the peaceful sky, the poetic mellowness of all the splendor, — who that has stood on the hills of West Seattle in a twilight of June can ever forget the scene? How did it happen that this beautiful region of the sea, this Vale of Tempe, this place worthy of the Golden Age, should have been the last in America to become settled!

The electric-car system in Seattle is the most rapid and daring that we have seen. The cars seem to race over the hills like horses, and stop on high hills with the ease of a flying deer.

From one of the far inland ranches a boy came to Seattle one day on a mule. When he had last seen the place it was a town. He entered West Seattle slowly, wondering at all he saw, when suddenly a car without horses went flying by, emitting lightning from its wheels, and sweeping over the hill. The mule saw it and fled, and the ranch-boy was as alarmed as the mule.

On reaching home, he told his father what he had seen, — a car without engine or horses.

"It was drawn by nothing," said he, "and its wheels were on fire."

"Jack," said the old ranchman, "I have always held you to be an honest boy until now. But no car was ever drawn by nothing, or ran over any hill in Seattle alone."

"It was spirits, father."

"Jack, if you were not a temperate boy, I should think it was spirits indeed. You have lost your senses, Jack."

The old man was greatly distressed. He had been proud of his boy's sense of honor and his sound mind.

In the course of a few weeks Jack met with an accident, and sickened and died.

"I never knew that boy to do wrong but once," said the old ranchman to the minister who attended the funeral, "and that was when he told me that he saw a car in Seattle drawn by nothing. He also said that Seattle was a great city. I could forgive him that, for he did not know what a great city is."

Jack was buried; but his supposed falsehood haunted the mind of his old father. Had Jack really lied?

"I will go and see," said the old ranchman at last.

He started away from the valley on the same mule that had borne the boy when he had seen the mysterious car that might have amazed Baron Munchausen. He rode slowly up the hill of West Seattle overlooking the surrounding country.

Suddenly the mule stopped; then began to back. A car glided by with flashing wheels, without horse or engine. The mule turned and ran.

"I have seen the Evil One with my own eyes," said the ranchman. "I don't know what the world has come to at last; but, thank Heaven! my boy Jack spoke the truth."

AN EVENING AT SEATTLE.

I shall never forget a scene I once saw in Seattle soon after the great fire.

The crimson flush of twilight quivered over Puget, Sound, and the crown of Mount Rainier lighted up for the last time in the afterglow of the dying day. There was the sound of a drum in the streets, a rattle and jingle of tambourines, and a red flag came sweeping by, followed by a procession of decently dressed men and women singing a lively tune. The musical company wheeled on to a plateau near the Hotel Belleview, planted their flag, and knelt down in a circle.

"The Salvation Army, I declare!" said a speculator. "They are a disgrace to Seattle;" and he put on his hat and left the veranda to enter a saloon.

It was Saturday night, after one of the great days of emigration, and the streets were filled with people, many of whom were taking their first view of wonderful Mount Rainier and the blue Puget Sound. There was a tramp of feet everywhere on the miles of wooden pavements. Saloons blazed; it was a harvest night for all those places which spring up so quickly in a new city, and from which Seattle — a moral city — is not free.

I passed from the hotel to the plateau. It was nearly nine o'clock, but still light, and the great tent of Mount Rainier still glistened in the high air. I expected to hear some minstrel songs, some comical and excited talking, and to witness sundry sensational performances such as I had witnessed under similar circumstances in the East.

The army was kneeling in a great circle in the open lot, under the northern twilight with its glimmering of stars. Orderly men and women were gathering around them, and the circle widened and widened until a great concourse of people was gathered, all reverent and devout as in a church. There were prayers, songs, and then came the "testimonies."

The pleasure-seeking critic from the East might have sneered at the scene. But brave men were here, — men who had faced the cannon in the old campaigns; men who had beaten down the wilderness and opened the highways of progress; and better yet, men who had overcome their own passions, the saloon, and all the ruinous excitements incident to pioneer life.

Indians were there, negroes, men who had been intemperate, and both men and women with whom passion had been stronger than conscience and will. One spirit animated all, — the desire to be free from the enchainment of sin.

It was ten o'clock when the great concourse dispersed. Puget Sound was a shadow, and Mount Rainier a ghost. The moon was shining.

"That was better than the saloon," said an observer to me.

"Yes; whatever may be thought of the Salvation Army *this* was better than the saloon."

TACOMA THE BEAUTIFUL.

Am I far from the truth when I say that Tacoma is the most beautifully situated of any city in the United States? So it seems to me, and I have been in most American cities. The poetry of the inland seas of Puget Sound and the Gulf of Georgia finds its most perfect expression in Commencement Bay. The high bluff on which Tacoma stands was covered by a most majestic forest before the city rose on the ashes of the giant trees, and it commanded the most glorious scenery of the places of the Sound. Here Mount Tacoma, like a bride from heaven, stands radiant before the eye, burning with jewels. Here flowers fill the winter, and Christmas roses bloom in the airs of Japanese seas. Here the woods are all pillared cathedrals, and the country all a wonderful park. Wherever one goes, Mount Tacoma glimmers on his vision. In fact, it is so for a hundred miles. Mount Tacoma is everywhere a white mountain of snow set on the imperial purple of the sky.

MOUNT TACOMA.

Says Joaquin Miller, in an article on Tacoma: —

"Sit, in fancy at least, with me here on the high hill, with the roar of hammers and the clatter of trowels at our backs. Let us turn our faces toward the east. Under the steep stone wall at our feet, hugging the precipice, which is hung with wild vines and countless wild flowers, steals the continuous car. These streams of cars pass so close under the precipice that you do not see them. You look straight down into the deep blue waters that tide in from the Japan seas. A common shot across, and a like precipice, with the ever crowding and ever crowning density of green. Then a little to the right the precipice melts down, and the green fir-trees touch the silver sands. Then the sands sweep in a crescent about the head of the sound; then sea-marsh; then the trees, dense, deep, tall, and imperious, for ten, twenty, thirty, forty miles! Up! up! up!

"You start to your feet, — you stand with your head uncovered; for above all this density of wood and out of and above all this blackness there gleam and flash, face to face, the everlasting snows of Mount Tacoma.

"Be silent, as I should be silent. It is an insolent thing that I should dare to dwell, even for a single paragraph, in the idle attempt to describe the indescribable.

"Out of the blackness and above the smoke, above the touch of pollution, above the clouds, companioned forever with the stars, Tacoma stands imperious and alone.

"You may watch the boat sail by at your feet for a little time, but somehow before you quite know it your head will turn to Tacoma.

"You may see a pretty woman pass by as you sit here on the high-built balcony of the new red city on the strong right arm of the sea of seas; but somehow she becomes a part of Tacoma, melts into the mountain of snow, and your face is again heavenward. You may hear a wise man speak of the actions of great men as you sit here; but somehow his utterances seem far, far away; your heart and your whole soul, — they have gone up into the mountains to pray. And it is well. You will come down to the world a truer and a better man. You will descend, but never entirely descend. Your soul will in some sort remain high and white and glorious. You can never again come quite down to the touch of that which is unworthy, for you have been companioned with the Eternal.

"The mountains of Mexico, and California as well, are mountains on top of mountains. Rather, I should say that the snow-peaks are set on the top of mountain ranges. Not so here in the northwest of our Republic. Mount Hood, or rather Mount Pat-twa, the true Indian name of Mount Hood, starts up from the water's edge of the Oregon River, and springs almost perpendicular in the air to its full height. It looks as if it might blow over, so steep and slim and lone and unsupported does it stand. The same might almost be said of Mount St. Helen's, and most especially of Mount Tacoma.

"As I may have said in this paper on a former occasion, the higher peaks of Mexico and California are merely the heads of well-raised families. But not so with these sublime snow-peaks of the north. They stand entirely alone. The foundation stones of Mount Tacoma are laid almost in the sea. And so you may write it down that the mountain scenery of Oregon and Washington surpasses that of either Mexico or California, so far as majesty and impressions are concerned.

"Come, then, and see the new world, and look up and wonder what fearful convulsions fashioned it. Sit with us in the wilderness, and get the balm and the balsam of the fir-trees in your fibre. It is good for the body as well as the soul to be here in the new red town with its girdle of good green wood."

One of the first questions that Charlie asked Mr. Lette, on landing at Tacoma, was, "Where is the pine-tree tower?"

"I had not heard of it," said Mr. Lette.

"It is the oldest church-tower in America," said Charlie.

"But Tacoma is the youngest city in America," said Mr. Lette.

"Yet it has the oldest church-tower in the States," said Charlie. "So I have read. Let us try to find it."

Charlie stopped a car. "Where is the church of the pine-tree tower?" he asked of the conductor.

"In old Tacoma. We go there."

"Let us go," said Charlie.

They rode out of the new city looking down on the islanded bay, and came to a quiet suburb, which was the original town.

"There it is," said the conductor. "Six hundred years old, they say. There, don't you see it, with ladder, bell, and cross?"

A little chapel half covered with ivy rose before them, attached to a leaning tower, on which was a bell

THE OLDEST CHURCH-TOWER IN AMERICA.

and cross. This tower had been a colossal pine or fir tree. It had been sawed off high in the air, and the chapel attached to it, and the bell hung upon it. The base was green with the most luxurious English ivy that Mr. Lette had ever seen. The altar also was covered with living ivy that had grown through the side of the building.

THE FOREST GIANTS.

Tacoma was once the seat of the great giants of the forest. One could hardly believe that these armies of trees had been overthrown, did not the stumps remain. A recent writer says of these giants of the Sound country: —

"Plying on Puget Sound is a boat one hundred and twenty-two feet long. The timbers of which the hull is built run from stem to stern, and not one is spliced. As a specimen product, a Washington lumberman sent to San Francisco last year a beam twenty-four inches thick and one hundred and fifty-two feet long, writes a correspondent of the St. Louis 'Globe-Democrat.' He explained that his intention was to make it one hundred and ninety feet long, but the end ran into a bank and the log had to be cut. Spars for ship-yards on the Clyde, in Scotland, are shipped from Puget Sound.

"At a mill in Portland you may see the timbers, sawed, mortised, painted, and numbered, for bridges to be put together in Michigan, Ohio, and Indiana. Puget Sound cedar shingles are used in New York State. Four ships are loading at a Sound wharf, all with lumber. One goes to London, the second to Melbourne, the third to Valparaiso, the fourth to San Francisco. A test was made not long ago of four-inch sticks of Washington fir, Michigan pine, and good white oak. The pine broke at seventeen hundred pounds, the white oak at thirty-five hundred pounds, and the Washington fir at forty-three hundred pounds. Engineers say the straining force and endurance of this fir lumber is greater than that of any other.

"When one of these monarchs of the coast forest goes down, it shakes the ground like an earthquake. Let it fall across a cañon, and it does n't snap under the tremendous shock, but lies intact and rigid. There is a bridge in Oregon across a ravine sixty feet deep, made by spiking a plank on a tree where it fell by accident. Where a windfall in the forest has occurred, these great timbers lie so thick that the only way to cross is to walk on the trunks from ten to thirty feet above the ground.

"Lumbermen tell of travelling for miles and not once putting their foot on the soil."

FOREST GIANTS.

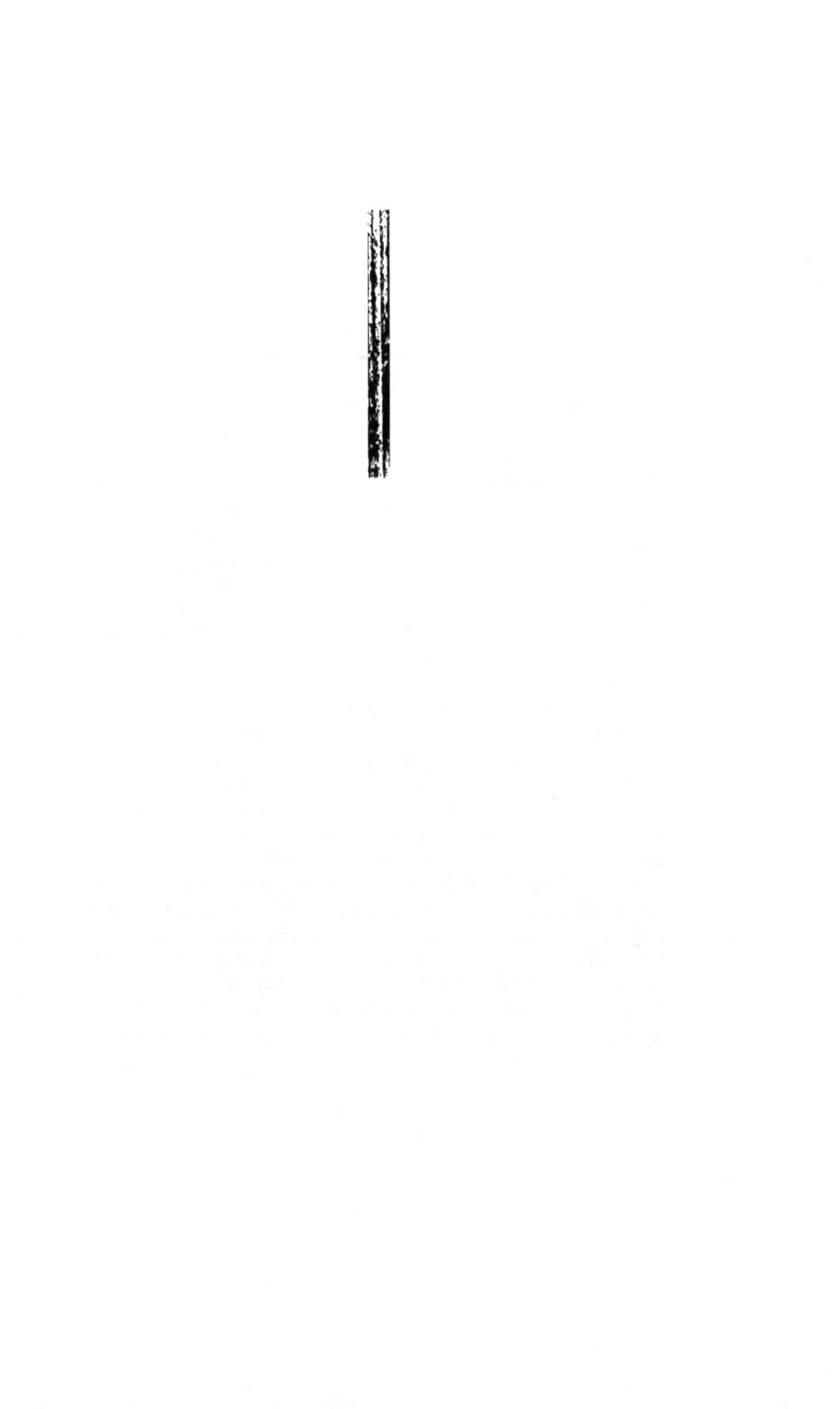

THE SURPRISE OF MOUNT HOOD.

The beautiful river of America is the Columbia, and no stream can bring to the traveller a greater surprise. Leaving Portland, Oregon, in an early morning boat, one is borne along past Vancouver, and the historic places of the old Hudson Bay Company and early United States trading-posts, into the calm waters of the salmon fisheries, and under bluffs of crumbling and ruined rock mountains. We will suppose the time to be June; for the Columbia River in June is in its glory. The beauty is continuous, and it becomes monotonous when one settles down to read or to doze in the sun. The boat halts anon to give bait to the fishermen. Suddenly the ourist starts. What is it that confronts him? Has a mountain come down to the shore to meet him? He might say, " There is God," half believing it. In a moment a mountain is brought to his vision, — a dead volcano, twelve thousand feet high, mantled with snow, and gleaming with glaciers. It is Mount Hood.

It is said that a State takes the character of its early settlers. The founders of Washington and Oregon were heroes, both the Protestant missionaries and the Jesuit fathers. The story of Whitman, the frontier missionary, is one of the grandest in the pioneer history of America. He crossed the Rocky Mountains with his young bride, — this one man who in himself was an army; Rev. Dr. Spaulding and his bride came with him. When they looked down from the Rockies and saw the valley of the Columbia, they opened the Bible, and raised over it the United States flag, and took formal possession of the whole land for liberty and God. Years passed. There was danger that the great region would become lost to the States by the diplomacy of the Hudson Bay Company. Whitman resolved to leave his mission station at Walla Walla, and make a circuitous route out of the way of hostile Indians to Washington, to tell the statesmen there how glorious this territory was. He made the ride alone. He was at first coolly received at the Capitol, but his famous ride saved to the States the vast empire. Whitman went back to Walla Walla, and was there killed by the Indians. A noble monument is to be erected over his remains, or near the old mission post.

In connection with these short accounts of the cities of the Pacific Coast we must not forget that early explorer of the Pacific Ocean and circumnavigator of the world, Sir Francis Drake, whose name recalls an interesting incident which occurred just before his defeat of the Spanish Armada.

SIR FRANCIS DRAKE.

Sir Francis Drake, the famous English explorer of the Elizabethan period, obtained a view of the Pacific Ocean from the Isthmus of Darien. Being imbued with the spirit of adventure, he returned to the Atlantic and there embarked in December, 1577, in five small vessels, on a buccaneering expedition to the Pacific. He sailed through the Straits of Magellan and obtained immense treasures by plundering along the coast of Chili and Peru. Sailing northward along the coast of California, he was overcome with the desire to discover a northwest passage to the Atlantic Ocean; but on arriving at the Island of Vancouver he retraced his way to San Francisco, and thence steered across the Pacific to the Moluccas, returning to England by the Cape of Good Hope in 1579, having circumnavigated the globe.

He was knighted by Queen Elizabeth, who in 1587 appointed him commander of a fleet and sent him to "singe the King of Spain's beard,"— meaning to burn his ships in the Spanish harbors.

The name of Vice-Admiral Drake is popularly associated with the splendid victory of the English fleet over the flower of Spain, the Invincible Armada. The opening incident of the short and

"THERE IS TIME ENOUGH TO FINISH THE GAME AND BEAT THE SPANIARDS TOO."

decisive struggle when the ships of the enemy were first sighted has always had a romantic interest so far as it applies to the courage and coolness of England's gallant defenders. The story is that the High Admiral, Lord Howard of Effingham, and his captains were playing a match on the bowling-green, on the well-known Hoe at Plymouth. One Fleming, the master of a Scotch privateer, — for the seamen of the land of John Knox were concerned in the coming conflict, — running before the wind, entered Plymouth Harbor, and learning where the Admiral was, hastened to announce that he had seen the Spanish fleet off the Cornish coast. Some of the captains, at this exciting information, were for ending the game, and a shouting for the boats was heard. Drake, however, did not show any excitement whatever, remarking, as he continued his play, "There is time enough to finish the game and beat the Spaniards too."

Such courage as this in the face of one of the greatest dangers that ever overshadowed good old England is indeed heroic, showing of what material the famous sea-king was made.

Charlie Hampden left Mr. Lette at Walla Walla. He crossed Montana, stopped awhile at the ranch-home of Helena, and then returned over the Northern Pacific to Rhode Island, visiting the National Park before taking the direct route home. He returned with the resolution to make a home for himself in the new empire.

"The next great American emigration," he said to Mr. Lette as they parted, "will be to Montana. I think I will go there."

His visit to the great inland empire, and the study of its prospects, confirmed the opinion that he had formed and the resolution that he had made. He assured Helena that he would return. She looked very happy at the declaration he had made, and her father seemed pleased.

"When you come again — " said Helena.

"I would like to stay," answered Charlie to the half sentence. "May I?"

"Yes," said Helena.

"Yes," said the ranchman.

It was a quiet fall evening in old Pokanoket. Aunt Mar and Helen were sitting by the rekindled fire, and Charlie was with them.

"I have a secret to tell you," said Aunt Mar. "I have found it. John Hampden did come to America."

"How do you know?" asked Charlie.

"I have found it so in Baylies' 'History of New Plymouth.' Let me read it to you."

Aunt Mar read: —

"When wandering about the woods of Pokanoket, or along the banks of Taunton River, or sleeping in Indian huts, little did Hampden dream of the fate which awaited him; little did he think that it was reserved for him to commence the overthrow of the British monarchy, and to shed his blood in the first daring attempt for a free constitution in England."

"Where did you find the History?"

"In my own library."

"Who was Baylies?"

"A Congressman and historian, who lived in the very place of the old tradition. He was born at Dighton, Mass., and was a Taunton lawyer."

"But he may have been misinformed."

"It is not likely; for his father, Dr. Baylies, lived to a great age, and he must have been familiar with the old settler's views and actual knowledge of the subject." Aunt Mar added, "And now I am happy."

"And so am I," said Charlie.

"You, why, — because the tradition is true?"

"No; because I am engaged."

"Engaged! To whom?"

"To Helena; and I am going to the Northwest next year."

"Well, well," said Aunt Mar, "you are rather young yet; but I do not object; it is a great country, and I think that you have great reason to be proud of your name and ancestry. I rather liked that Montana girl and her mother; and when you go, I think Helen and I will go too."

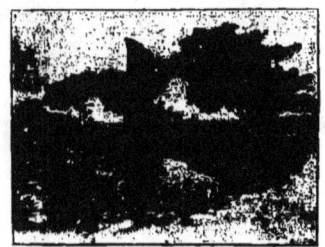

NATURE'S MONUMENT, CANADIAN PACIFIC COAST.

CELEBRATED WAR STORIES.

THE BOYS OF '61.
 OR FOUR YEARS OF FIGHTING. A record of personal observation with the Army and Navy from the battle of Bull Run to the fall of Richmond. By CHARLES CARLETON COFFIN, author of "The Boys of '76," "Our New Way 'Round the World," "The Story of Liberty," "Winning His Way," "Old Times in the Colonies," etc. With numerous illustrations.
 1 vol., 8vo, chromo-lithographed board covers and linings $1.75
 1 vol., 8vo, cloth, gilt 2.50

THE SAILOR BOYS OF '61.
 By Prof. J. RUSSELL SOLEY, author of "The Boys of 1812," etc. This volume contains an accurate and vivid account of the naval engagements of the great Civil War, and the deeds of its heroes. Elaborately and beautifully illustrated from original drawings.
 1 vol., 8vo, chromo-lithographed board covers, ... $1.75
 1 vol., 8vo, cloth gilt, . . 2.50

THE BOYS OF 1812.
 By Prof. J. RUSSELL SOLEY, author of "Blockaders and Cruisers," "The Sailor Boys of '61," etc., etc. This "most successful war book for the young, issued last year," is now made boards with an illustrated cover designed by Barnes.
 1 vol., 8vo, chromo-lithographed board covers $1.75
 1 vol., 8vo, cloth gilt, . . 2.50

"Prof. SOLEY'S books should be read by every American boy, who cares for the honor of his country." — *Boston Beacon.*

"He must be a dull boy who can read such records of heroism without a quickening of the pulses." — *San Francisco Chronicle.*

"We are in no danger of cultivating too much patriotism, and such a book as this is an excellent educator along an excellent line of thought." — *Chicago Daily Inter-Ocean.*

The Sixth Mass. Regiment passing through Baltimore.

MY DAYS AND NIGHTS ON THE BATTLEFIELD.
 By CHARLES CARLETON COFFIN. With eighteen full-page plates. Small quarto. Bound in illuminated board covers, ... $1.25

FOLLOWING THE FLAG.
 By CHARLES CARLETON COFFIN. With eighteen full-page plates. Small quarto. Bound in illuminated board covers, ... $1.25

WINNING HIS WAY.
 By CHARLES CARLETON COFFIN. With twenty-one full-page plates. Small quarto. Bound in illuminated board covers, ... $1.25

THE CARLETON SERIES OF JUVENILES,
CONSISTING OF
WINNING HIS WAY, FOLLOWING THE FLAG, MY DAYS AND NIGHTS ON THE BATTLEFIELD.
 3 vols., 16mo, cloth, in a box, ... $3.75
 Any volume sold separately, ... 1.25

ESTES & LAURIAT, Publishers, BOSTON, MASS.

THE FOUR GREAT ANNUALS.

CHATTERBOX FOR 1891.

This name, a household word in every home in the land, has become endeared in the hearts of two generations, and the readers of the early volumes are now men and women, who know that no books will delight their children more, or instruct them to a greater extent, than these dear old annual volumes, whose sales have long since mounted above the million mark.

This author is print from duplicates of the original English plates, contains a large amount of copyright Ameri   ter, which cannot be reprinted by any other firm.

The Genuine Ch.. box contains a great variety of original stories, sketches and poems for the young, and every illustration which appears in it is expressly designed for this work, by the most eminent English artists. It has over 200 full-page original illustrations.

This year, to add to the enormous sales, no expense or trouble have been spared in securing a paper that would do entire justice to this royal juvenile, and make the illustrations appear to their best advantage, and if possible, bring the book nearer the zenith of juvenile perfection.

1 vol., quarto, illuminated board covers,	$1.25
1 vol., quarto, cloth, black and gold stamps,	1.75
1 vol., quarto, cloth, extra, chromo, gilt side and edges,	2.25

LITTLE ONES ANNUAL.

Illustrated Stories and Poems for the Little Ones Edited by WILLIAM T. ADAMS (Oliver Optic). This beautiful volume consists of original stories and poems by the very best writers of juvenile literature, carefully selected and edited. It is embellished with 370 entirely original illustrations, drawn expressly for the work by the most celebrated book illustrators in America, and engraved on wood in the highest style, under the superintendence of George T. Andrew.

1 vol., quarto, illuminated board covers,	$1.75
1 vol., quarto, cloth and gilt,	2.25

"Little Ones Annual is by all odds the best thing of the season for children from five to ten years old."— *Boston Journal*.

THE NURSERY — T.

For 26 years the Nur y has been welcomed in thousands of families as the favorite picture book for our little folks, and the best of it is it improves in quality every year. It is now enlarged in size and crowded with charming stories and original artistic illustrations. Edited by OLIVER OPTIC

1 vol., royal octavo, illuminated covers, ... $1.25

OLIVER OPTIC'S ANNUAL, 1891.

A volume edited by OLIVER OPTIC appeals at once to the heart of every boy and girl, with all of whom his name is a synonym for everything bright and entertaining in juvenile literature. This is the leading book of its kind of the year, with original illustrations.

1 vol., quarto, illuminated board covers and frontispiece, . . . $1.50

ESTES & LAURIAT, Publishers, BOSTON, MASS

ENTERTAINING JUVENILES.

SCHOOLBOYS OF ROOKESBURY;
Or, The Boys of the Fourth Form. An entertaining story of the mishaps and adventures of several boys during a term at an English school. Edited by LAWRENCE H. FRANCIS. Fully illustrated with original drawings.
1 vol., small quarto, illuminated board cover $1.25

QUEEN HILDEGARDE;
By LAURA E. RICHARDS, author of "Four Feet, Two Feet, and No Feet." A new edition of this popular girl's book, — a second "Little Women," — containing nineteen illustrations from new and original drawings.
1 vol., small quarto, illuminated board covers $1.50
"We should like to see the sensible, heroine loving girl in her early teens who would not like this book. Not to like it would simply argue a screw loose somewhere." — BOSTON POST.

THE DAYS OF CHIVALRY;
Or, Page, Squire and Knight. A highly interesting and instructive, historical romance of the Middle Ages. Edited by W. H. Davenport Adams, author of "Success in Life," "The Land of the Incas," etc. Thoroughly illustrated with 113 drawings.
1 vol., small quarto, illuminated board covers $1.50

THE RED MOUNTAIN OF ALASKA.
By WILLIS BOYD ALLEN. An exciting narrative of a trip through this most interesting but little known country, with accurate description of the same. Full of adventures, vividly portrayed by choice, original illustrations, by F. T. Merrill and others.
1 vol., 8vo, cloth, gilt, ... $2.50
"It throws 'Robinson Crusoe', the 'Swiss Family Robinson', and all those fascinating phantasies, hopelessly into the shade, and will hold many a boy spellbound, through many an evening, of many a winter." — CHICAGO TRIBUNE.

HUNTING IN THE JUNGLE
With Gun and Guide. From Les Animaux Sauvages, by WARREN F. KELLOGG. An exciting and amusing series of adventures in search of large game — gorillas, elephants, tigers and lions — fully illustrated with over a hundred original drawings by celebrated artists, engraved on wood by the best modern book illustrators.
1 vol., 8vo, chromo-lithographed board covers $1.75
1 vol., 8vo, cloth, gilt, ... 2.50

OUR NEW WAY 'ROUND THE WORLD.
By CHARLES CARLETON COFFIN, author of "The Story of Liberty," "The Boys of '61," "Following the Flag," "The Boys of '76," "Winning His Way," "My Days and Nights on the Battlefield," etc., etc. A new REVISED edition of this standard book of travel, which is interesting and useful to young and old; with a large number of additional illustrations.
1 vol., 8vo, chromo-lithographed board covers, ... $1.75
1 vol., 8vo, cloth, gilt, ... 2.50

TRAVELS IN MEXICO.
By F. A. OBER. A brilliant record of a remarkable journey from Yucatan to the Rio Grande Historic ruins, tropic wilds, silver hills are described with eloquence. No country possesses so rich a field for the historian, antiquarian, fortune-hunter, and traveller.
1 vol., 8vo, chromo-lithographed board covers $1.50
1 vol., 8vo, cloth, gilt, ... 2.50

DICKENS'S CHILD'S HISTORY OF ENGLAND.
Holiday edition, with 100 fine illustrations, by De Neuville, Emile Bayard, F. Liz, and others.
1 vol., 8vo, chromo-lithographed board covers $1.75
1 vol., 8vo, cloth, gilt, ... 2.50

THE YOUNG MOOSE HUNTERS.
By C. A. STEPHENS, author of the "Knockabout Club in the Tropics," etc., etc. With numerous full-page original illustrations made expressly for this edition. An exciting account of a hunting trip through the Maine woods.
1 vol., small quarto, illuminated board covers $1.50

SIX GIRLS.
By FANNY BELLE IRVING. A charming story of every-day home life, pure in sentiment and healthy in tone. A beautiful book for girls. Fully illustrated from original designs.
1 vol., small quarto, illuminated board covers and linings, ... $1.50

HANS CHRISTIAN ANDERSEN'S FAIRY TALES.
The standard authorized edition. A new translation from the original Danish edition, complete and unabridged, fully illustrated with engravings made from the original drawings, with an appropriate cover designed by L. S. IPSEN.
1 vol., quarto, cloth, ... $2.25

FEATHERS, FURS AND FINS;
Or Stories of Animal Life for Children. A collection of the most fascinating stories about birds, fishes and animals, both wild and domestic, with illustrations drawn by the best artists, and engraved in the finest possible style by Andrew.
1 vol., quarto, chromo-lithographed board covers, ... $1.75
1 vol., quarto, cloth and gilt, ... 2.50

ESTES & LAURIAT, Publishers, BOSTON, MASS.

THE FAMOUS ZIGZAG SERIES.

The Most Entertaining and Instructive, the Most Successful and Universally Popular Series of Books for the Young Ever Issued in America.

Over Three Hundred Thousand Volumes of the Series have already been sold in this Country alone.

Zigzag Journeys in Australia,
Or, a Visit to the Ocean World. Describing the wonderful resources and natural advantages of the fifth continent, giving an insight into the social relations of the people and containing stories of gold discoveries and of the animals peculiar to this fascinating country.

1 vol., small quarto, illuminated board covers and linings, - - - - - - - $1.75
1 vol., small quarto, cloth, bevelled and gilt, - 2.25

Uniform in style and price with the above, the other volumes of the series can be had as follows:

Zigzag Journeys in the Great North-West;
Or, a Trip to the American Switzerland. Giving an account of the marvelous growth of our Western Empire, with legendary tales of the early explorers. Full of interesting, instructive and entertaining stories of the New Northwest, the country of the future.

Zigzag Journeys in the British Isles.
With excursions among the lakes of Ireland and the hills of Scotland. Replete with legend and romance. Over 100 illustrations.

Zigzag Journeys in the Antipodes.
This volume takes the reader to Siam, and with delightful illustration and anecdote, tells him of the interesting animal worship of the country. Ninety-six illustrations.

Zigzag Journeys in India;
Or, the Antipodes of the Far East. A collection of Zenana Tales. With nearly 100 fine original illustrations.

Zigzag Journeys in the Sunny South.
In which the Zigzag Club visits the Southern States and the Isthmus of Panama. With romantic stories of early voyagers and discoverers of the American continent. Seventy-two illustrations.

Zigzag Journeys in the Levant.
An account of a tour of the Zigzag Club through Egypt and the Holy Land, including a trip up the Nile, and visit to the ruins of Thebes, Memphis, etc. 114 illustrations.

Zigzag Journeys in Acadia & New France.
In which the Zigzag Club visits Nova Scotia and Acadia — "the Land of Evangeline," — New Brunswick, Canada, the St. Lawrence, Montreal, Quebec, etc., with romantic stories and traditions connected with the early history of the country. 109 illustrations.

Zigzag Journeys in Northern Lands.
From the Rhine to the Arctic Circle. Zigzag Club in Holland, Belgium, Germany, Denmark, Norway, and Sweden, with picturesque views, entertaining stories, etc. 119 illustrations.

Zigzag Journeys in the Occident.
A trip of the Zigzag Club from Boston to the Golden Gate; including visits to the wheat-fields of Dakota, the wonders of the Yellowstone and Yosemite. 148 illustrations.

Zigzag Journeys in the Orient.
A journey of the Zigzag Club from Vienna to the Golden Horn, the Euxine, Moscow, and St. Petersburg; containing a description of the Great Fair at Nijni-Novgorod, etc. 147 illustrations.

Zigzag Journeys in Classic Lands;
Or, Tommy Toby's Trip to Parnassus. An account of a tour of the Zigzag Club in France, Italy, Greece, Spain, and Portugal. 124 illustrations.

Zigzag Journeys in Europe;
Or, Vacation Rambles in Historic Lands. In which the Zigzag Club travels through England, Scotland, Belgium, and France; with interesting stories and legends. 126 illustrations.

ESTES & LAURIAT, Publishers, BOSTON, MASS.

THE FAMOUS VASSAR GIRL SERIES.

☞ "Mrs. Champney's fame as the authoress of the delightful series of travels by the 'Three Vassar Girls,' has extended throughout the English-speaking world."

Three Vassar Girls in the Tyrol.
An entertaining description of the travels of our Vassar friends through this well-known country, giving an interesting account of the Passion Play at Ober Ammergau. Illustrated by "Champ" and others.
1 vol., small quarto, illuminated board covers and linings, - - - - - - $1.50
1 vol., small quarto, cloth, bevelled and gilt, - 2.00

Uniform in style and price with the above, the other volumes of the series can be had as follows:

Three Vassar Girls in Switzerland.
By ELIZABETH W. CHAMPNEY. An exceedingly interesting story interwoven with bits of Swiss life, historic incidents, and accounts of happenings at Geneva, Lucerne, and the Great St. Bernard. Illustrated by "Champ" and others.

Three Vassar Girls in Russia and Turkey.
During the exciting scenes and events of the late Turko-Russian war, with many adventures, both serious and comic. Profusely illustrated from original designs, by "CHAMP" and others.

Three Vassar Girls in France.
A story of the siege of Paris. A thrilling account of adventures when Germany and France were engaged in their terrible struggle. Ninety-seven illustrations by "CHAMP," DETAILLE, and DE NEUVILLE.

Three Vassar Girls at Home.
Travels through some of our own States and Territories, with many interesting adventures. Ninety-seven illustrations by "CHAMP."

Three Vassar Girls on the Rhine.
Full of amusing incidents of the voyage and historic stories of the castles and towns along the route. 128 Illustrations by "CHAMP" and others.

Three Vassar Girls in Italy.
Travels through the vineyards of Italy, visiting all the large cities, and passing some time in Rome, in the Vatican, the Catacombs, etc. 107 illustrations.

Three Vassar Girls in South America.
A trip through the heart of South America, up the Amazon, across the Andes, and along the Pacific coast to Panama. 112 illustrations.

Three Vassar Girls in England.
Sunny memories of a holiday excursion of three college girls in the mother country, with visits to historic scenes and notable p' es. Ninety-eight illustrations.

Three Vassar Girls Abroad.
The vacation rambles of three college girls on a European trip for amusement and instruction, with their haps and mishaps. Ninety-two illustrations.

THE NEW SERIES.

Great Grandmother's Girls in New Mexico.
By ELIZABETH W. CHAMPNEY. This is the second volume of this delightful series describing incidents in the life of a quaint little maiden who lived in the time of the Spanish adventurers. Illustrated by "CHAMP."
1 vol., 8vo, chromo-lithographed board covers - $1.75
1 vol., 8vo, cloth, gilt - - - - - 2.50

Great Grandmother's Girls in France.
By ELIZABETH W. CHAMPNEY. A charming volume for girls, consisting of romantic stories of the heroines in the early colonial days—their privations and courage.
1 vol., 8vo, chromo-lithographed board covers - $1.75
1 vol., 8vo, cloth, gilt, - - - - 2.50

"A beautiful volume and one that cannot fail to arouse intense interest."—*Toledo Blade.*

"An excellent present for a boy or girl."—*Boston Transcript.*

ESTES & LAURIAT, Publishers, BOSTON, MASS.

THE FAMOUS "KNOCKABOUT CLUB" SERIES.

"Delightful and wholesome books of stirring out-door adventure for healthy American boys; books whose steadily increasing popularity is but a well-earned recognition of intrinsic merit."

THE KNOCKABOUT CLUB ON THE SPANISH MAIN.
By FRED A. OBER. In which the Knockabout Club visits Caracas, La Guayra, Lake Maracaibo, etc. Containing stories of the exploits of the pirates of the Spanish Main. Fully illustrated.
1 vol., small quarto, illuminated board covers and linings, ... $1.50
1 vol., small quarto, cloth, bevelled and gilt, ... $2.00

Uniform in style and price with the above, the other volumes of the series can be had as follows:

THE KNOCKABOUT CLUB IN NORTH AFRICA.
By FRED A. OBER. An account of a trip along the coast of the Dark Continent, caravan journeys, and a visit to a pirate city, with stories of lion hunting and life among the Moors. Fully illustrated.

THE KNOCKABOUT CLUB IN SPAIN.
By FRED A. OBER. A panorama of Seville, the Guadalquivir, the Palaces of the Moors, the Alhambra, Madrid, Bull-fights, etc. Full of original illustrations, many full-page.

THE KNOCKABOUT CLUB IN THE ANTILLES.
By FRED A. OBER. A visit to the delightful islands that extend in a graceful line from Florida to South America, accompanied by a "Special Artist." 78 illustrations.

THE KNOCKABOUT CLUB IN THE EVERGLADES.
By FRED A. OBER. A visit to Florida for the purpose of exploring Lake Okechobee, on which trip the boys encounter various obstacles and adventures with alligators, etc. 55 illustrations.

THE KNOCKABOUT CLUB IN THE TROPICS.
By C. A. STEPHENS. From the ice-fields of the North to the plains of New Mexico, thence through the "Land of the Aztecs," and the wonderful ruins of Central America, to the "Queen of the Antilles." 105 illustrations.

THE KNOCKABOUT CLUB ALONGSHORE.
By C. A. STEPHENS. A journey alongshore from Boston to Greenland, with descriptions of seal-fishing, Arctic Scenery, and stories of the ancient Northmen. 137 illustrations.

THE KNOCKABOUT CLUB IN THE WOODS.
By C. A. STEPHENS. A boy's book of anecdotes and adventures in the wilds of Maine and Canada. An account of a vacation spent in healthy amusement, fascinating adventure, and instructive entertainment. 117 illustrations.

ESTES & LAURIAT, Publishers, BOSTON, MASS.

YOUNG FOLKS' HISTORIES

YOUNG FOLKS' HISTORY OF THE NETHERLANDS.
A concise history of Holland and Belgium, from the earliest times, in which the author goes over the ground covered by Motley in his standard histories of these most interesting countries, and brings the narrative down to the present time. By ALEXANDER YOUNG. 150 illustrations.

YOUNG FOLKS' HISTORY OF AMERICA.
From the earliest times to the present. A new edition. With a chapter and additional illustrations on the Life and Death of President Garfield. Edited by H. BUTTERWORTH, author of "Zigzag Journeys." With 157 illustrations. Over 10,000 copies sold in one year.

YOUNG FOLKS' HISTORY OF MEXICO.
Comprising the principle events from the sixth century to the present time. By FRED. A. OBER, author of "Camps in the Caribbees." With 100 illustrations.
The intimate relations of our country with Mexico, which the railroads and mines are developing, make this volume one of the most important in the entire series.

YOUNG FOLKS' HISTORY OF RUSSIA.
By NATHAN HASKELL DOLE. With 110 illustrations.

THE GREAT CITIES OF THE WORLD.

YOUNG FOLKS' HISTORY OF LONDON.
With graphic stories of its historic landmarks. By W. H. RIDEING. With 100 illustrations.

YOUNG FOLKS' HISTORY OF BOSTON.
By H. BUTTERWORTH, author of "Zigzag Journeys," etc. With 140 illustrations.

CHARLOTTE M. YONGE. YOUNG FOLKS' HISTORIES.

YOUNG FOLKS' BIBLE HISTORY. With 132 illustrations.
YOUNG FOLKS' HISTORY OF ENGLAND. With 60 illustrations by De Neuville, E. Bayard and others.
YOUNG FOLKS' HISTORY OF FRANCE. With 84 illustrations by A. De Neuville, E. Bayard and others.
YOUNG FOLKS' HISTORY OF ROME. With 114 illustrations.
YOUNG FOLKS' HISTORY OF GREECE. With 51 illustrations.
YOUNG FOLKS' HISTORY OF GERMANY. With 82 illustrations.

YOUNG FOLKS' EPOCHS OF HISTORY.

YOUNG FOLKS' HISTORY OF THE CIVIL WAR.
A concise and impartial account of the late war, for young people, from the best authorities both North and South. By MRS. C. EMMA CHENEY. Illustrated with 100 engravings, maps and plans.

YOUNG FOLKS' HISTORY OF THE REFORMATION.
IN GERMANY, FRANCE, ENGLAND AND OTHER COUNTRIES. By FRED H. ALLEN. A graphic account of the men and the movements by which the great religious revolution which resulted in the establishment of Protestantism was carried on, from the early centuries of Christianity to the end of the Reformation. Fully Illustrated.

YOUNG FOLKS' HISTORY OF THE QUEENS OF SCOTLAND.
These valuable books are condensed from Strickland's Queens of Scotland by ROSALIE KAUFMAN, and are at once reliable and entertaining to both old and young folks. Fully illustrated. 2 vols., 16mo, cloth. . . $3.00.

YOUNG FOLKS' HISTORY OF THE QUEENS OF ENGLAND.
From the Norman Conquest. Founded on Strickland's Queens of England. Abridged, adapted and continued to the present time. By ROSALIE KAUFMAN. With nearly 300 illustrations. 3 vols., 16mo, cloth . $4.50.

LIBRARY OF ENTERTAINING HISTORY.
Edited by Arthur Gilman, M. A.

INDIA.	By FANNIE ROPER FEUDGE. With 100 illustrations, . . .	$1.50
EGYPT.	By Mrs. CLARA ERSKINE CLEMENT. With 108 illustrations,	1.50
SPAIN.	By Prof. JAMES HERBERT HARRISON. With 111 illustrations, . .	1.50
SWITZERLAND.	By Miss HARRIET D. S. MACKENZIE. With 100 illustrations, .	1.50
HISTORY OF AMERICAN PEOPLE.	With 175 illustrations, . . .	1.50

All the above volumes are published as 16mos, in cloth, at $1.50.

ESTES & LAURIAT, PUBLISHERS,
BOSTON, MASS.

HOUSEHOLD NECESSITIES.

SOCIAL CUSTOMS.

New edition, REDUCED IN PRICE. Complete Manual of American Etiquette. By FLORENCE HOWE HALL, daughter of Mrs. Julia Ward Howe. Handsomely printed, and neatly bound in extra cloth, gilt top, uncut. Small 8vo. - - - - - - - - $1.75

DO YOU ALWAYS KNOW JUST WHAT TO DO? Do you know how to encourage Mrs. D. Lightful, accept and return her courtesies, as they deserve; and politely but firmly avoid and defeat Mrs. Bore in her inroads on your privacy and more agreeable engagements? If you do not, let us recommend for EVERY SOCIAL QUESTION the above entertaining and instructive book, or its new baby relative, "THE CORRECT THING," mentioned below, for with these two books, one can make no mistake in life, as every possible question may be answered from their combined wisdom. They are *comprehensive, practical, reliable and authoritative*.

THE CORRECT THING.

By FLORENCE HOWE HALL, author of "Social Customs." 18mo. Very neatly bound in extra cloth, gilt top, - - - - - - - - - - - - $0.75

Same, Bound in full flexible morocco, gilt edges (in a box). - - - - - $1.25

This new manual is neatly printed in a size not too large to be slipped into the pocket, and is arranged so that one page reminds the reader that "IT IS THE CORRECT THING" to do this, while *per contra* the opposite page tells him that "IT IS NOT THE CORRECT THING" to do that. Its conciseness recommends it to many who would not take the time to master any more comprehensive manual.

"It is, indeed, a treasure of good counsel, and, like most advice, it has the merit of not being expensive."—*Montreal Gazette*.

PARLOA'S KITCHEN COMPANION.

A GUIDE FOR ALL WHO WOULD BE GOOD HOUSEKEEPERS.

Handsomely printed, and very fully illustrated. Large 8vo. (nearly 1000 pages). Neatly bound in extra cloth or in waterproof binding. - - - - - - - - $2.50

☞ It is thoroughly practical; it is perfectly reliable; it is marvellously comprehensive; it is copiously illustrated. It is, in short, overflowing with good qualities, and is just the book that all housekeepers need to guide them.

Miss Parloa's new book has proved a remarkable success, and it could hardly have been otherwise. Exhaustive in its treatment of a subject of the highest importance to all, the result of years of conscientious study and labor upon the part of one who has been called "the apostle of the *renaissance* in domestic service," it could not be otherwise than welcome to every intelligent housekeeper in the land.

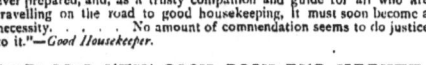

"This is the most comprehensive volume that Miss Parloa has ever prepared, and, as a trusty companion and guide for all who are travelling on the road to good housekeeping, it must soon become a necessity. . . . . No amount of commendation seems to do justice to it."—*Good Housekeeper*.

PARLOA'S NEW COOK BOOK AND MARKETING GUIDE.

12mo. Cloth. - - - - - - - - - $1.50

This is one of the most popular Cook Books ever printed, containing 1724 receipts and items of instruction. The directions are clear and concise, and the chapters on marketing and kitchen furnishing very useful.

ESTES & LAURIAT, PUBLISHERS,
BOSTON, MASS.

www.ingramcontent.com/pod-product-compliance
Lightning Source LLC
Chambersburg PA
CBHW021200230426
43667CB00006B/479